D1034668

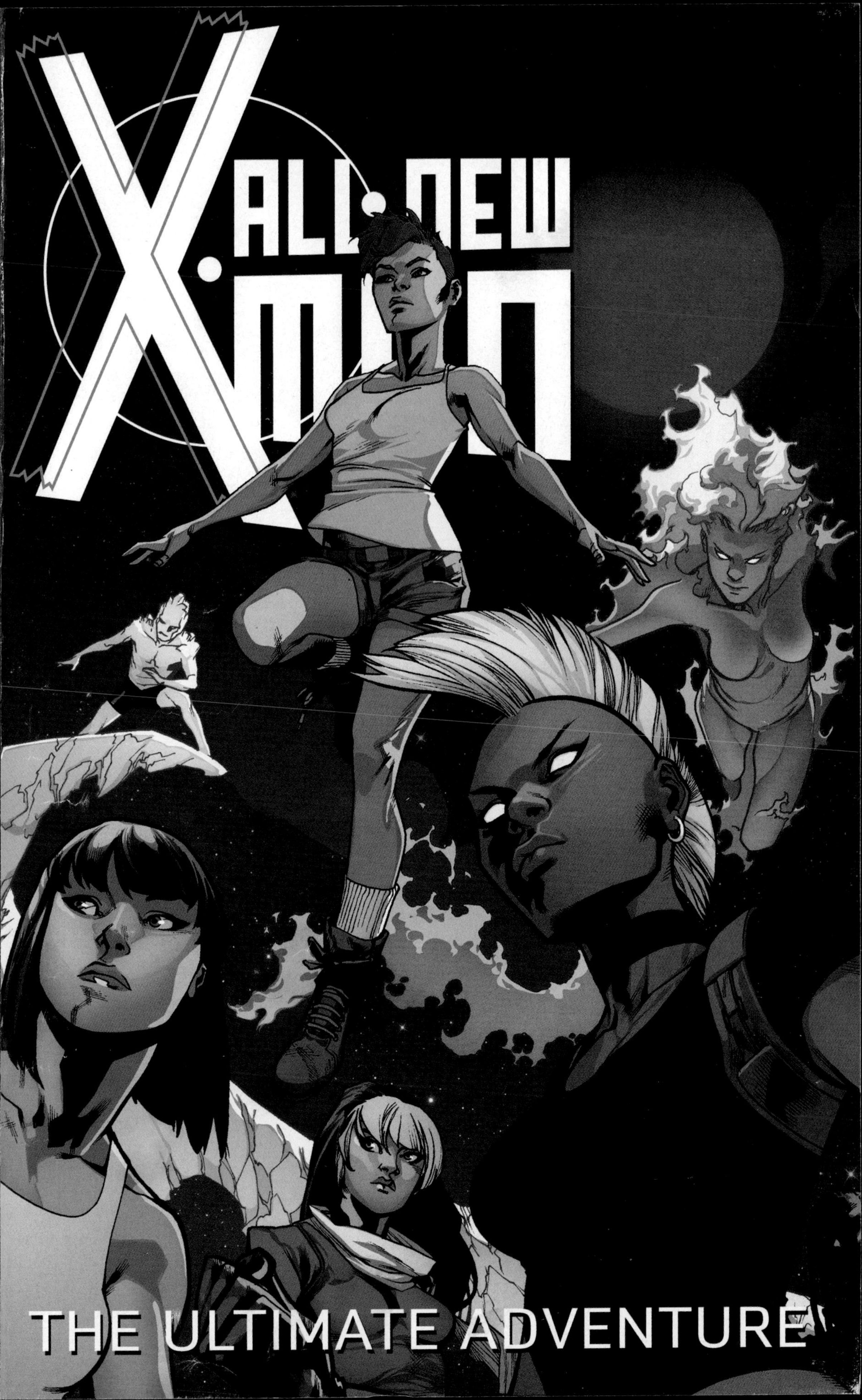
ALL-NEW X-MEN
THE ULTIMATE ADVENTURE

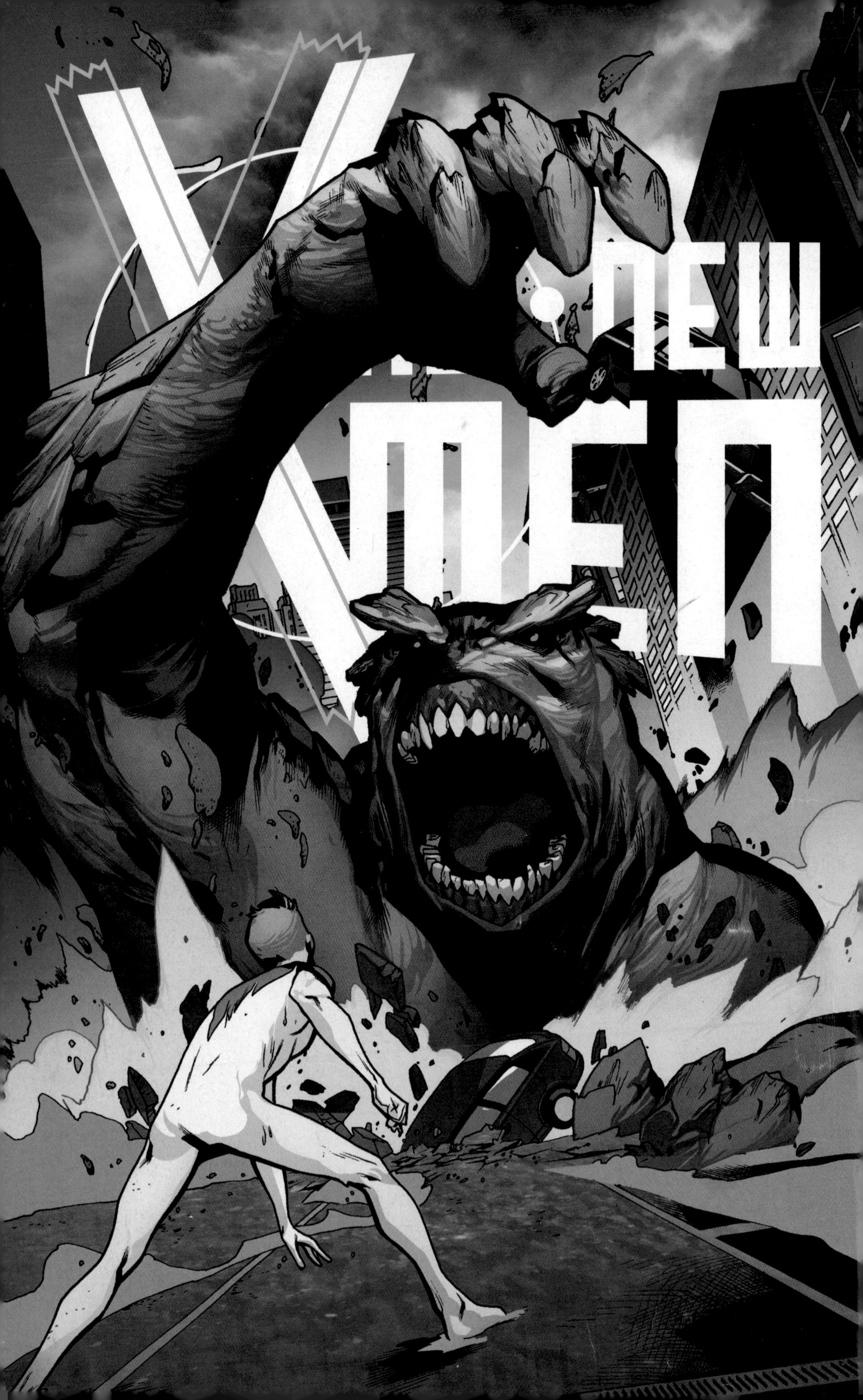
X
NEW
MEN

BEAST
HANK McCOY

MARVEL GIRL
JEAN GREY

CYCLOPS
SCOTT SUMMERS

ANGEL
WARREN WORTHINGTON III

ICEMAN
BOBBY DRAKE

THE ULTIMATE ADVENTURE

BRIAN MICHAEL
BENDIS
WRITER

MAHMUD
ASRAR
ARTIST

MARTE
GRACIA
COLORISTS
WITH **JASON KEITH** (#31)

CORY
PETIT
LETTERER

XANDER
JAROWEY
ASSISTANT EDITOR

MIKE
MARTS
EDITOR

COVER ART: **STUART IMMONEN, WADE VON GRAWBADGER & MARTE GRACIA** (#31),
SARA PICHELLI & MARTE GRACIA (#32 & #35) AND **MAHMUD ASRAR & MARTE GRACIA** (#33-34 & #36)

X-MEN CREATED BY **STAN LEE & JACK KIRBY**

COLLECTION EDITOR: **JENNIFER GRÜNWALD** ASSOCIATE MANAGING EDITOR: **ALEX STARBUCK**
EDITOR, SPECIAL PROJECTS: **MARK D. BEAZLEY** SENIOR EDITOR, SPECIAL PROJECTS: **JEFF YOUNGQUIST**
SVP PRINT, SALES & MARKETING: **DAVID GABRIEL** BOOK DESIGNER: **RODOLFO MURAGUCHI**

EDITOR IN CHIEF: **AXEL ALONSO** CHIEF CREATIVE OFFICER: **JOE QUESADA**
PUBLISHER: **DAN BUCKLEY** EXECUTIVE PRODUCER: **ALAN FINE**

ALL-NEW X-MEN VOL. 6: THE ULTIMATE ADVENTURE. Contains material originally published in magazine form as ALL-NEW X-MEN #31-36. First printing 2015. ISBN# 978-0-7851-5434-1. Published by
MARVEL WORLDWIDE, INC., a subsidiary of MARVEL ENTERTAINMENT, LLC. OFFICE OF PUBLICATION: 135 West 50th Street, New York, NY 10020. Copyright © 2015 Marvel Characters, Inc. All rights reserved. All
characters featured in this issue and the distinctive names and likenesses thereof, and all related indicia are trademarks of Marvel Characters, Inc. No similarity between any of the names, characters, persons,
and/or institutions in this magazine with those of any living or dead person or institution is intended, and any such similarity which may exist is purely coincidental. **Printed in the U.S.A.** ALAN FINE, EVP - Office
of the President, Marvel Worldwide, Inc. and EVP & CMO Marvel Characters B.V.; DAN BUCKLEY, Publisher & President - Print, Animation & Digital Divisions; JOE QUESADA, Chief Creative Officer; TOM BREVOORT,
SVP of Publishing; DAVID BOGART, SVP of Operations & Procurement, Publishing; C.B. CEBULSKI, SVP of Creator & Content Development; DAVID GABRIEL, SVP Print, Sales & Marketing; JIM O'KEEFE, VP of
Operations & Logistics; DAN CARR, Executive Director of Publishing Technology; SUSAN CRESPI, Editorial Operations Manager; ALEX MORALES, Publishing Operations Manager; STAN LEE, Chairman Emeritus. For
information regarding advertising in Marvel Comics or on Marvel.com, please contact Niza Disla, Director of Marvel Partnerships, at ndisla@marvel.com. For Marvel subscription inquiries, please call 800-217-
9158. **Manufactured between 1/19/2015 and 3/2/2015 by R.R. DONNELLEY, INC., SALEM, VA, USA.**
10 9 8 7 6 5 4 3 2 1

Born with genetic mutations that gave them abilities beyond those of normal humans, mutants are the next stage in evolution. As such, they are feared and hated by humanity. A group of mutants known as the X-Men fight for peaceful coexistence between mutants and humankind. But not all mutants see peaceful coexistence as a reality.

ALL·NEW X·MEN

The original X-Men — Jean Grey, Cyclops, Iceman, Angel and Beast — were brough to the present in an attempt to shine a light on the errors of the present day X-Men. Unable to return to the past, the All-New X-Men have taken up residence at the New Xavier School along with new teammate X-23, and their leader, Professor Kitty Pryde. However, the team recently lost the young Scott Summers, when he left to explore space with his father, Corsair, whom he long thought dead.

Having defeated the future Brotherhood of Mutants, the All-New X-Men have been left to lick their wounds and collect their thoughts. Seeking some rest and relaxation, Angel and X-23 took their leave of the school to spend a night out together. Meanwhile, Jean Grey began to receive training from Emma Frost in the use of her new psionic powers. Though they initially locked horns, the training process began to heal the rift between the two, bringing about a surprising revelation — Jean and Emma are becoming friends. However, Jean's training was interrupted by the arrival of Storm and the present-day versions of Iceman and Beast. And they have brought startling news — they've come to collect Scott Summers for the reading of Charles Xavier's will!

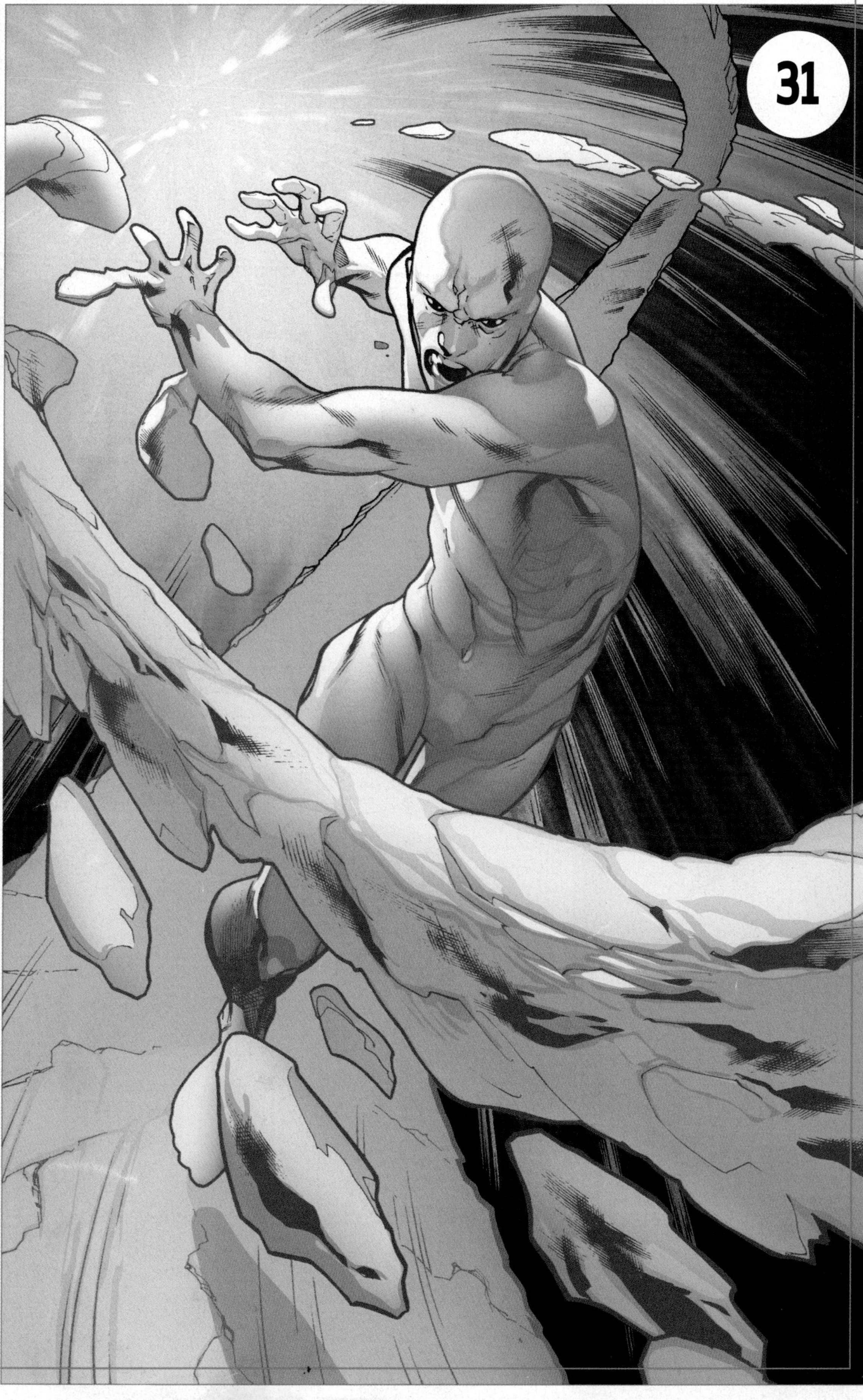
31

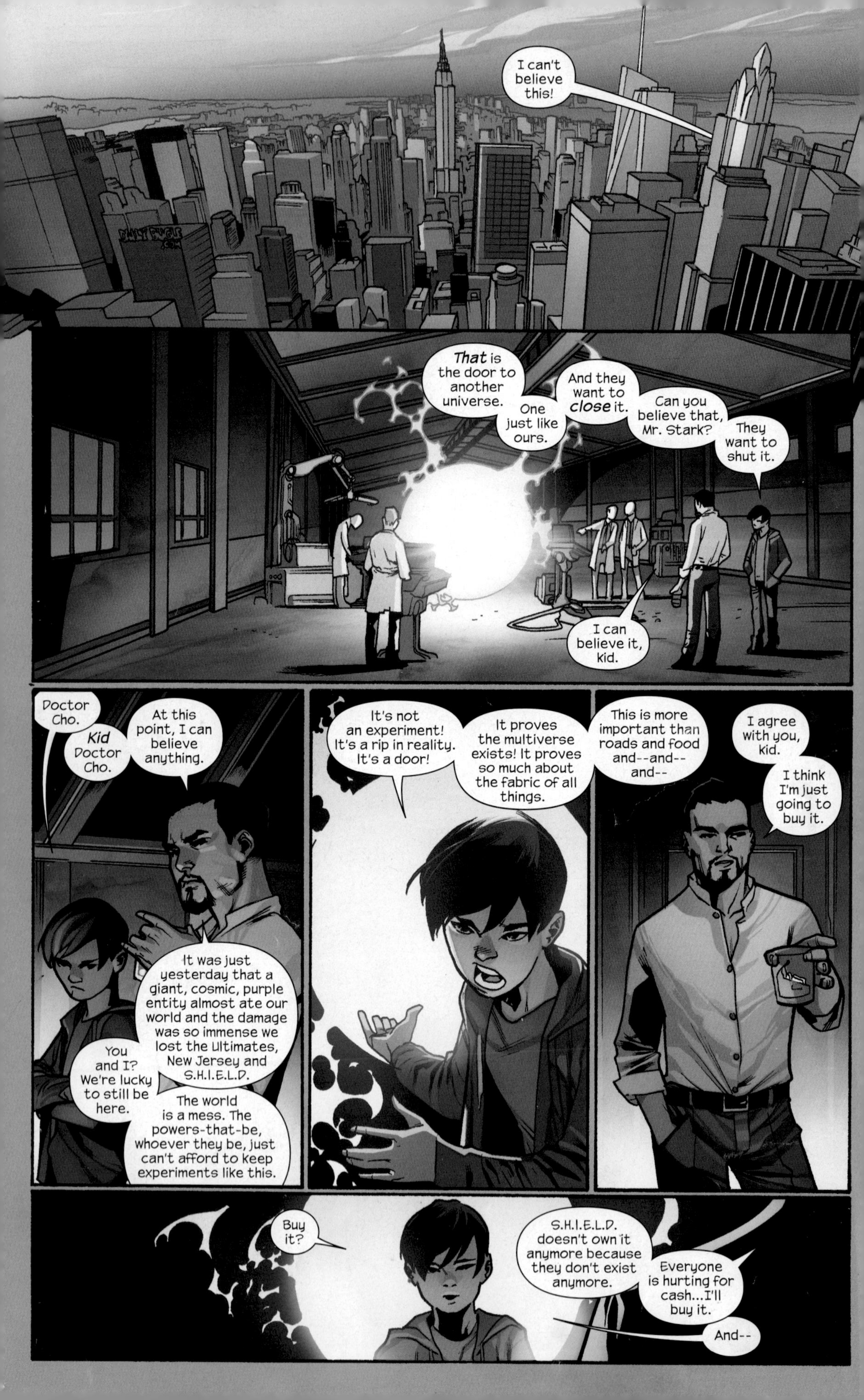
I can't believe this!
That is the door to another universe.
One just like ours.
And they want to close it.
Can you believe that, Mr. Stark?
They want to shut it.
I can believe it, kid.
Doctor Cho.
Kid Doctor Cho.
At this point, I can believe anything.
It was just yesterday that a giant, cosmic, purple entity almost ate our world and the damage was so immense we lost the Ultimates, New Jersey and S.H.I.E.L.D.
You and I? We're lucky to still be here.
The world is a mess. The powers-that-be, whoever they be, just can't afford to keep experiments like this.
It's not an experiment! It's a rip in reality. It's a door!
It proves the multiverse exists! It proves so much about the fabric of all things.
This is more important than roads and food and--and-- and--
I agree with you, kid.
I think I'm just going to buy it.
Buy it?
S.H.I.E.L.D. doesn't own it anymore because they don't exist anymore.
Everyone is hurting for cash...I'll buy it.
And--

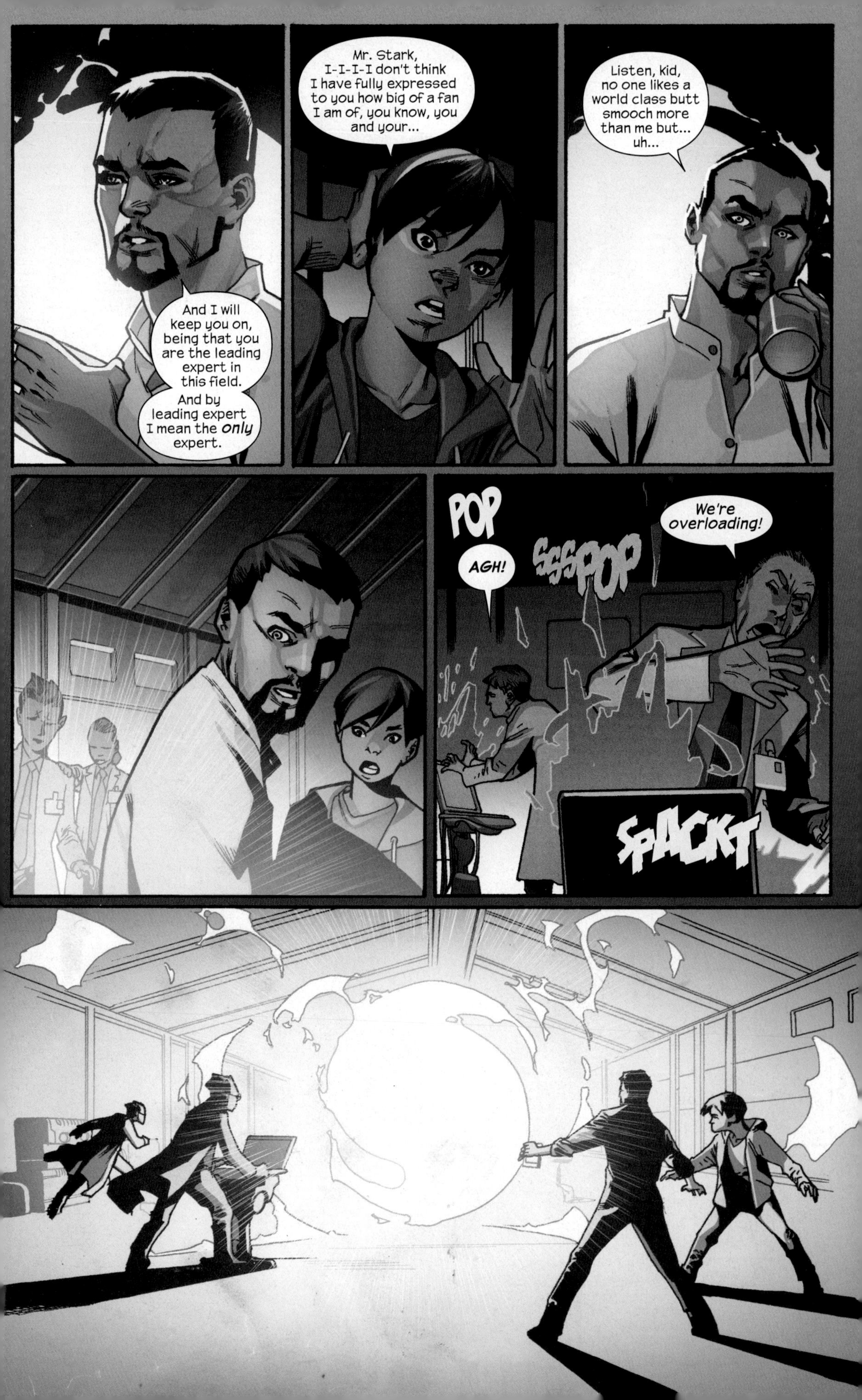
And I will keep you on, being that you are the leading expert in this field.
And by leading expert I mean the only expert.
Mr. Stark, I-I-I-I don't think I have fully expressed to you how big of a fan I am of, you know, you and your...
Listen, kid, no one likes a world class butt smooch more than me but... uh...
POP
AGH!
SSSPOP
We're overloading!
SPACKT

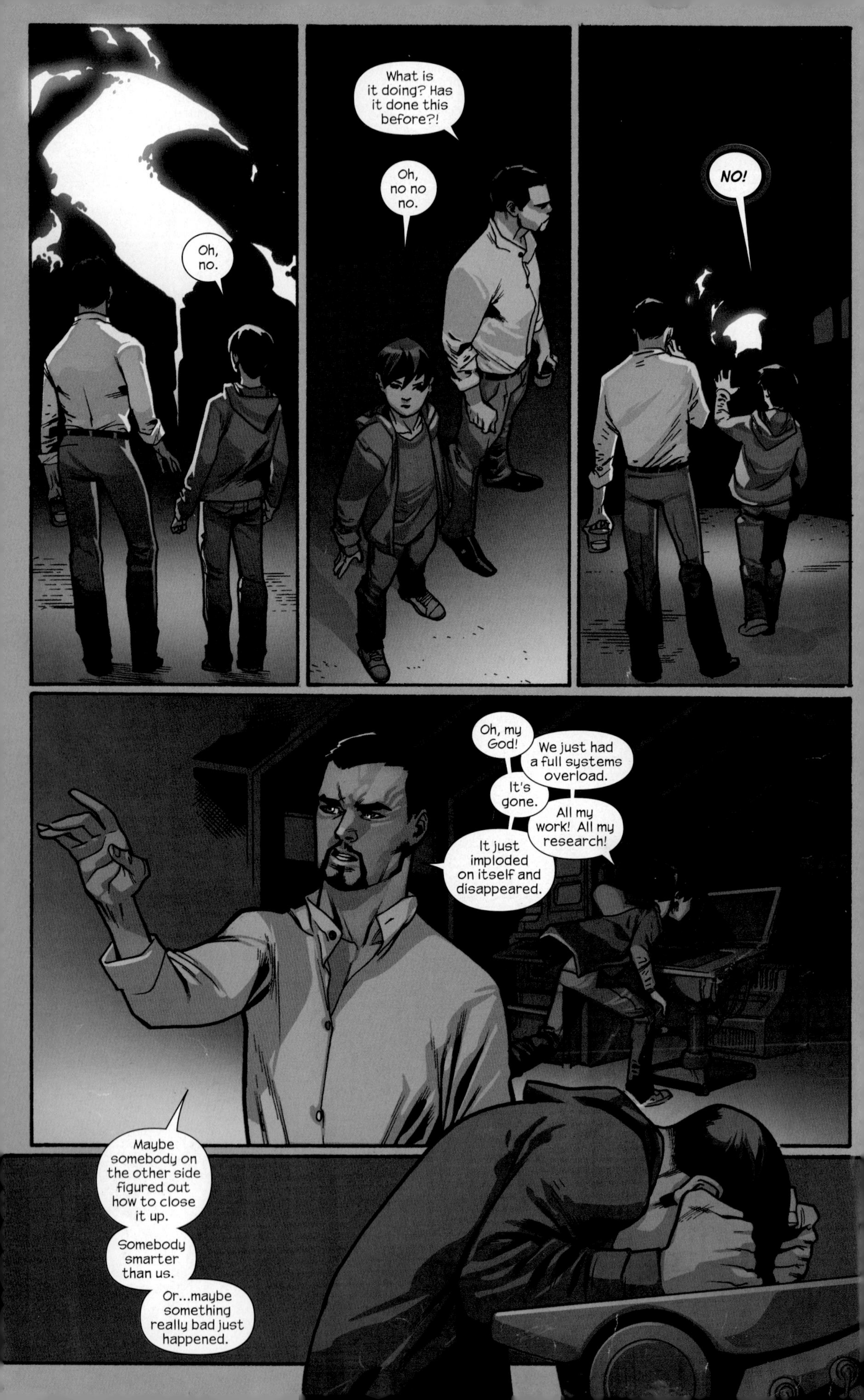
Oh,
no.
What is
it doing? Has
it done this
before?!
Oh,
no no
no.
NO!
Oh, my
God!
We just had
a full systems
overload.
It's
gone.
All my
work! All my
research!
It just
imploded
on itself and
disappeared.
Maybe
somebody on
the other side
figured out
how to close
it up.
Somebody
smarter
than us.
Or...maybe
something
really bad just
happened.

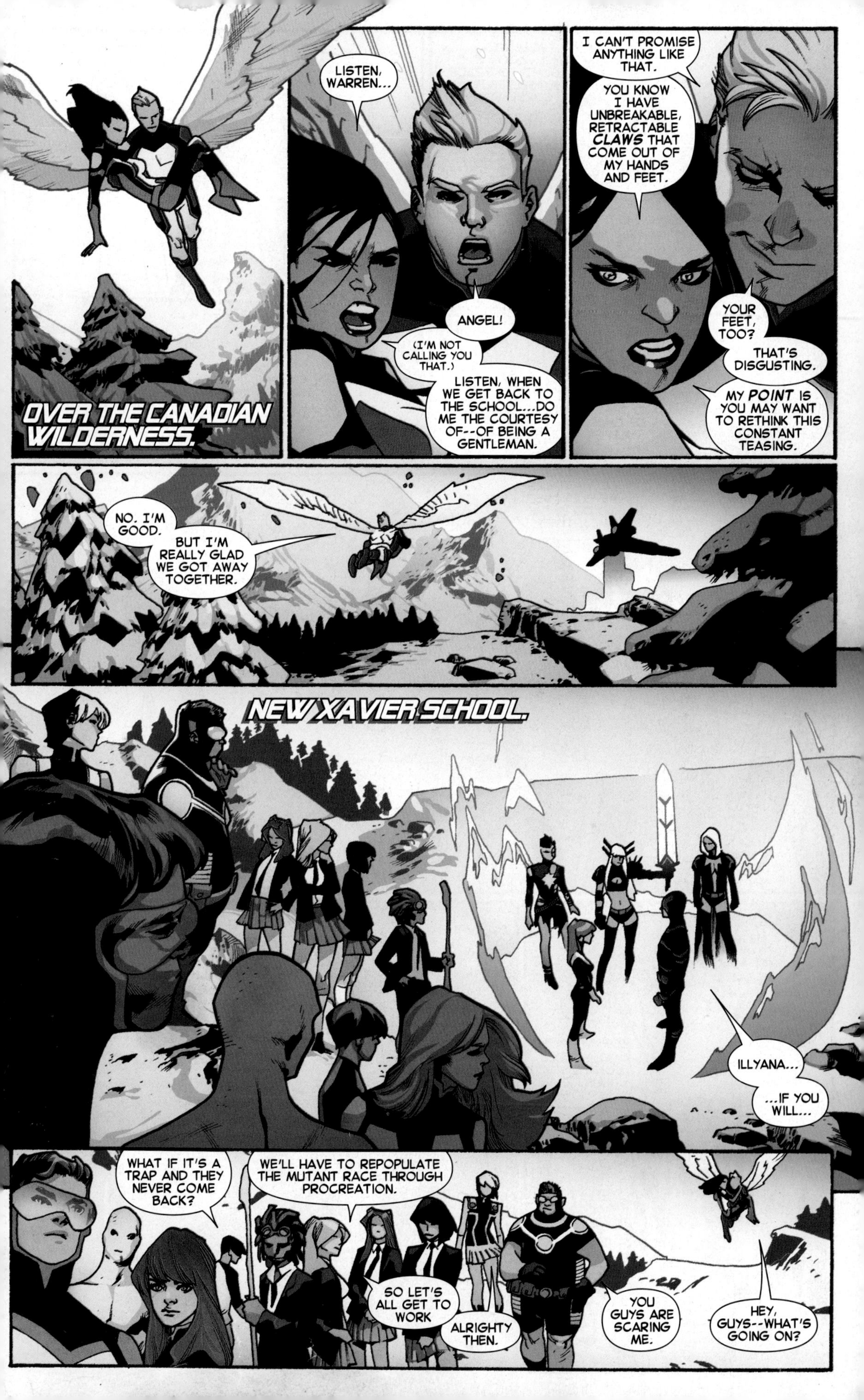
OVER THE CANADIAN WILDERNESS.
LISTEN, WARREN...
ANGEL!
(I'M NOT CALLING YOU THAT.)
LISTEN, WHEN WE GET BACK TO THE SCHOOL...DO ME THE COURTESY OF--OF BEING A GENTLEMAN.
I CAN'T PROMISE ANYTHING LIKE THAT.
YOU KNOW I HAVE UNBREAKABLE, RETRACTABLE CLAWS THAT COME OUT OF MY HANDS AND FEET.
YOUR FEET, TOO?
THAT'S DISGUSTING.
MY POINT IS YOU MAY WANT TO RETHINK THIS CONSTANT TEASING.
NO. I'M GOOD.
BUT I'M REALLY GLAD WE GOT AWAY TOGETHER.
NEW XAVIER SCHOOL.
ILLYANA...
...IF YOU WILL...
WHAT IF IT'S A TRAP AND THEY NEVER COME BACK?
WE'LL HAVE TO REPOPULATE THE MUTANT RACE THROUGH PROCREATION.
SO LET'S ALL GET TO WORK
ALRIGHTY THEN.
YOU GUYS ARE SCARING ME.
HEY, GUYS--WHAT'S GOING ON?

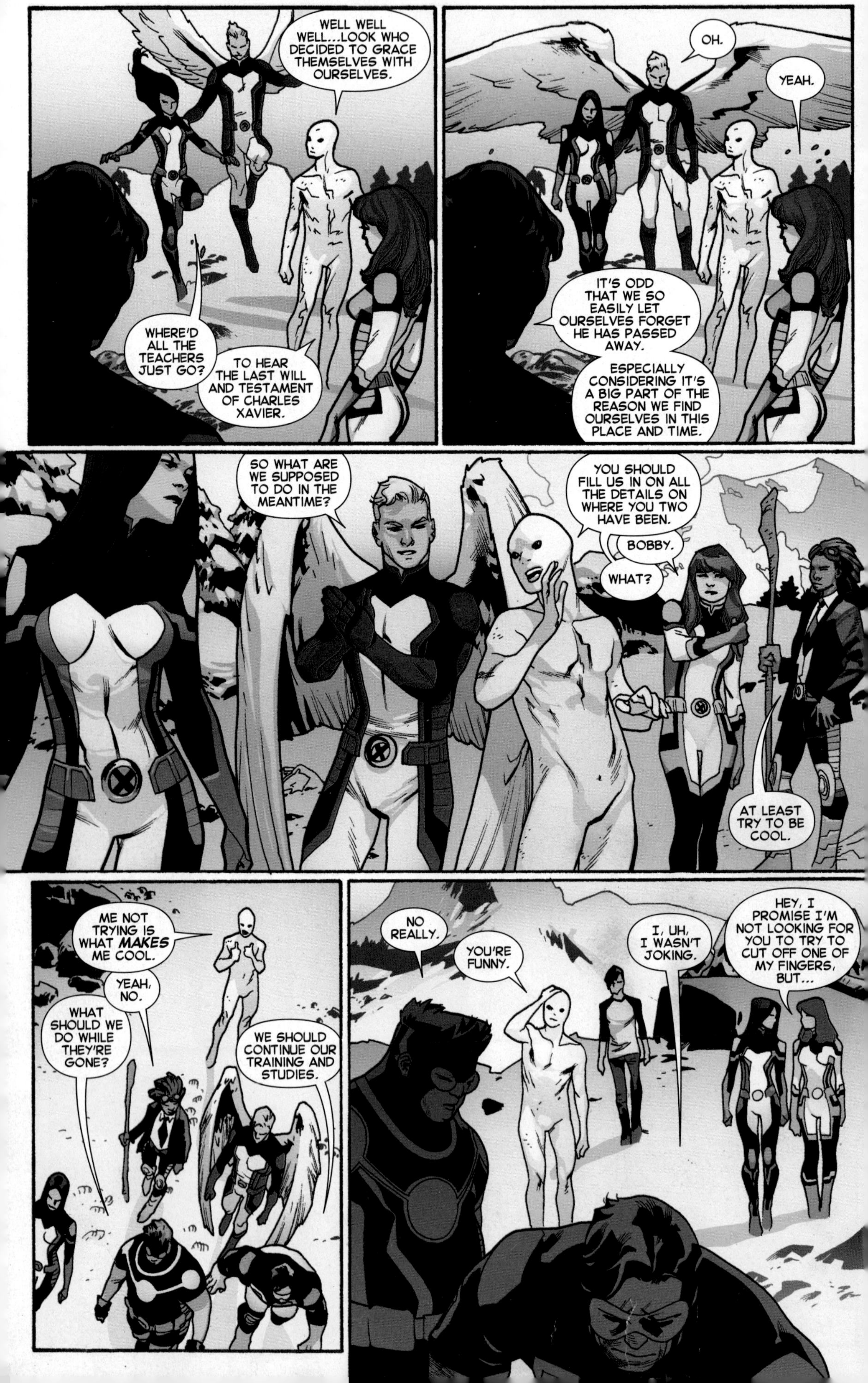
WELL WELL WELL...LOOK WHO DECIDED TO GRACE THEMSELVES WITH OURSELVES.
WHERE'D ALL THE TEACHERS JUST GO?
TO HEAR THE LAST WILL AND TESTAMENT OF CHARLES XAVIER.
OH.
YEAH.
IT'S ODD THAT WE SO EASILY LET OURSELVES FORGET HE HAS PASSED AWAY.
ESPECIALLY CONSIDERING IT'S A BIG PART OF THE REASON WE FIND OURSELVES IN THIS PLACE AND TIME.
SO WHAT ARE WE SUPPOSED TO DO IN THE MEANTIME?
YOU SHOULD FILL US IN ON ALL THE DETAILS ON WHERE YOU TWO HAVE BEEN.
BOBBY.
WHAT?
AT LEAST TRY TO BE COOL.
ME NOT TRYING IS WHAT *MAKES* ME COOL.
YEAH, NO.
WHAT SHOULD WE DO WHILE THEY'RE GONE?
WE SHOULD CONTINUE OUR TRAINING AND STUDIES.
NO REALLY.
YOU'RE FUNNY.
I, UH, I WASN'T JOKING.
HEY, I PROMISE I'M NOT LOOKING FOR YOU TO TRY TO CUT OFF ONE OF MY FINGERS, BUT...

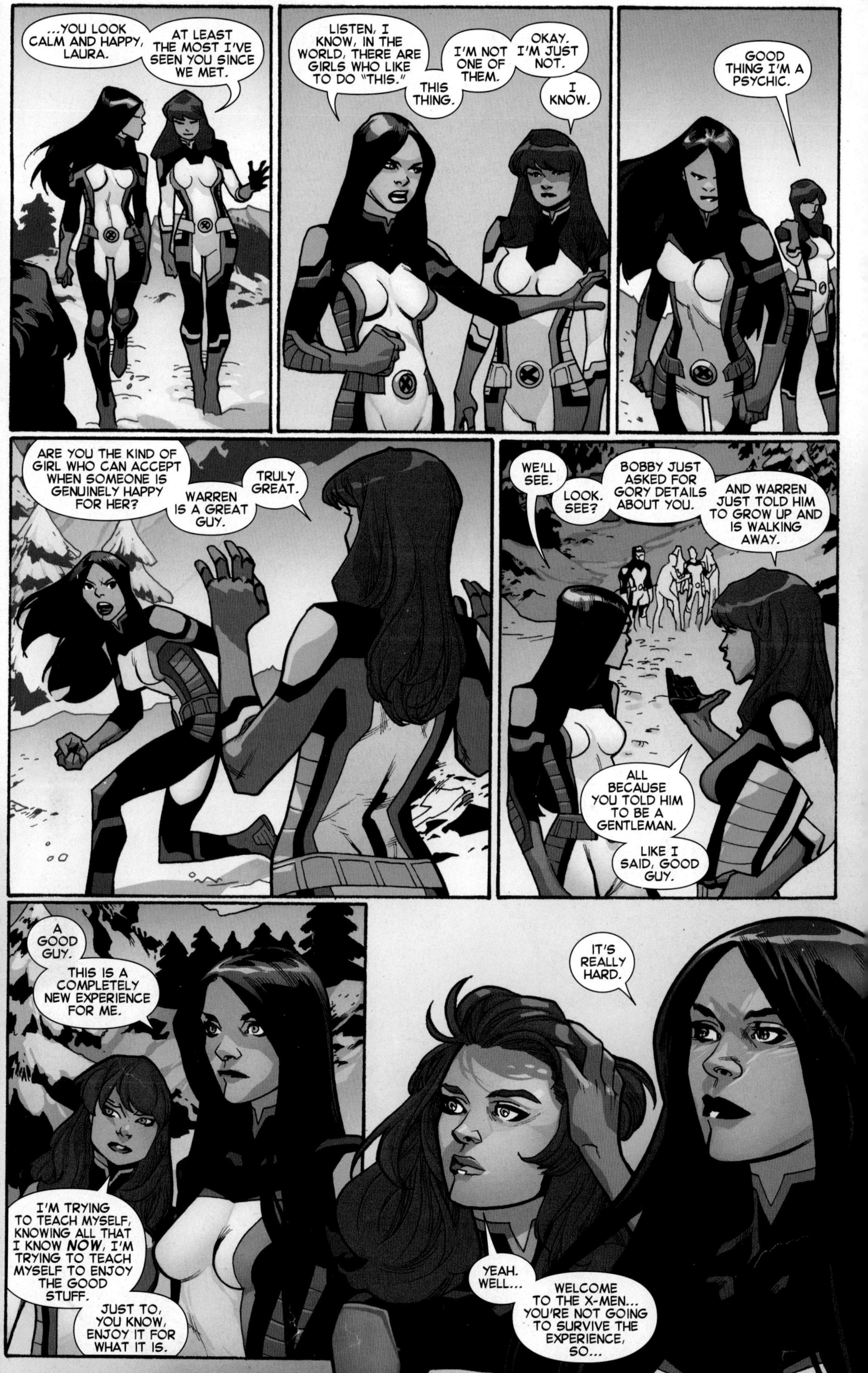
...YOU LOOK CALM AND HAPPY, LAURA.
AT LEAST THE MOST I'VE SEEN YOU SINCE WE MET.
LISTEN, I KNOW, IN THE WORLD, THERE ARE GIRLS WHO LIKE TO DO "THIS."
THIS THING.
I'M NOT ONE OF THEM.
OKAY. I'M JUST NOT.
I KNOW.
GOOD THING I'M A PSYCHIC.
ARE YOU THE KIND OF GIRL WHO CAN ACCEPT WHEN SOMEONE IS GENUINELY HAPPY FOR HER?
WARREN IS A GREAT GUY.
TRULY GREAT.
WE'LL SEE.
LOOK. SEE?
BOBBY JUST ASKED FOR GORY DETAILS ABOUT YOU.
AND WARREN JUST TOLD HIM TO GROW UP AND IS WALKING AWAY.
ALL BECAUSE YOU TOLD HIM TO BE A GENTLEMAN.
LIKE I SAID, GOOD GUY.
A GOOD GUY.
THIS IS A COMPLETELY NEW EXPERIENCE FOR ME.
I'M TRYING TO TEACH MYSELF, KNOWING ALL THAT I KNOW *NOW*, I'M TRYING TO TEACH MYSELF TO ENJOY THE GOOD STUFF.
JUST TO, YOU KNOW, ENJOY IT FOR WHAT IT IS.
IT'S REALLY HARD.
YEAH. WELL...
WELCOME TO THE X-MEN... YOU'RE NOT GOING TO SURVIVE THE EXPERIENCE, SO...

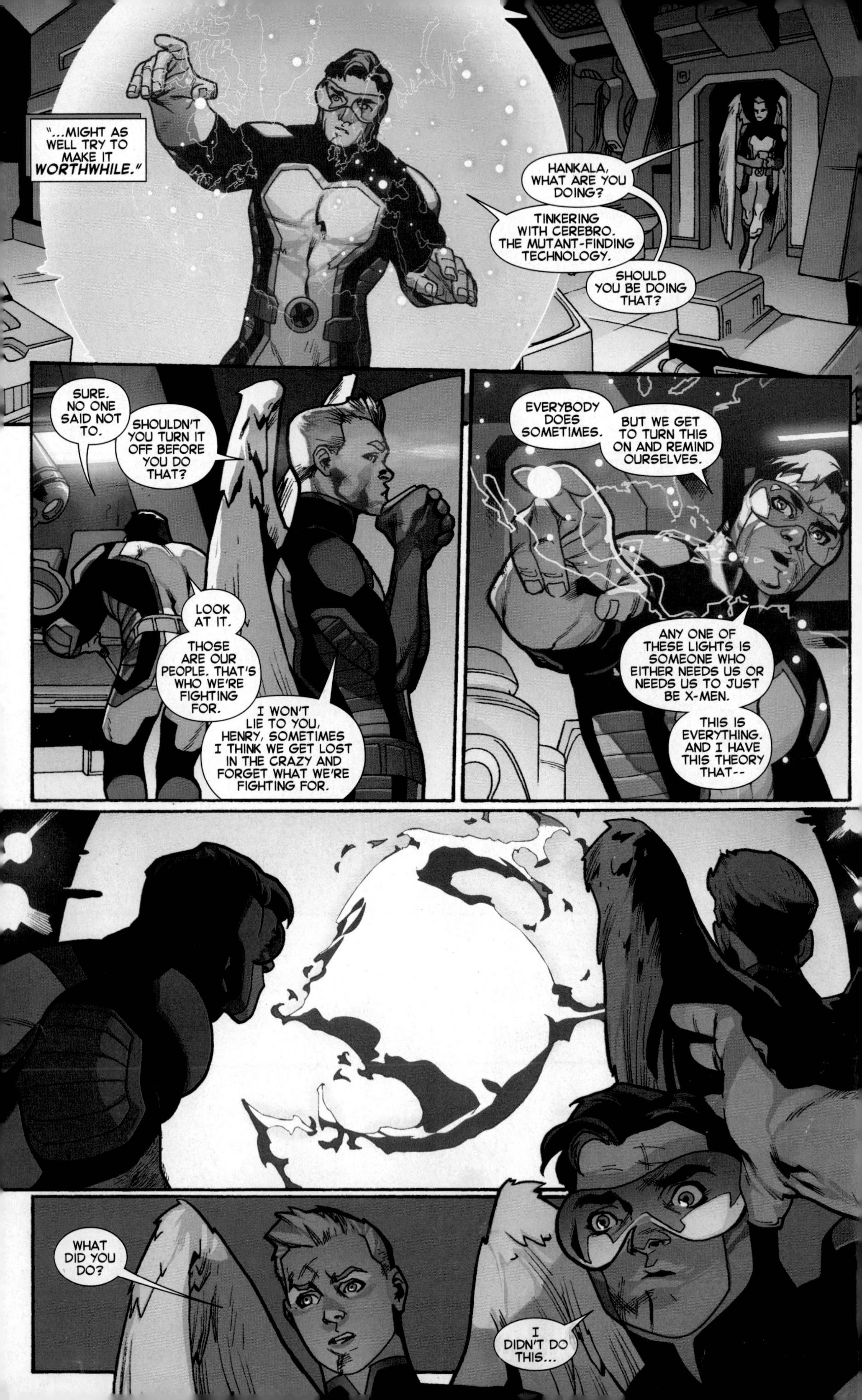
"...MIGHT AS WELL TRY TO MAKE IT *WORTHWHILE.*"
HANKALA, WHAT ARE YOU DOING?
TINKERING WITH CEREBRO. THE MUTANT-FINDING TECHNOLOGY.
SHOULD YOU BE DOING THAT?
SURE. NO ONE SAID NOT TO.
SHOULDN'T YOU TURN IT OFF BEFORE YOU DO THAT?
LOOK AT IT.
THOSE ARE OUR PEOPLE. THAT'S WHO WE'RE FIGHTING FOR.
I WON'T LIE TO YOU, HENRY, SOMETIMES I THINK WE GET LOST IN THE CRAZY AND FORGET WHAT WE'RE FIGHTING FOR.
EVERYBODY DOES SOMETIMES.
BUT WE GET TO TURN THIS ON AND REMIND OURSELVES.
ANY ONE OF THESE LIGHTS IS SOMEONE WHO EITHER NEEDS US OR NEEDS US TO JUST BE X-MEN.
THIS IS EVERYTHING. AND I HAVE THIS THEORY THAT--
WHAT DID YOU DO?
I DIDN'T DO THIS...

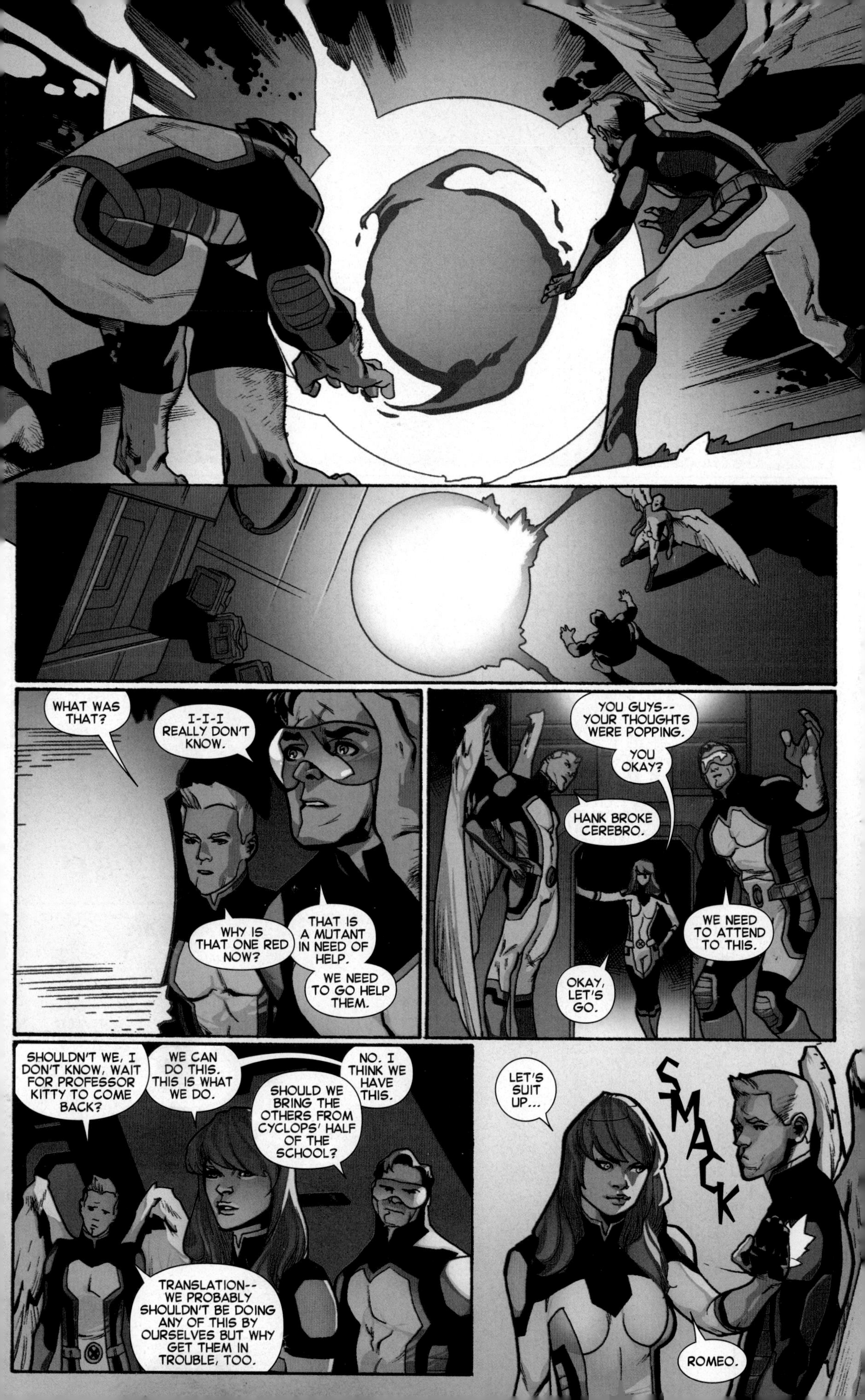

WHAT WAS THAT?
I-I-I REALLY DON'T KNOW.
WHY IS THAT ONE RED NOW?
THAT IS A MUTANT IN NEED OF HELP.
WE NEED TO GO HELP THEM.
YOU GUYS-- YOUR THOUGHTS WERE POPPING.
YOU OKAY?
HANK BROKE CEREBRO.
WE NEED TO ATTEND TO THIS.
OKAY, LET'S GO.
SHOULDN'T WE, I DON'T KNOW, WAIT FOR PROFESSOR KITTY TO COME BACK?
WE CAN DO THIS. THIS IS WHAT WE DO.
NO. I THINK WE HAVE THIS.
SHOULD WE BRING THE OTHERS FROM CYCLOPS' HALF OF THE SCHOOL?
TRANSLATION-- WE PROBABLY SHOULDN'T BE DOING ANY OF THIS BY OURSELVES BUT WHY GET THEM IN TROUBLE, TOO.
LET'S SUIT UP...
SMACK
ROMEO.

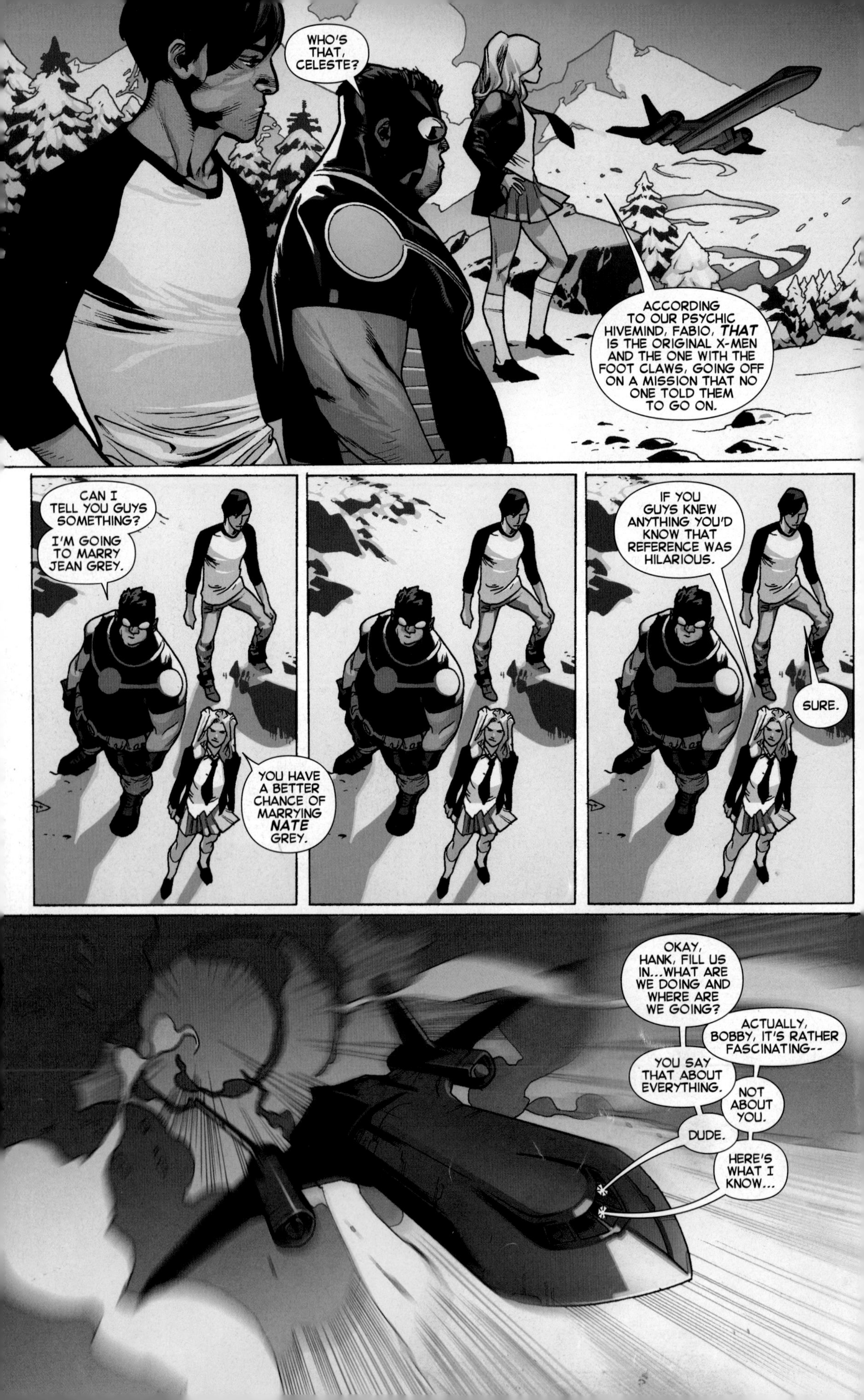
WHO'S THAT, CELESTE?
ACCORDING TO OUR PSYCHIC HIVEMIND, FABIO, THAT IS THE ORIGINAL X-MEN AND THE ONE WITH THE FOOT CLAWS, GOING OFF ON A MISSION THAT NO ONE TOLD THEM TO GO ON.
CAN I TELL YOU GUYS SOMETHING?
I'M GOING TO MARRY JEAN GREY.
YOU HAVE A BETTER CHANCE OF MARRYING NATE GREY.
IF YOU GUYS KNEW ANYTHING YOU'D KNOW THAT REFERENCE WAS HILARIOUS.
SURE.
OKAY, HANK, FILL US IN...WHAT ARE WE DOING AND WHERE ARE WE GOING?
ACTUALLY, BOBBY, IT'S RATHER FASCINATING--
YOU SAY THAT ABOUT EVERYTHING.
NOT ABOUT YOU.
DUDE.
HERE'S WHAT I KNOW...

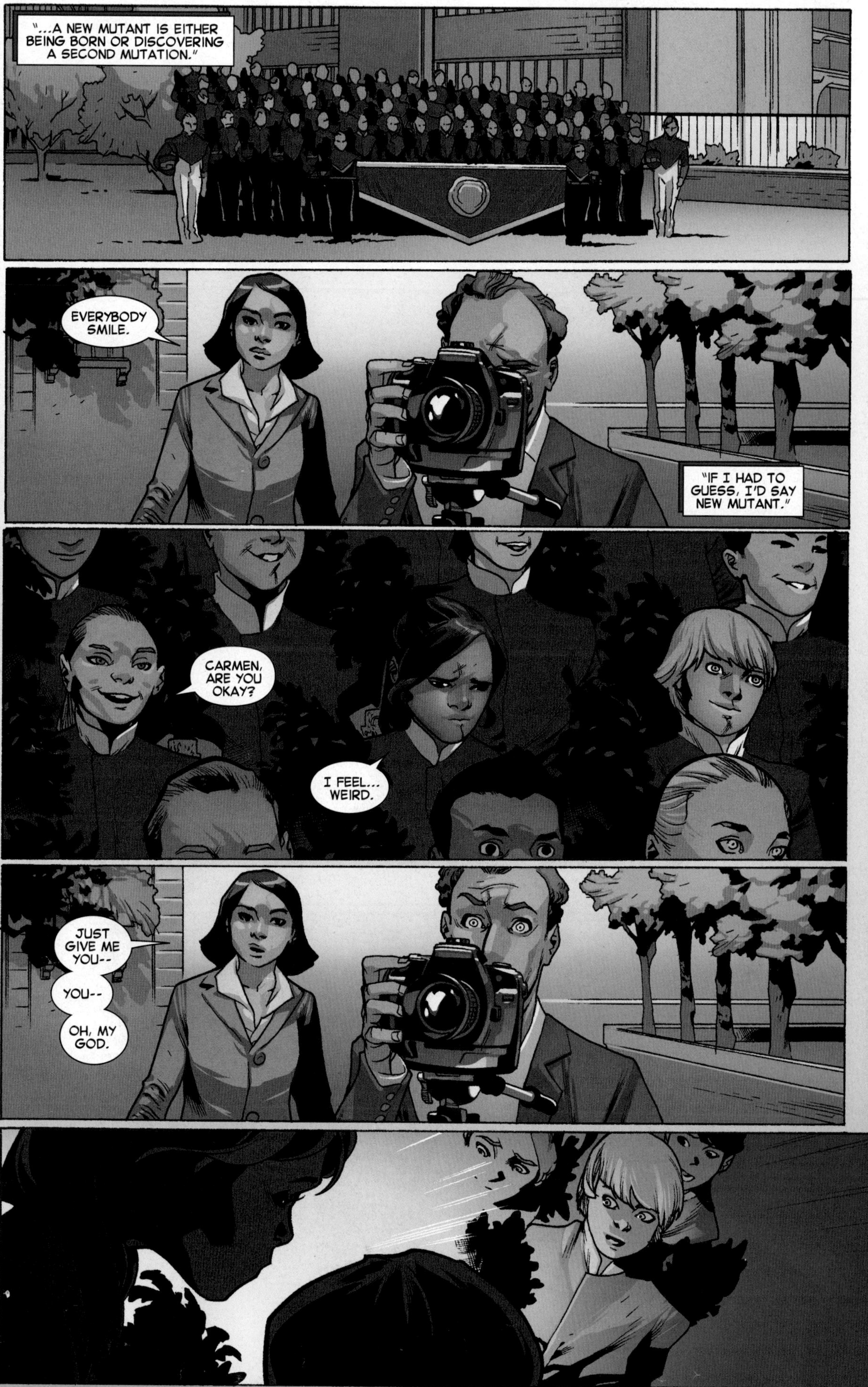
"...A NEW MUTANT IS EITHER BEING BORN OR DISCOVERING A SECOND MUTATION."
EVERYBODY SMILE.
"IF I HAD TO GUESS, I'D SAY NEW MUTANT."
CARMEN, ARE YOU OKAY?
I FEEL... WEIRD.
JUST GIVE ME YOU--
YOU--
OH, MY GOD.

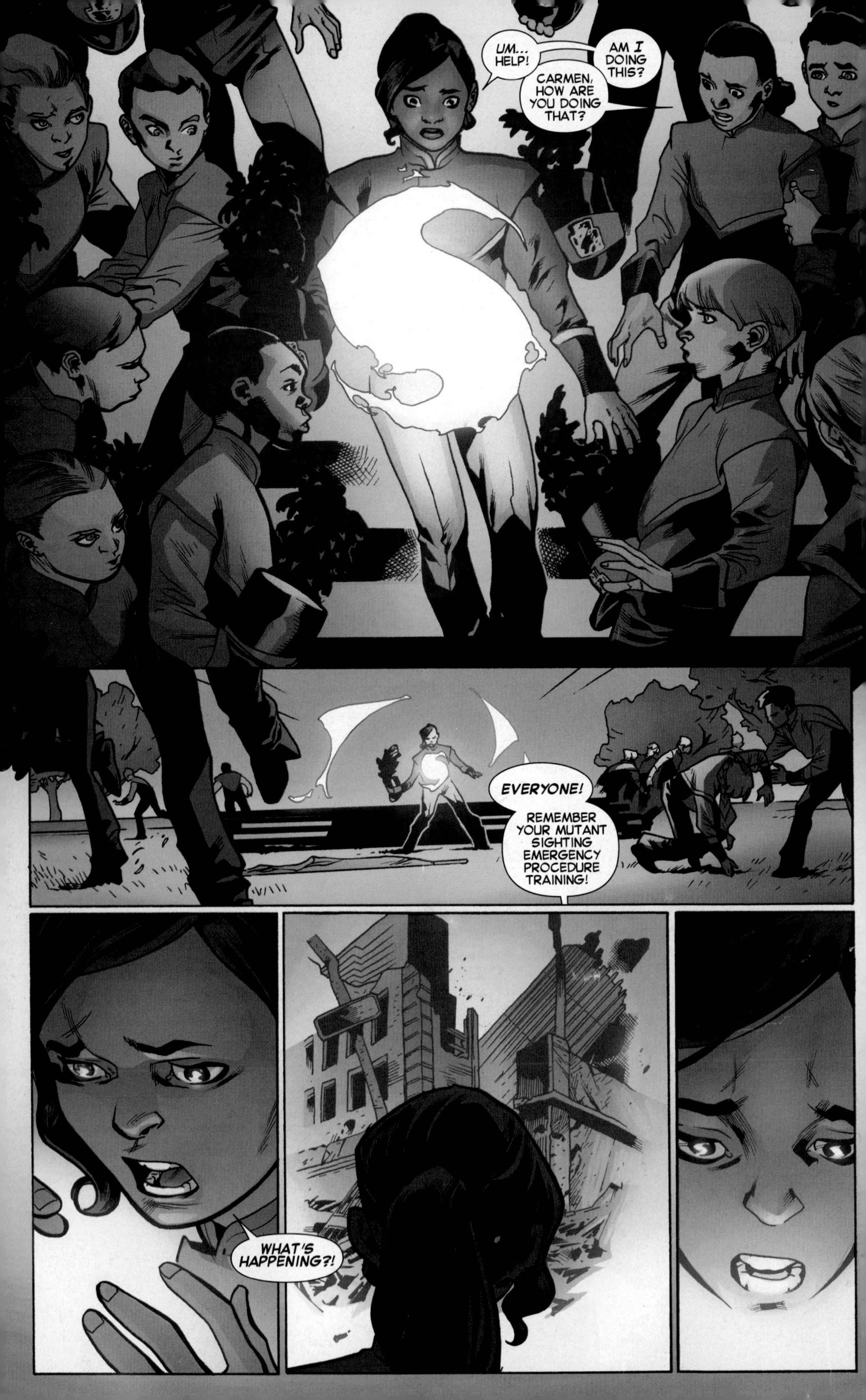
UM... HELP!
AM I DOING THIS?
CARMEN, HOW ARE YOU DOING THAT?
EVERYONE!
REMEMBER YOUR MUTANT SIGHTING EMERGENCY PROCEDURE TRAINING!
WHAT'S HAPPENING?!

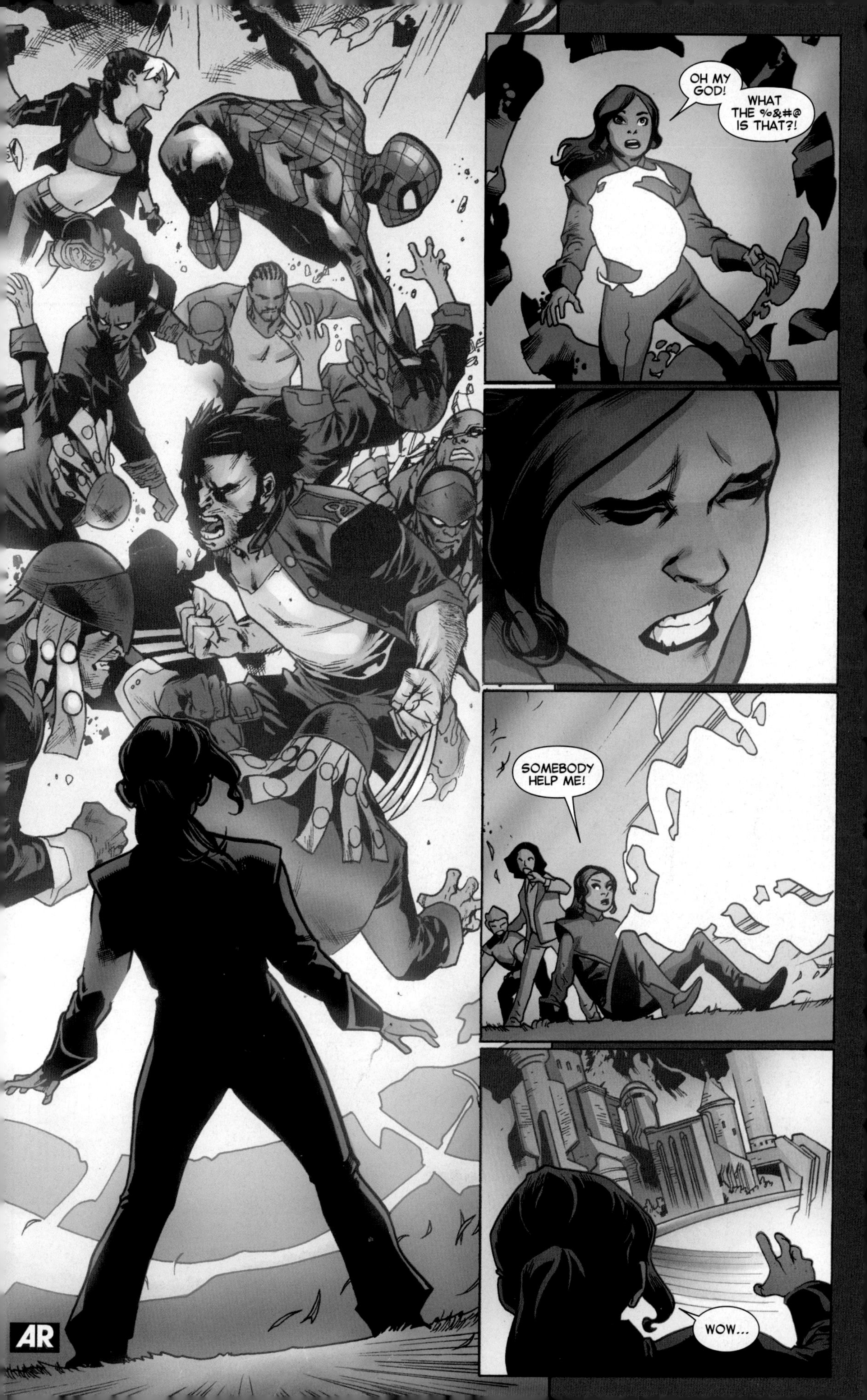
OH MY GOD!
WHAT THE %&#@ IS THAT?!
SOMEBODY HELP ME!
WOW...
AR

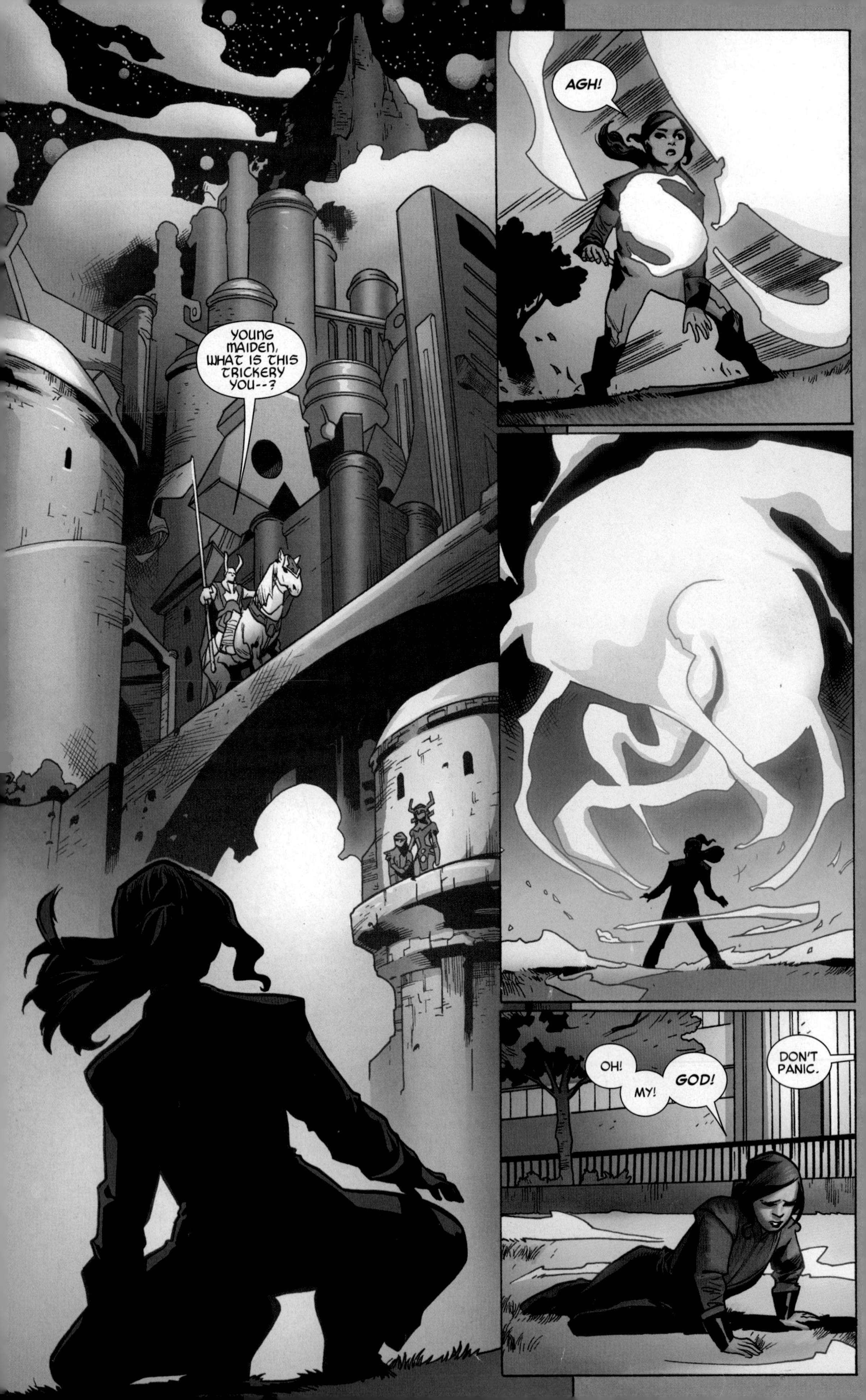
YOUNG MAIDEN, WHAT IS THIS TRICKERY YOU--?
AGH!
OH!
MY!
GOD!
DON'T PANIC.

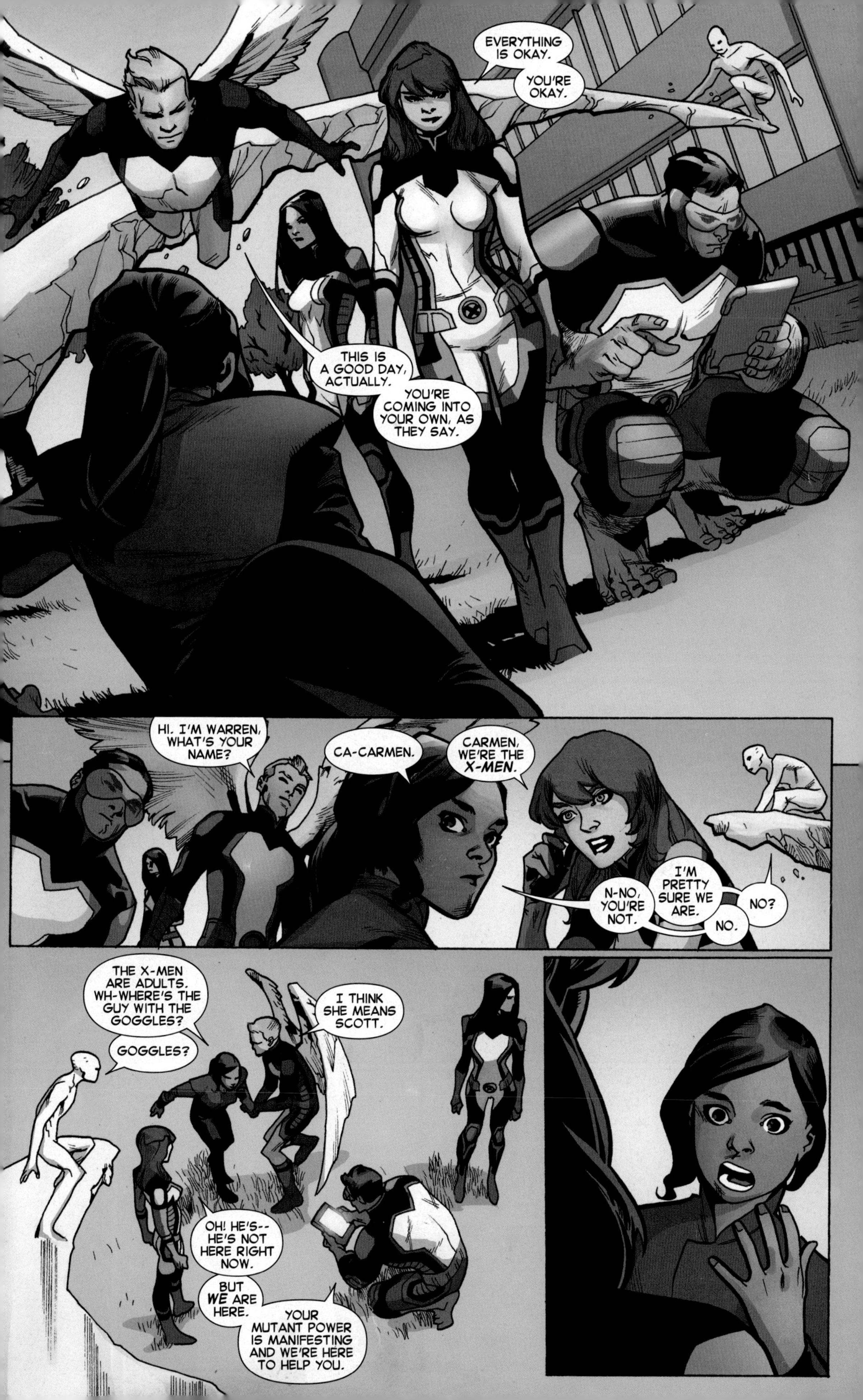
EVERYTHING IS OKAY.
YOU'RE OKAY.
THIS IS A GOOD DAY, ACTUALLY.
YOU'RE COMING INTO YOUR OWN, AS THEY SAY.
HI. I'M WARREN, WHAT'S YOUR NAME?
CA-CARMEN.
CARMEN, WE'RE THE *X-MEN*.
N-NO, YOU'RE NOT.
I'M PRETTY SURE WE ARE.
NO?
NO.
THE X-MEN ARE ADULTS. WH-WHERE'S THE GUY WITH THE GOGGLES?
GOGGLES?
I THINK SHE MEANS SCOTT.
OH! HE'S-- HE'S NOT HERE RIGHT NOW.
BUT *WE* ARE HERE.
YOUR MUTANT POWER IS MANIFESTING AND WE'RE HERE TO HELP YOU.

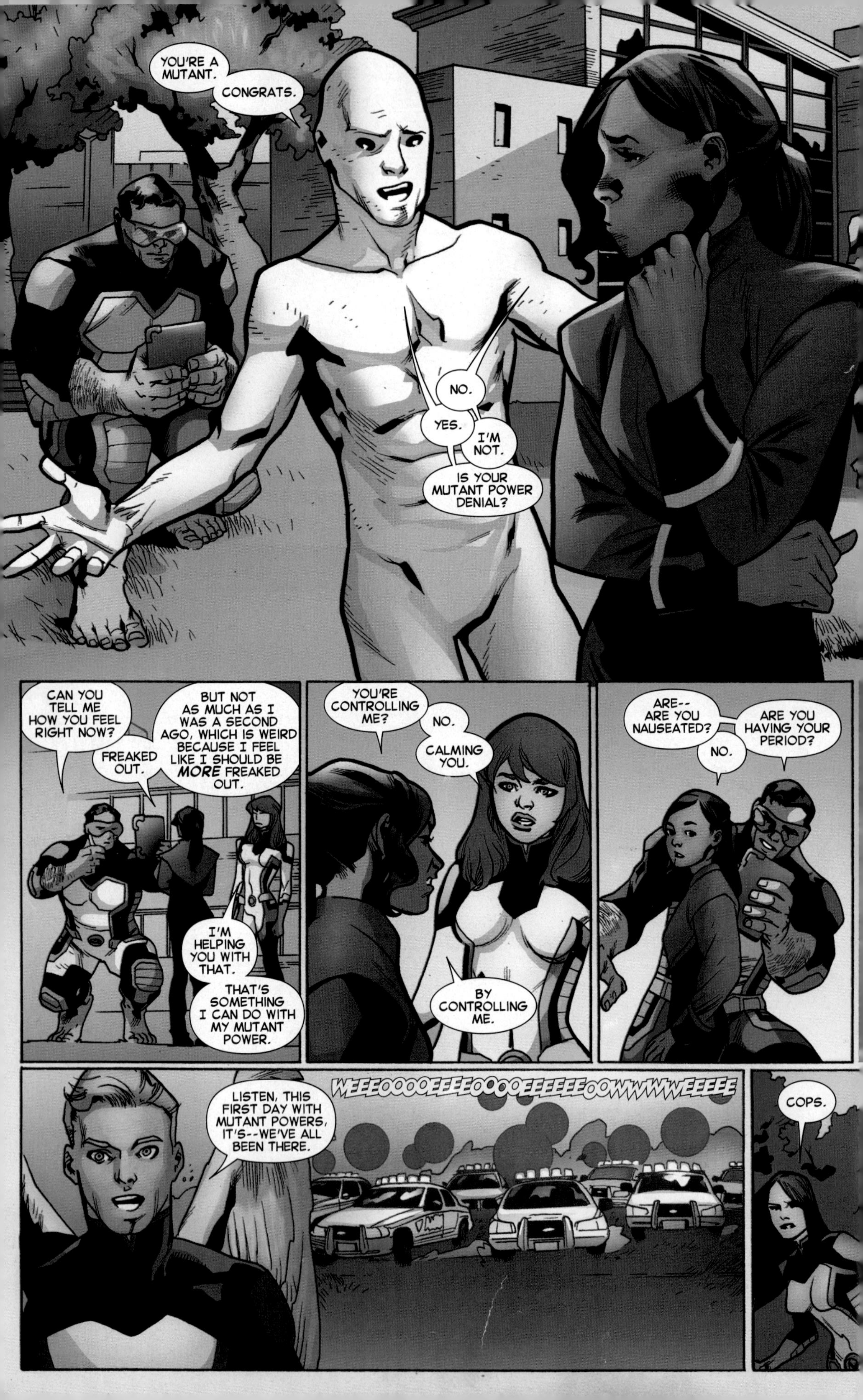
YOU'RE A MUTANT.
CONGRATS.
NO.
YES.
I'M NOT.
IS YOUR MUTANT POWER DENIAL?
CAN YOU TELL ME HOW YOU FEEL RIGHT NOW?
FREAKED OUT.
BUT NOT AS MUCH AS I WAS A SECOND AGO, WHICH IS WEIRD BECAUSE I FEEL LIKE I SHOULD BE *MORE* FREAKED OUT.
I'M HELPING YOU WITH THAT.
THAT'S SOMETHING I CAN DO WITH MY MUTANT POWER.
YOU'RE CONTROLLING ME?
NO.
CALMING YOU.
BY CONTROLLING ME.
ARE-- ARE YOU NAUSEATED?
NO.
ARE YOU HAVING YOUR PERIOD?
LISTEN, THIS FIRST DAY WITH MUTANT POWERS, IT'S--WE'VE ALL BEEN THERE.
WEEEOOOOEEEEOOOOEEEEEEOOWWWWEEEEE
COPS.

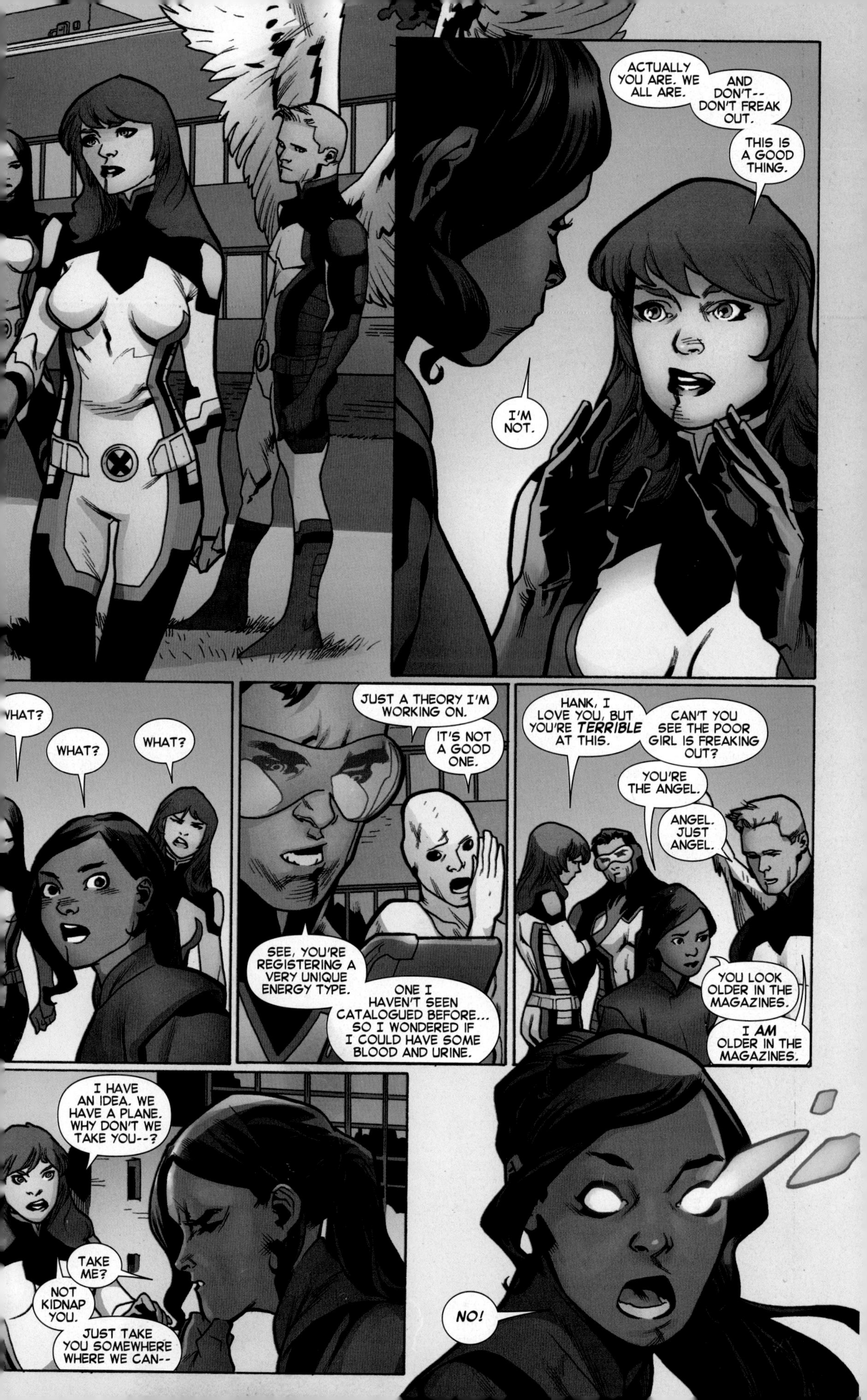
ACTUALLY YOU ARE. WE ALL ARE.
AND DON'T-- DON'T FREAK OUT.
THIS IS A GOOD THING.
I'M NOT.
WHAT?
WHAT?
WHAT?
JUST A THEORY I'M WORKING ON.
IT'S NOT A GOOD ONE.
SEE, YOU'RE REGISTERING A VERY UNIQUE ENERGY TYPE.
ONE I HAVEN'T SEEN CATALOGUED BEFORE... SO I WONDERED IF I COULD HAVE SOME BLOOD AND URINE.
HANK, I LOVE YOU, BUT YOU'RE TERRIBLE AT THIS.
CAN'T YOU SEE THE POOR GIRL IS FREAKING OUT?
YOU'RE THE ANGEL.
ANGEL. JUST ANGEL.
YOU LOOK OLDER IN THE MAGAZINES.
I AM OLDER IN THE MAGAZINES.
I HAVE AN IDEA. WE HAVE A PLANE. WHY DON'T WE TAKE YOU--?
TAKE ME?
NOT KIDNAP YOU.
JUST TAKE YOU SOMEWHERE WHERE WE CAN--
NO!

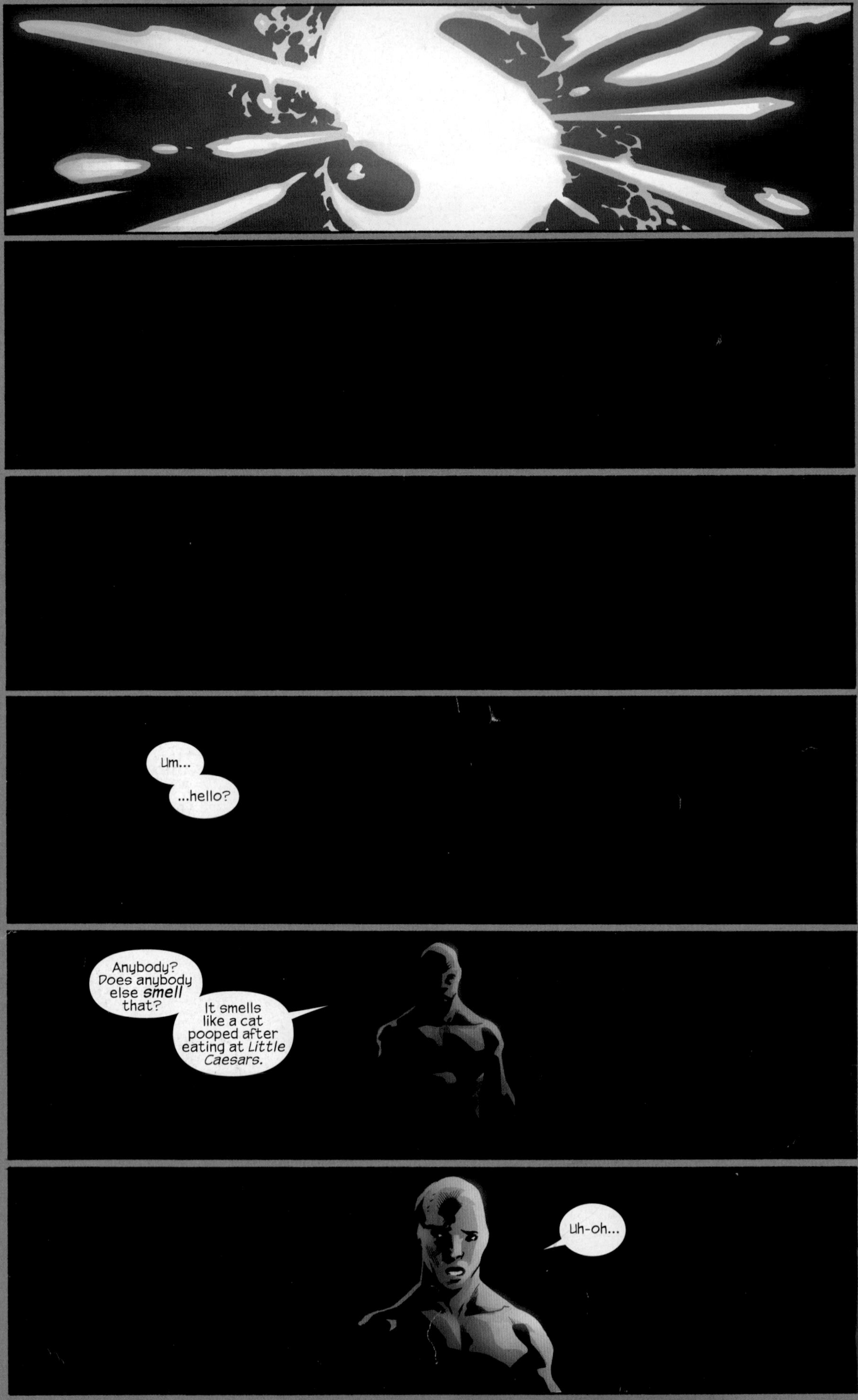
Um...
...hello?
Anybody? Does anybody else smell that?
It smells like a cat pooped after eating at Little Caesars.
Uh-oh...

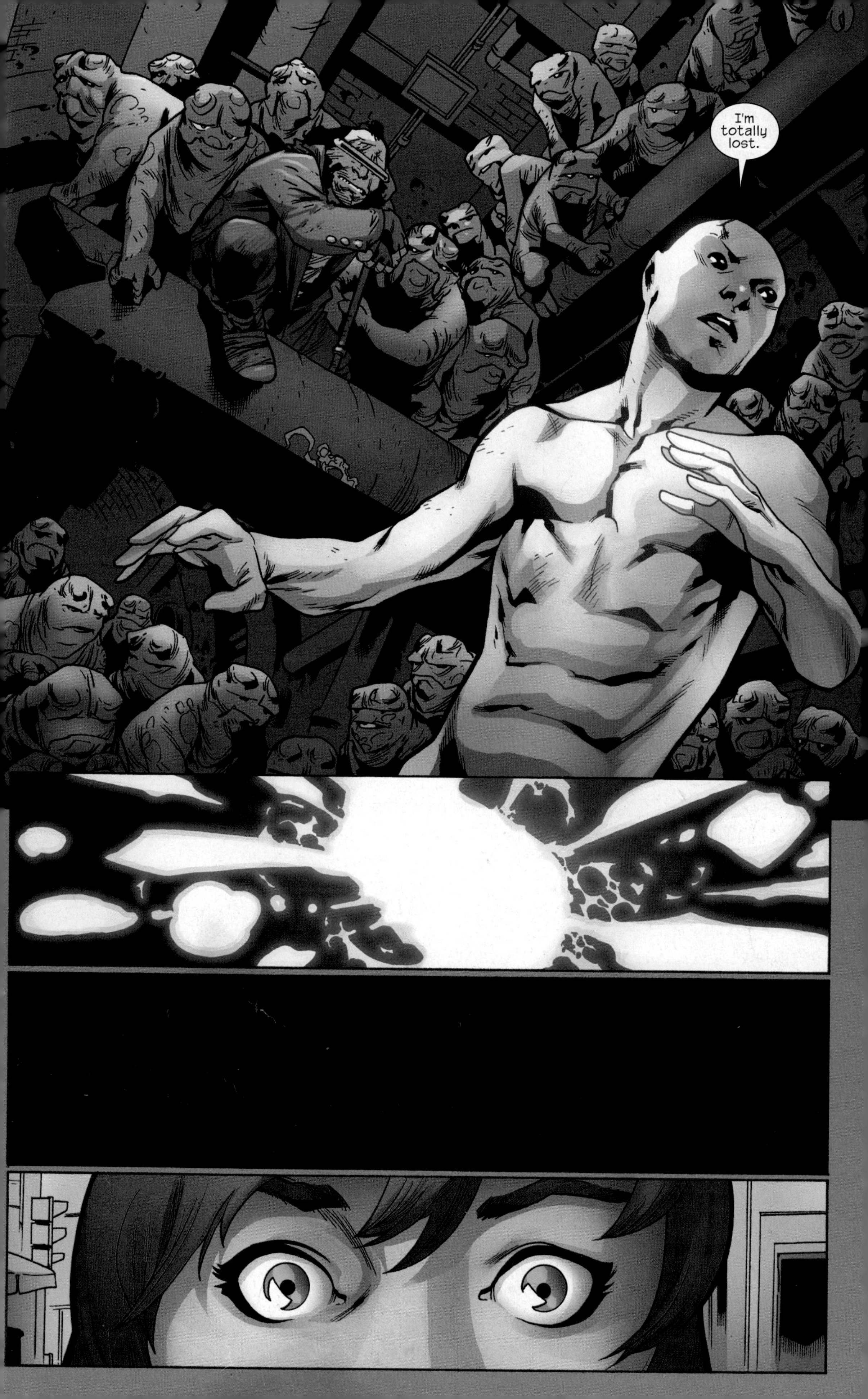
I'm totally lost.

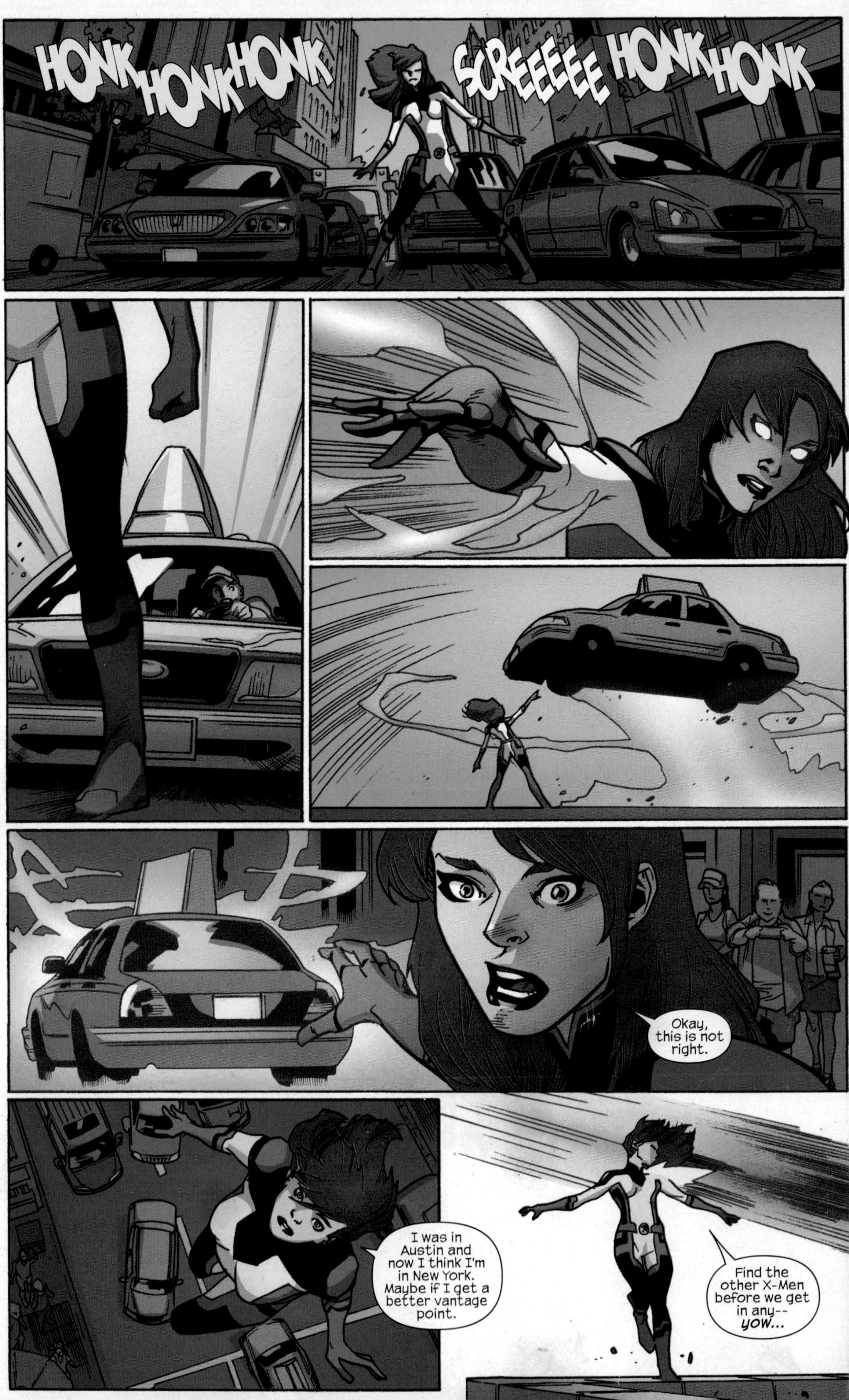
HONK HONK HONK
SCREEEEE HONK HONK
Okay, this is not right.
I was in Austin and now I think I'm in New York. Maybe if I get a better vantage point.
Find the other X-Men before we get in any-- YOW...

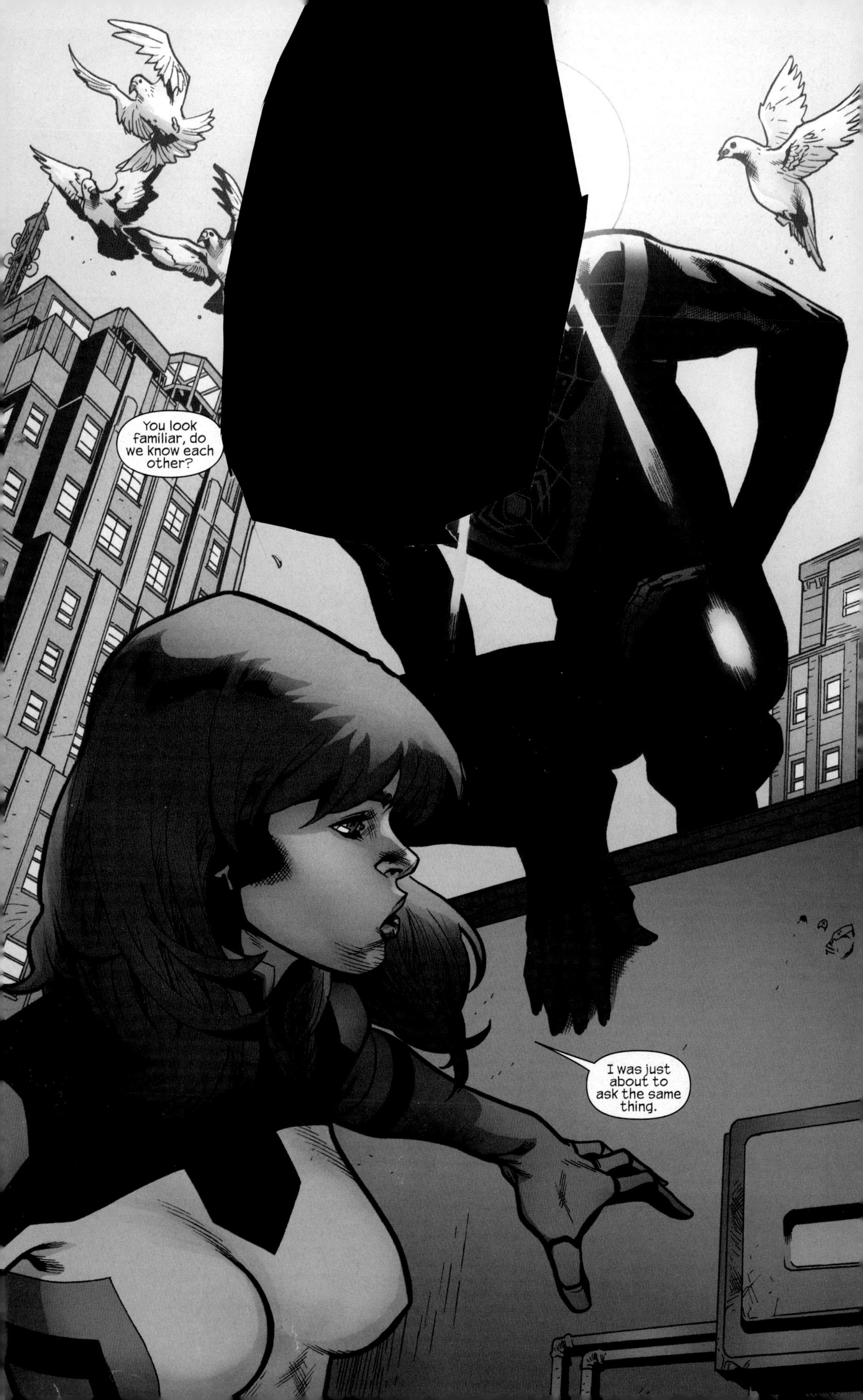
You look familiar, do we know each other?
I was just about to ask the same thing.

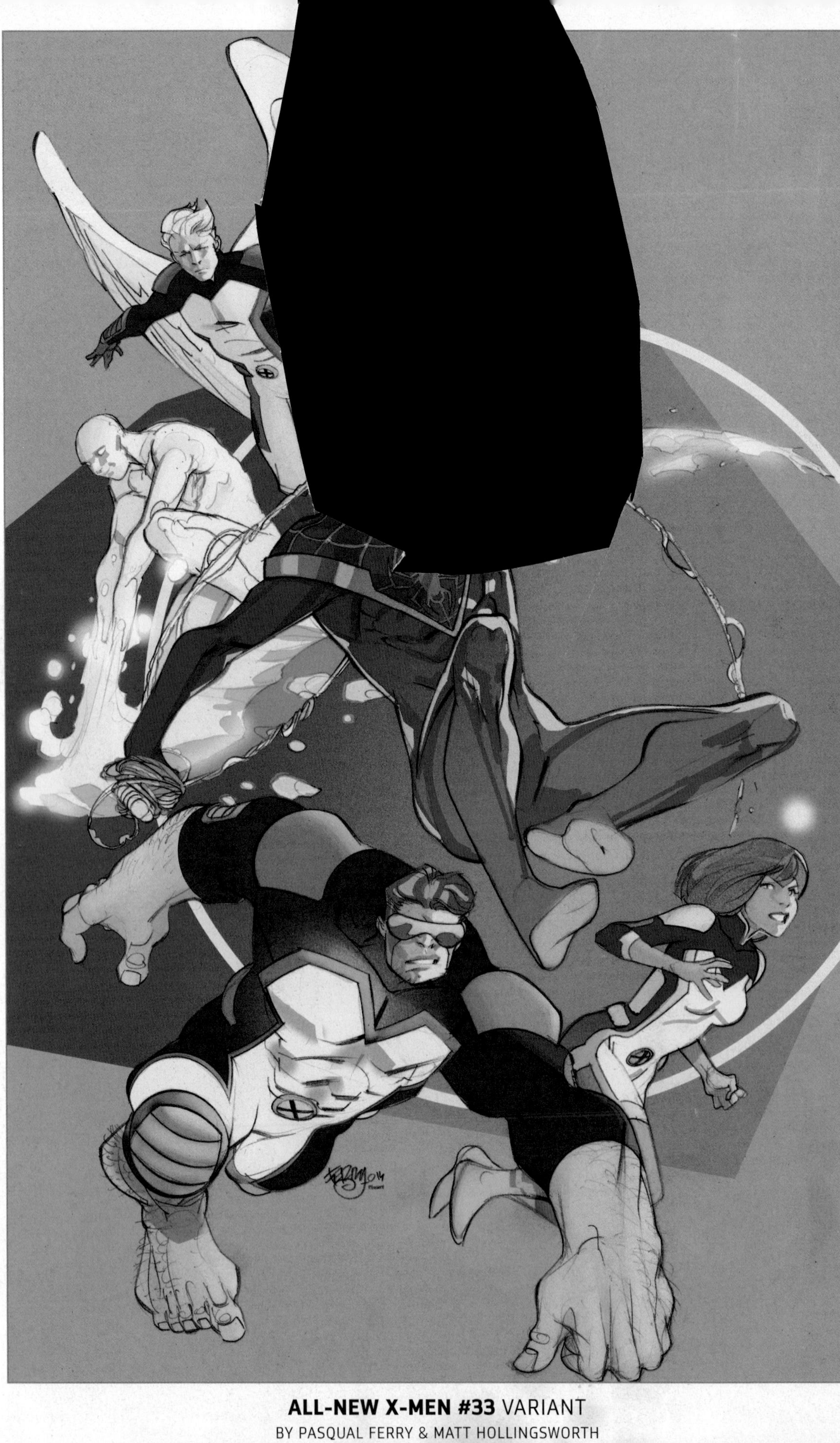

ALL-NEW X-MEN #33 VARIANT

BY PASQUAL FERRY & MATT HOLLINGSWORTH

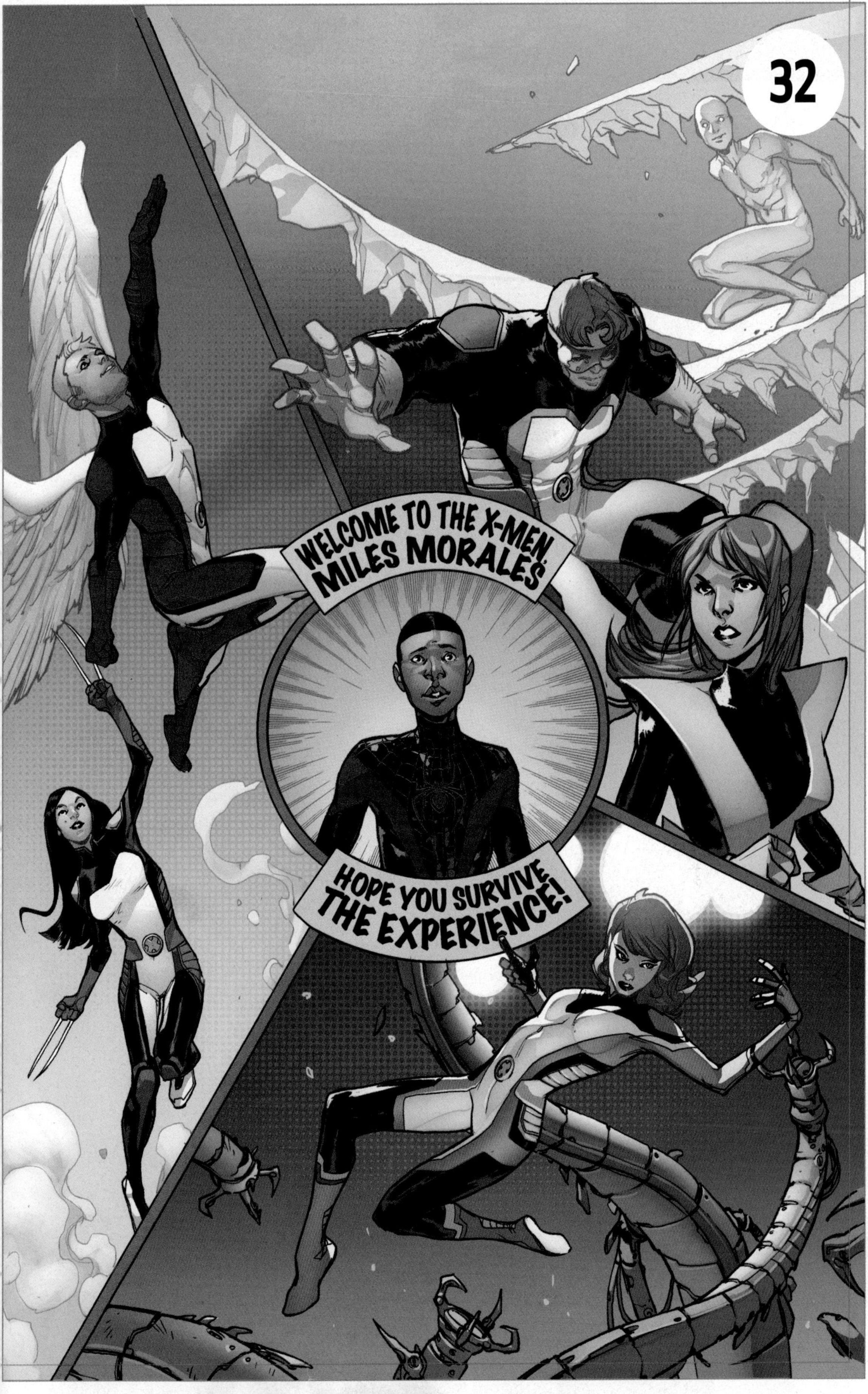
32
WELCOME TO THE X-MEN, MILES MORALES
HOPE YOU SURVIVE THE EXPERIENCE!

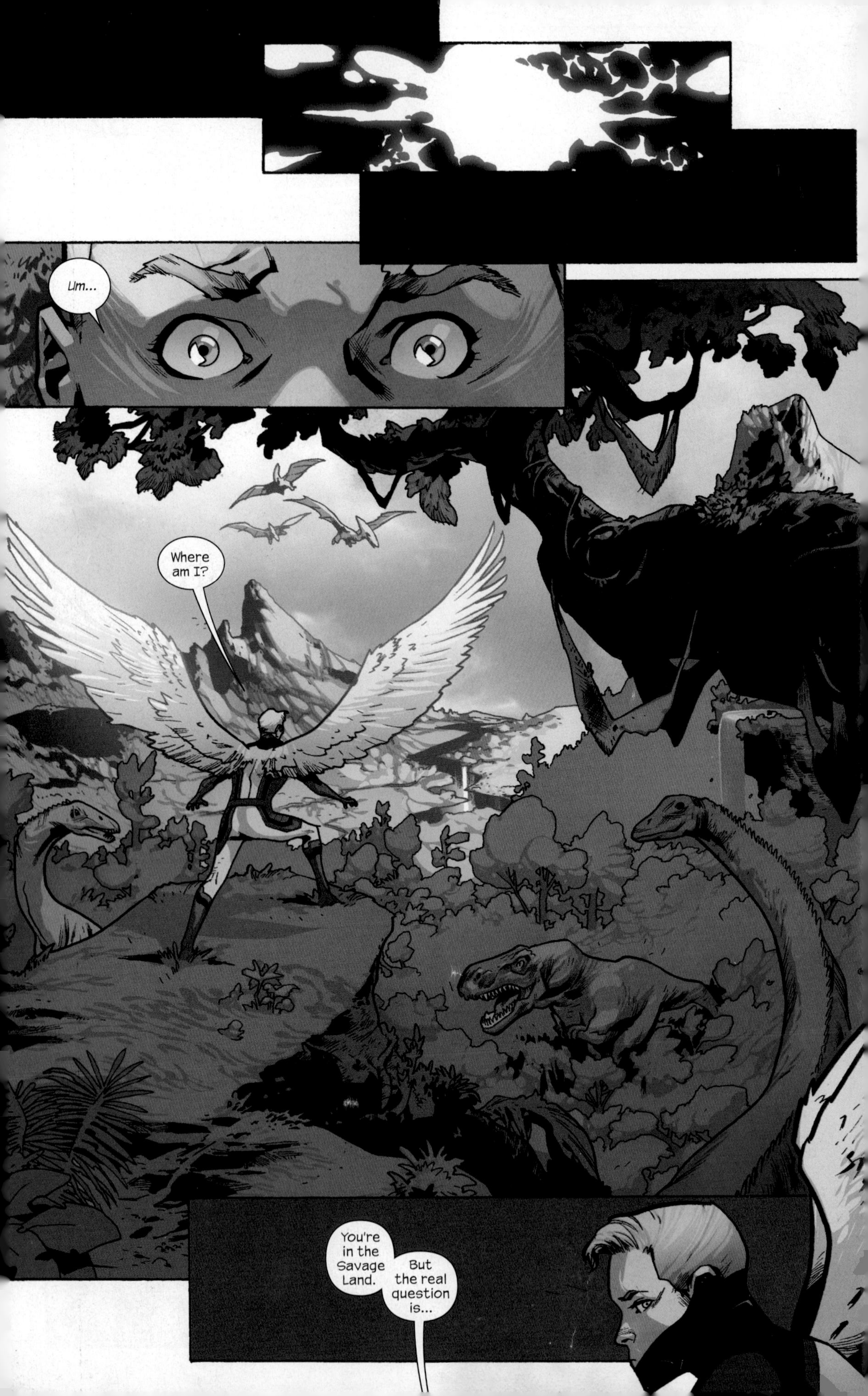
Um...
Where am I?
You're in the Savage Land.
But the real question is...

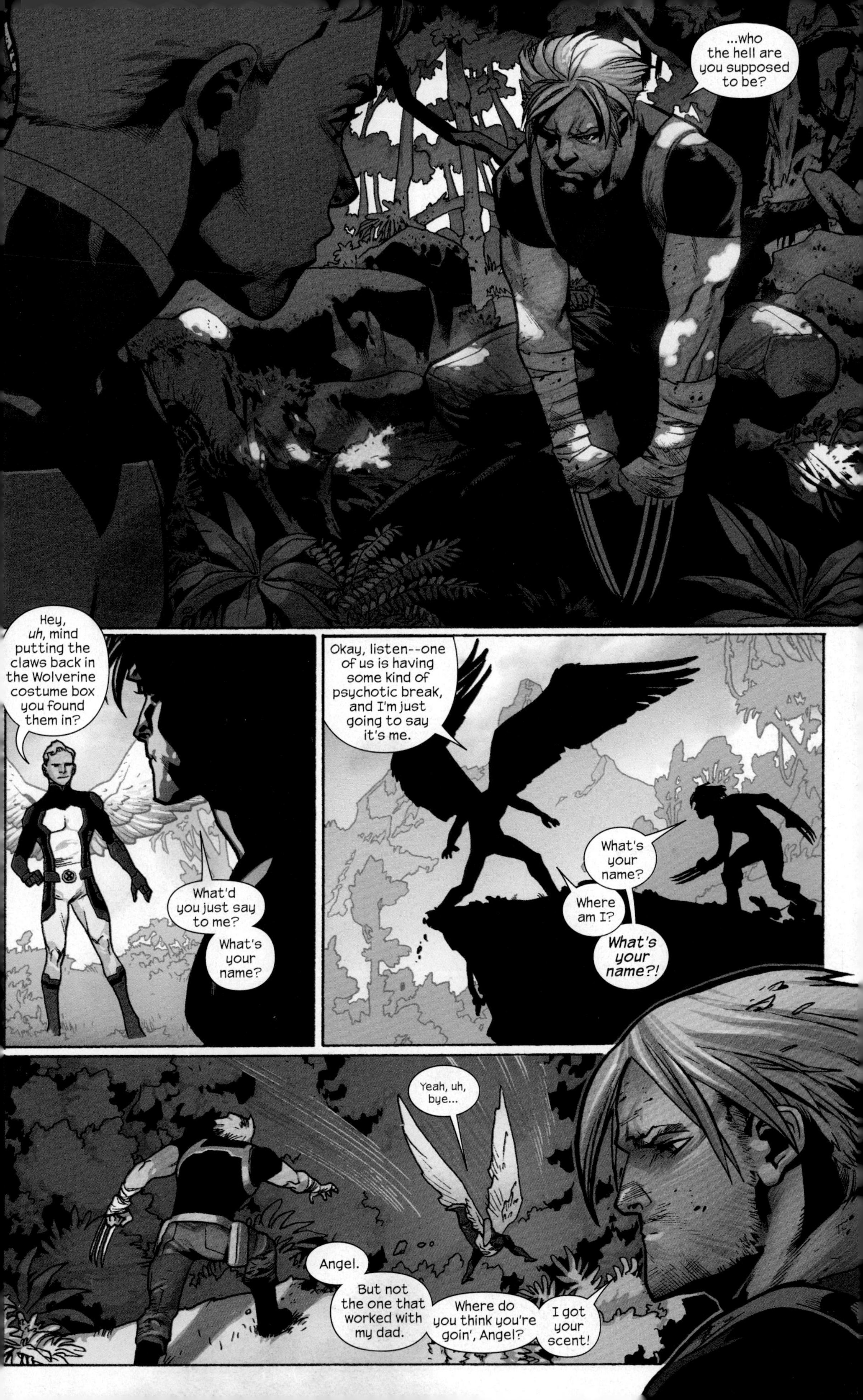
...who the hell are you supposed to be?
Hey, *uh*, mind putting the claws back in the Wolverine costume box you found them in?
What'd you just say to me?
What's your name?
Okay, listen--one of us is having some kind of psychotic break, and I'm just going to say it's me.
What's your name?
Where am I?
What's your name?!
Yeah, uh, bye...
Angel.
But not the one that worked with my dad.
Where do you think you're goin', Angel?
I got your scent!

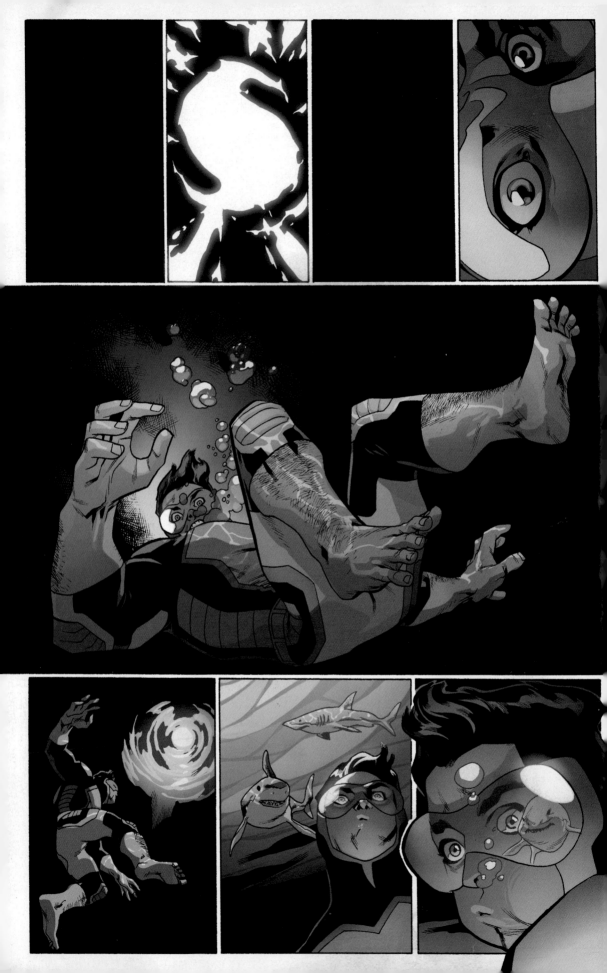

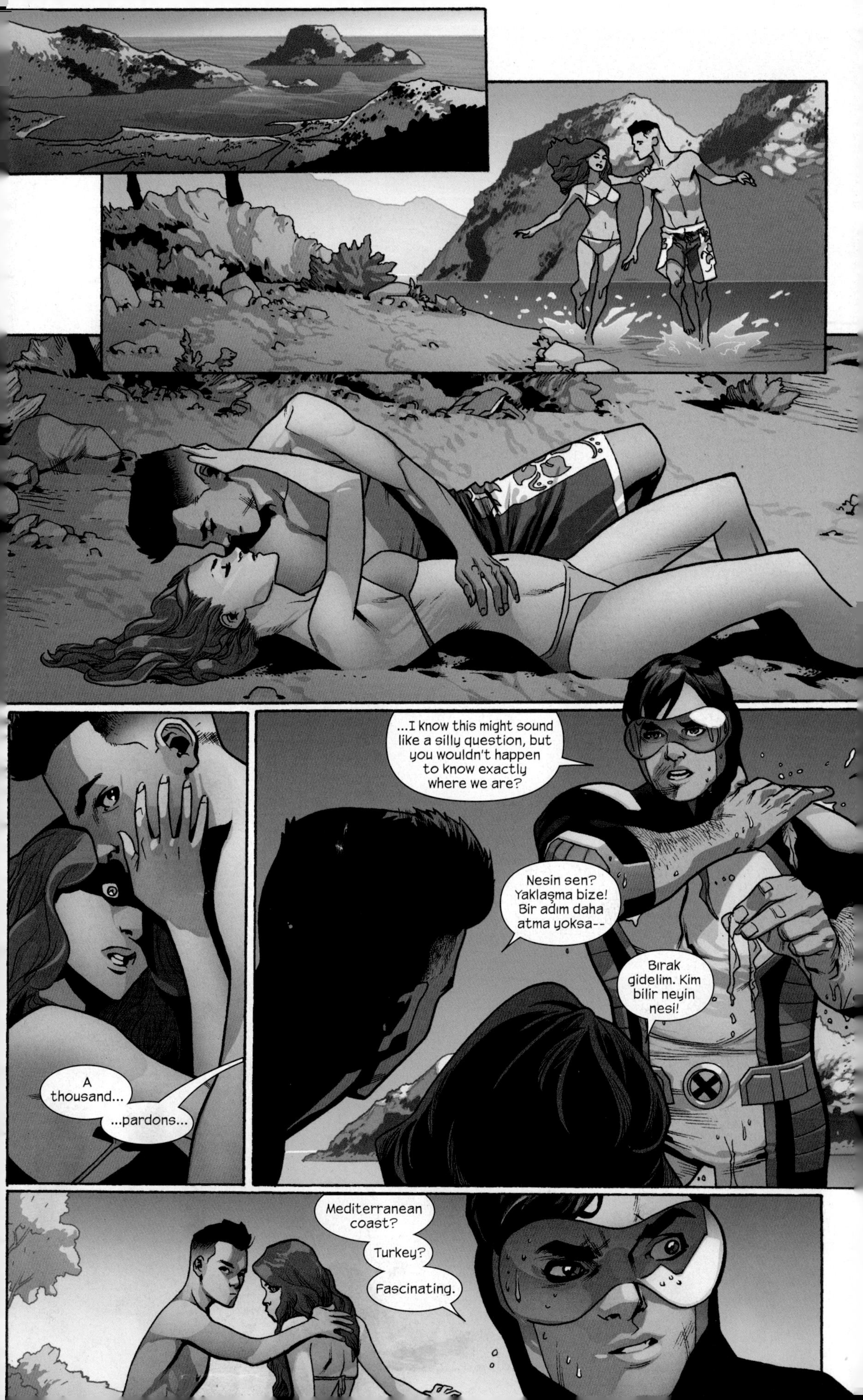

...I know this might sound like a silly question, but you wouldn't happen to know exactly where we are?
A thousand...
...pardons...
Nesin sen? Yaklaşma bize! Bir adım daha atma yoksa--
Bırak gidelim. Kim bilir neyin nesi!
Mediterranean coast?
Turkey?
Fascinating.

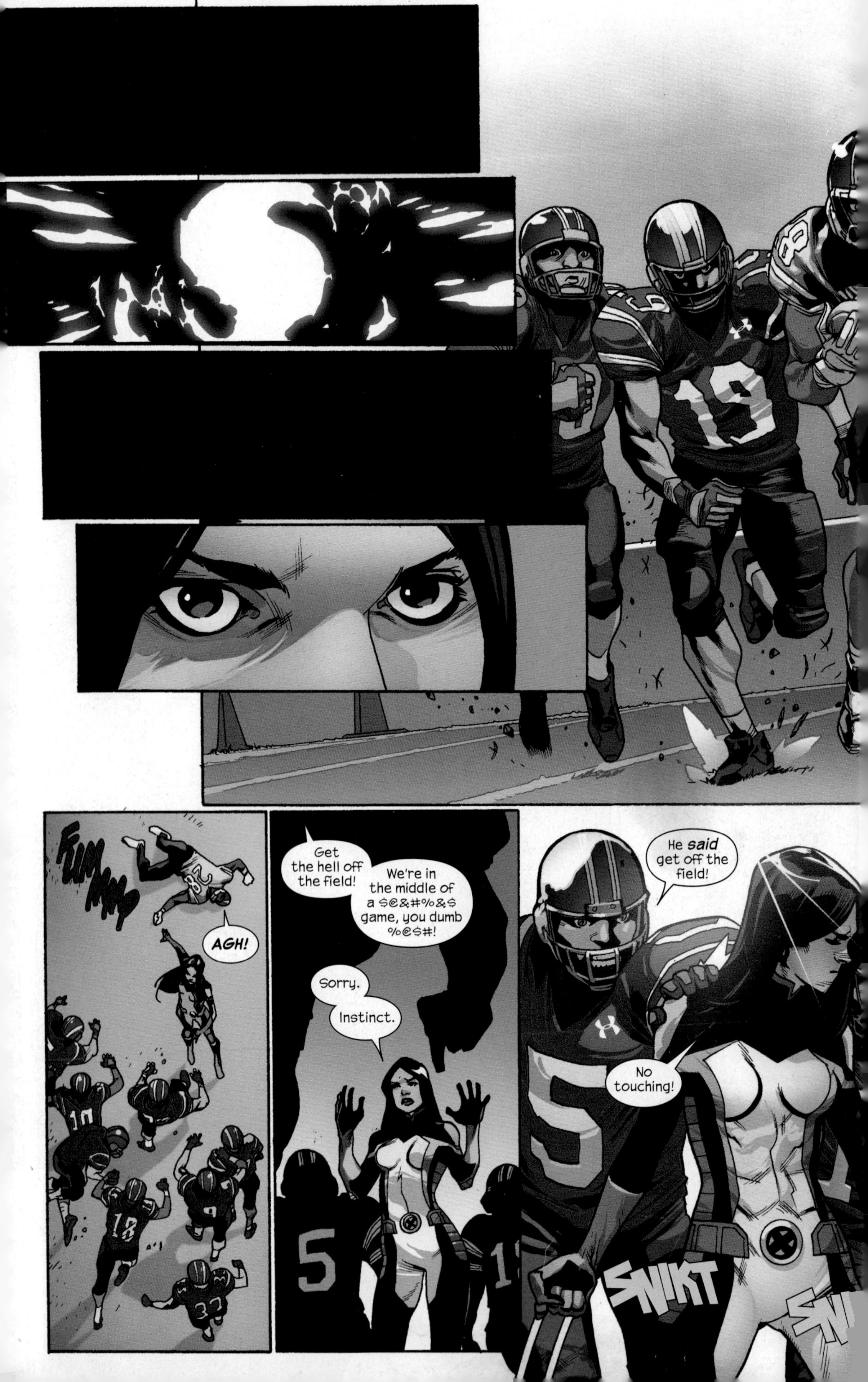
AGH!
Get the hell off the field!
We're in the middle of a $@&#%&$ game, you dumb %@$#!
Sorry.
Instinct.
He *said* get off the field!
No touching!
SNIKT

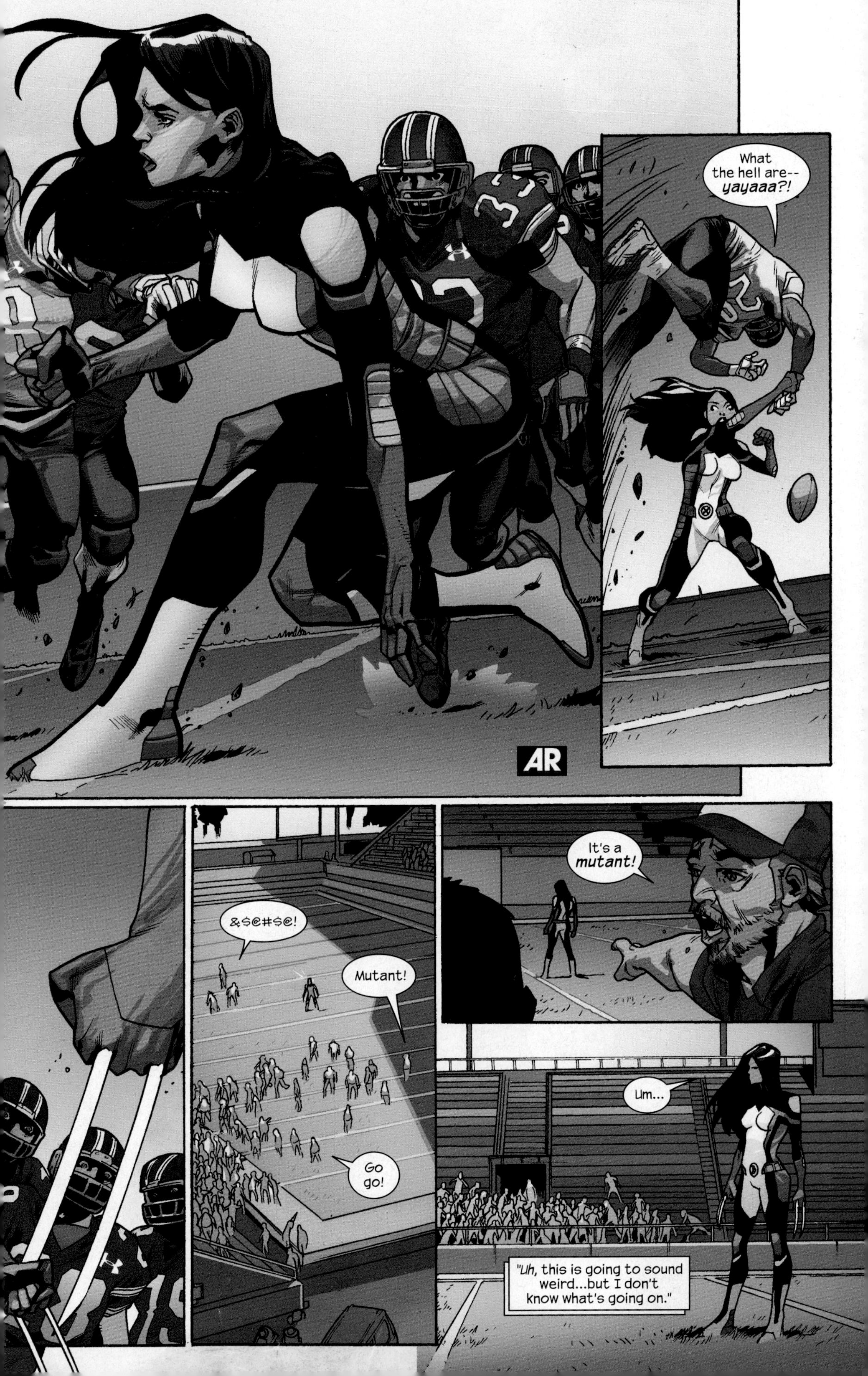
What the hell are-- yayaaa?!
&$@#$@!
Mutant!
Go go!
It's a mutant!
Um...
"Uh, this is going to sound weird...but I don't know what's going on."

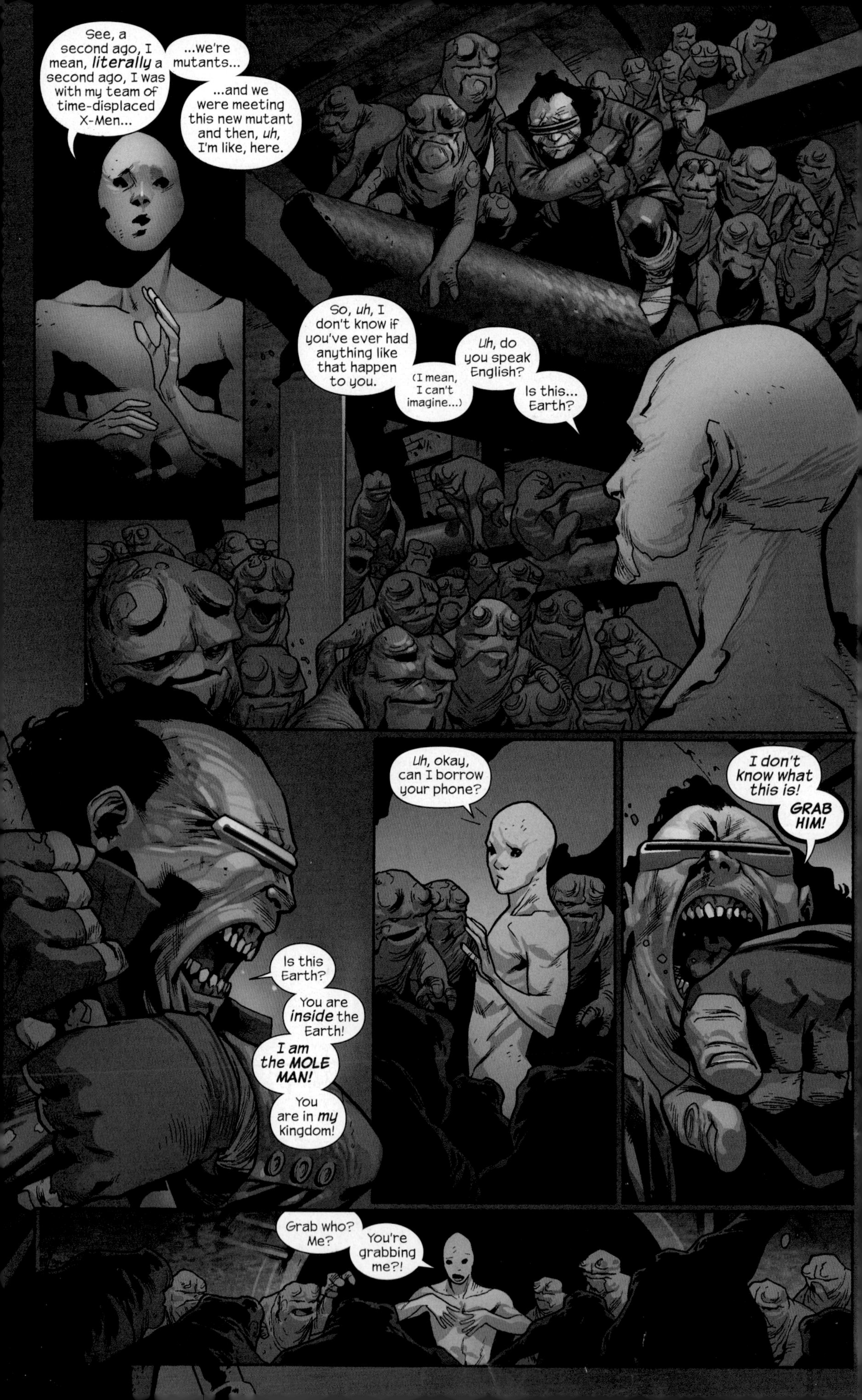
See, a second ago, I mean, literally a second ago, I was with my team of time-displaced X-Men...
...we're mutants...
...and we were meeting this new mutant and then, uh, I'm like, here.
So, uh, I don't know if you've ever had anything like that happen to you.
(I mean, I can't imagine...)
Uh, do you speak English?
Is this... Earth?
Is this Earth?
You are inside the Earth!
I am the MOLE MAN!
You are in my kingdom!
Uh, okay, can I borrow your phone?
I don't know what this is!
GRAB HIM!
Grab who? Me?
You're grabbing me?!

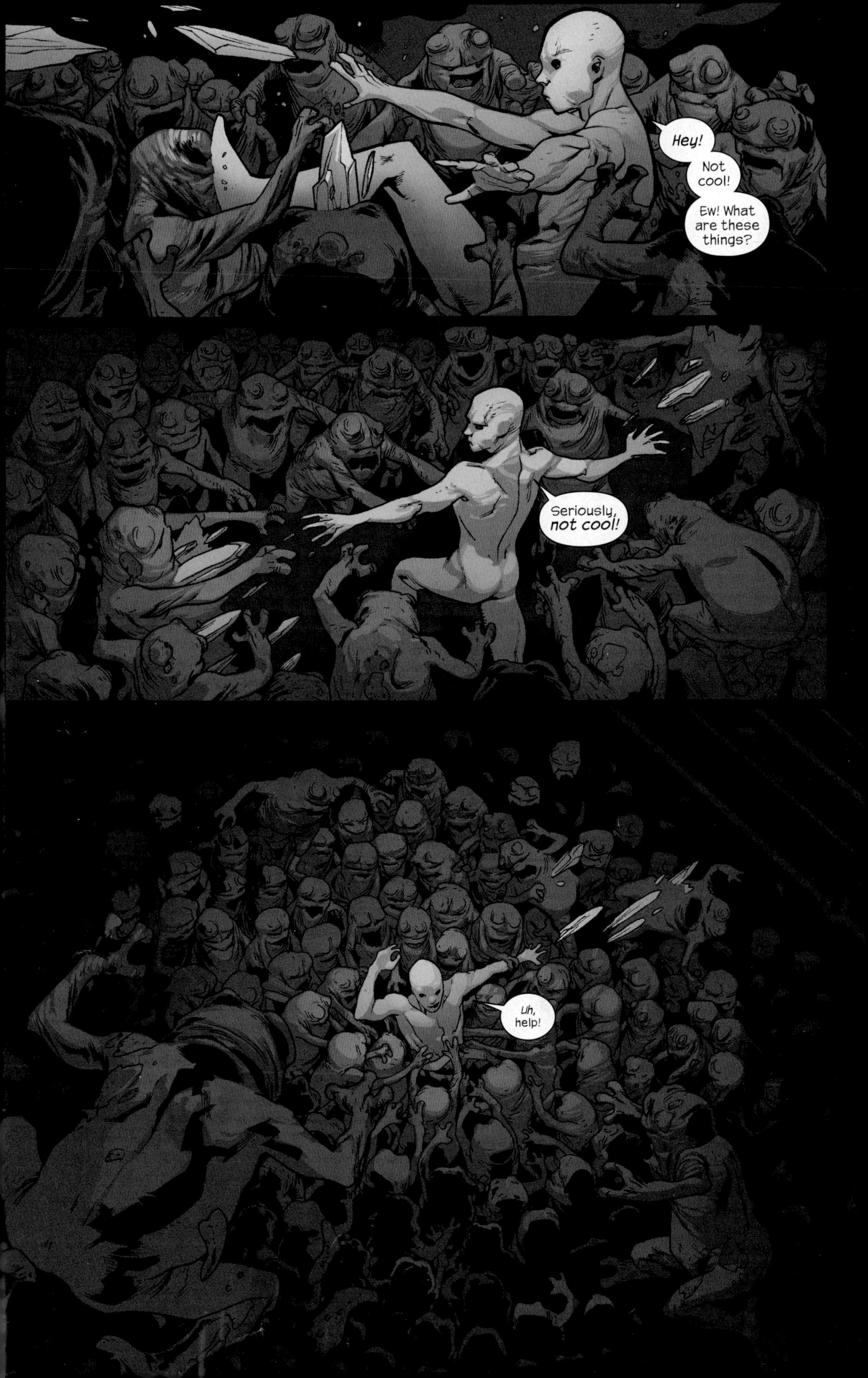
Hey!
Not cool!
Ew! What are these things?
Seriously, not cool!
Uh, help!

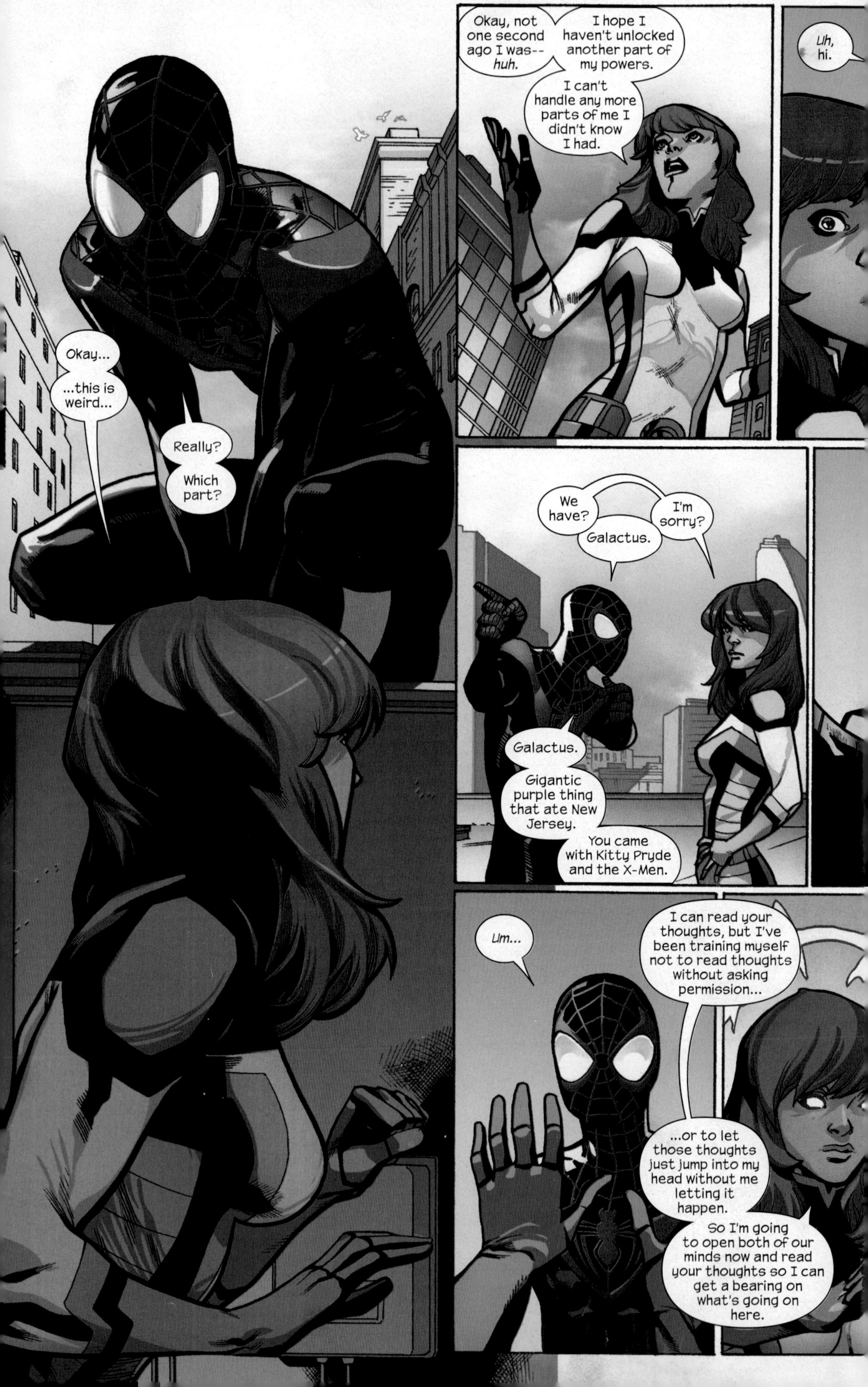
Okay...
...this is weird...
Really?
Which part?
Okay, not one second ago I was-- huh.
I hope I haven't unlocked another part of my powers.
I can't handle any more parts of me I didn't know I had.
Uh, hi.
We have?
I'm sorry?
Galactus.
Galactus.
Gigantic purple thing that ate New Jersey.
You came with Kitty Pryde and the X-Men.
Um...
I can read your thoughts, but I've been training myself not to read thoughts without asking permission...
...or to let those thoughts just jump into my head without me letting it happen.
So I'm going to open both of our minds now and read your thoughts so I can get a bearing on what's going on here.

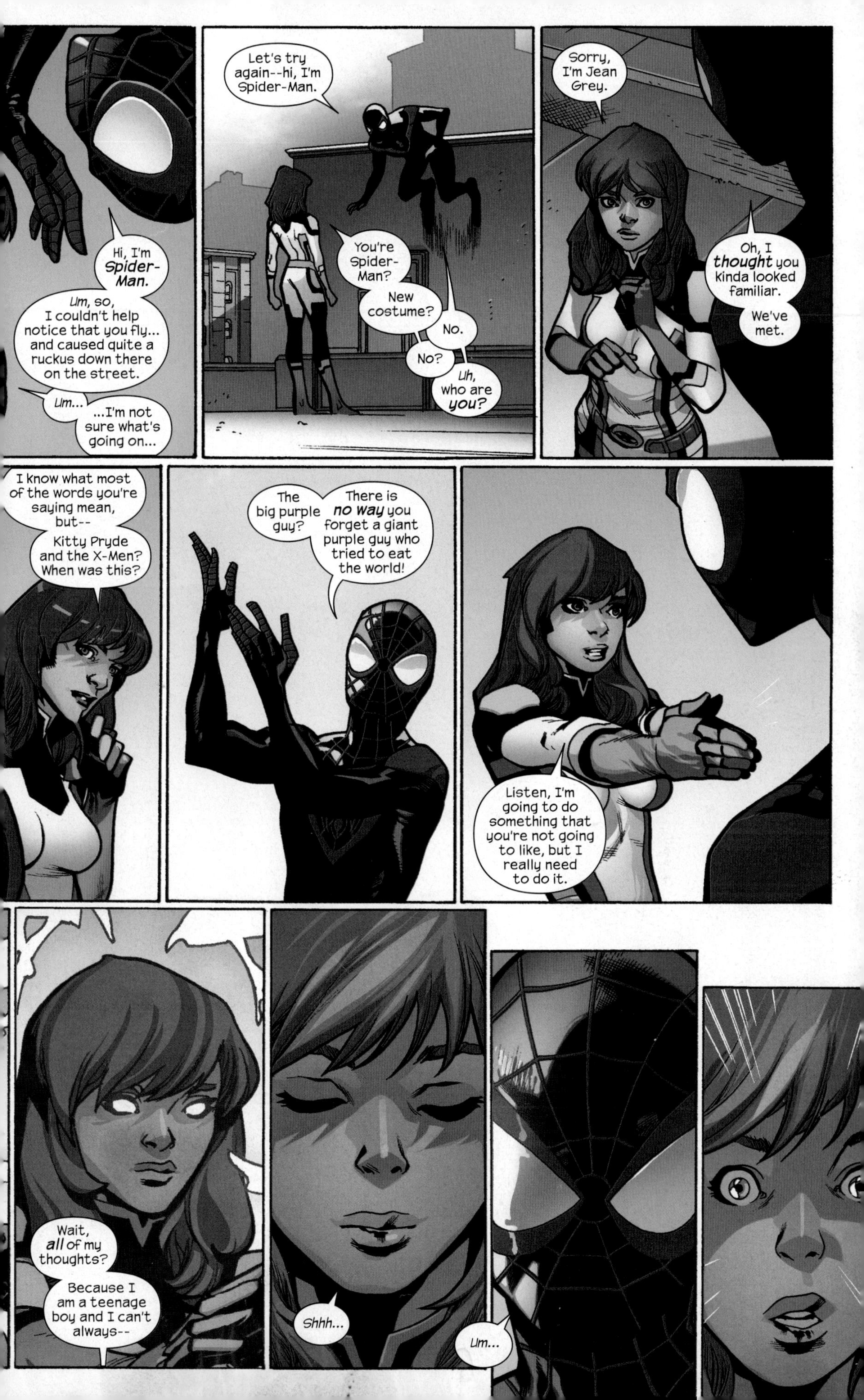
Hi, I'm *Spider-Man.*
Um, so, I couldn't help notice that you fly... and caused quite a ruckus down there on the street.
Um...
...I'm not sure what's going on...
Let's try again--hi, I'm Spider-Man.
You're Spider-Man?
New costume?
No.
No?
Uh, who are *you?*
Sorry, I'm Jean Grey.
Oh, I *thought* you kinda looked familiar.
We've met.
I know what most of the words you're saying mean, but--
Kitty Pryde and the X-Men? When was this?
The big purple guy?
There is *no way* you forget a giant purple guy who tried to eat the world!
Listen, I'm going to do something that you're not going to like, but I really need to do it.
Wait, *all* of my thoughts?
Because I am a teenage boy and I can't always--
Shhh...
Um...

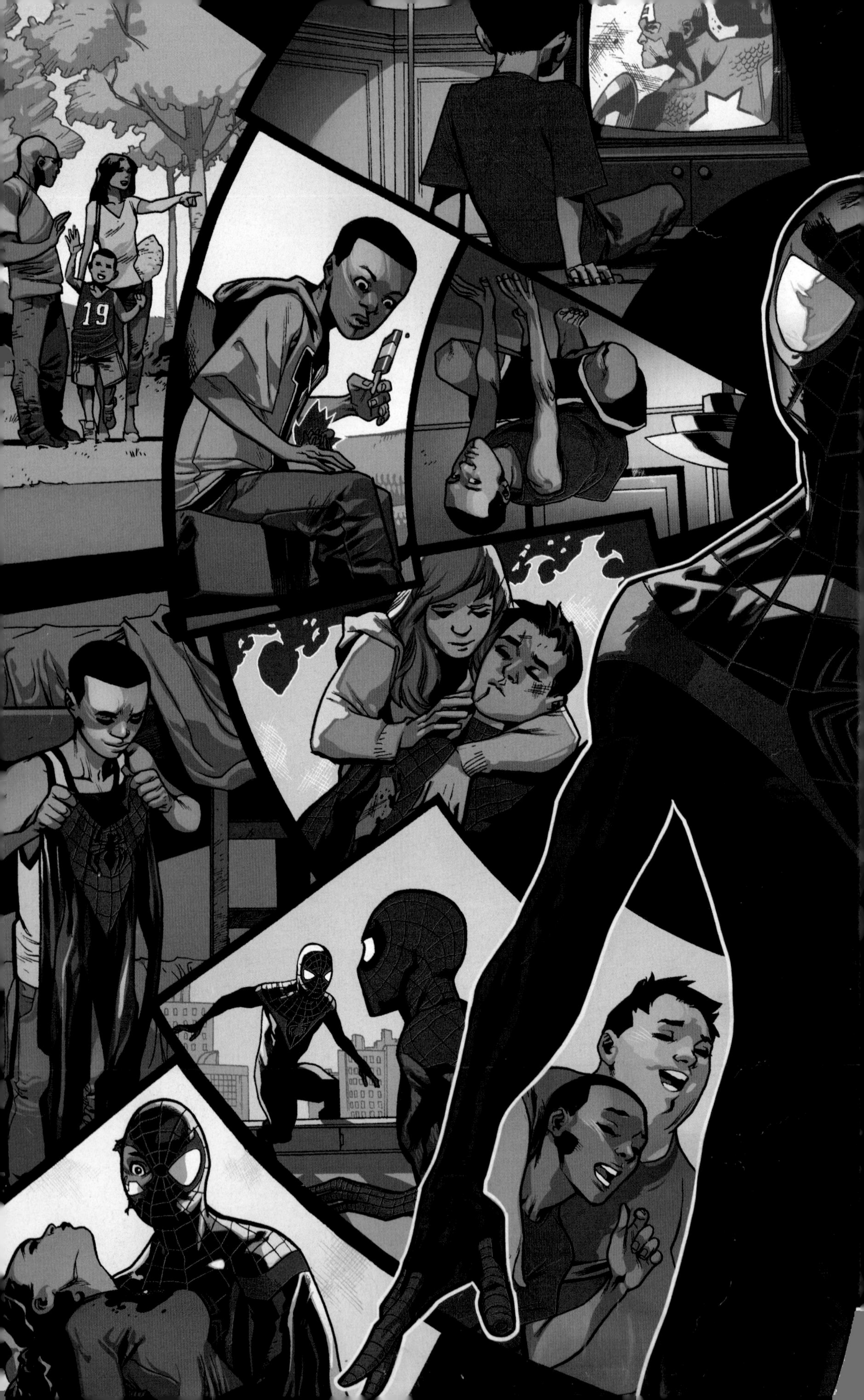
19

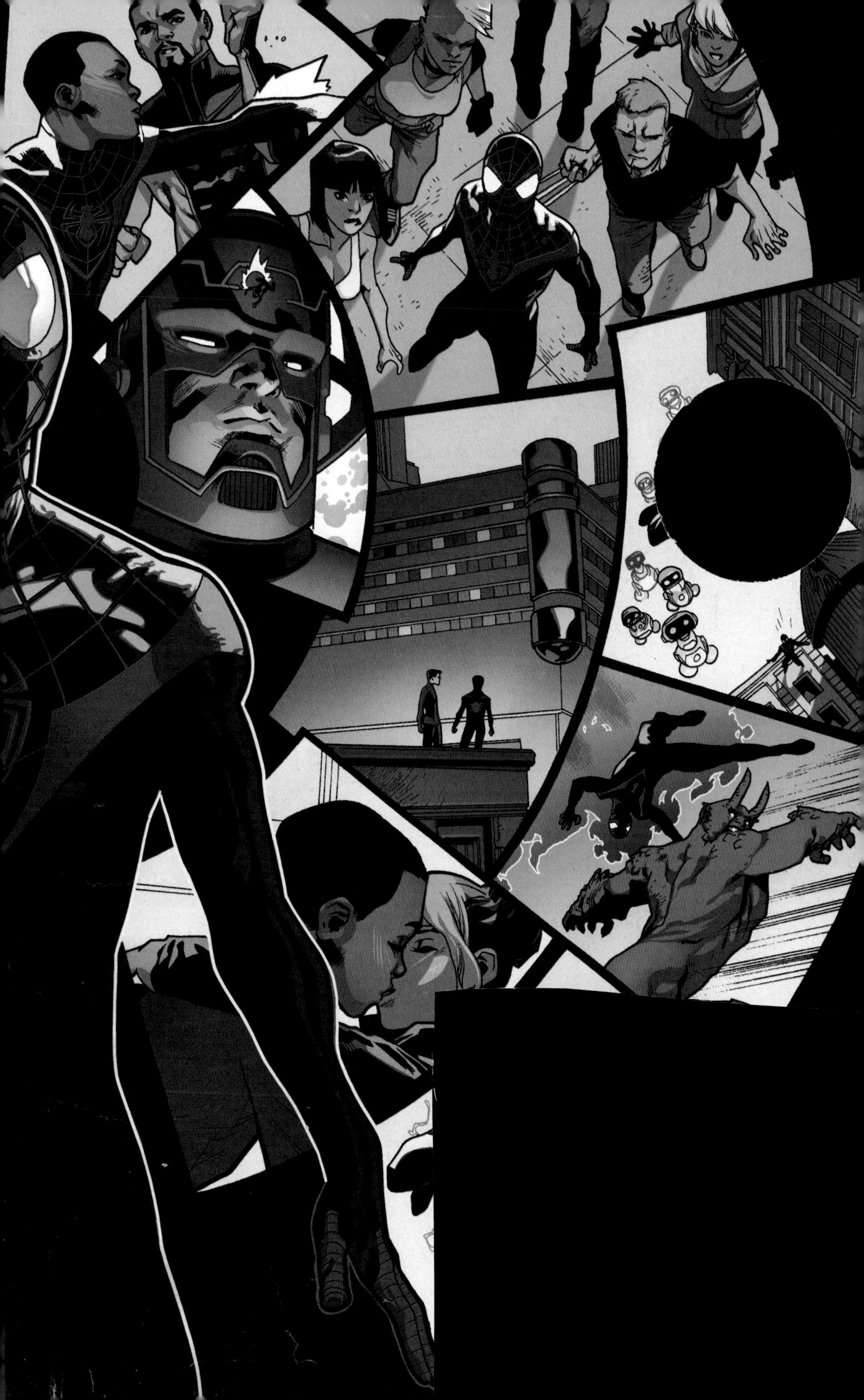

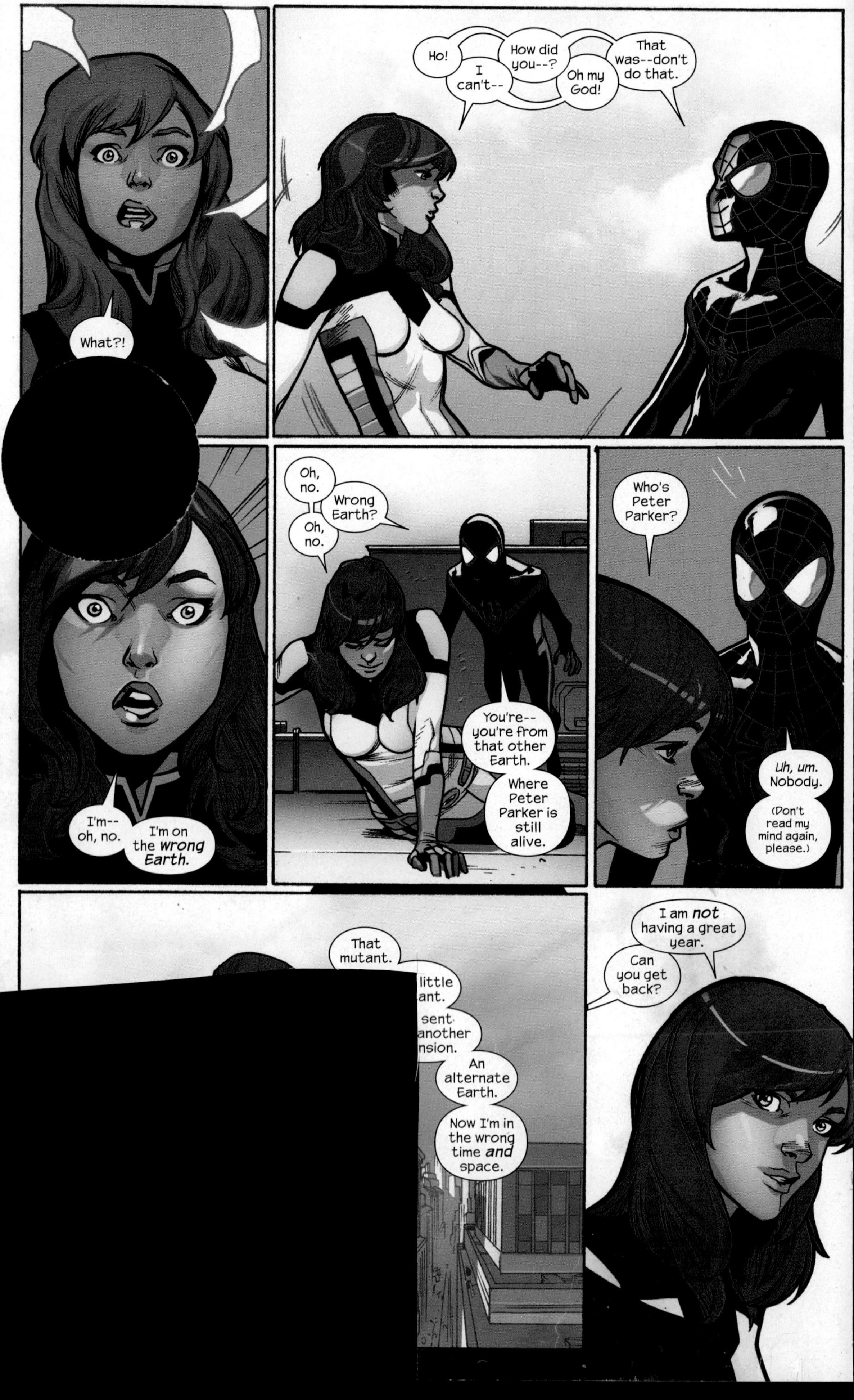
What?!
Ho!
I can't--
How did you--?
Oh my God!
That was--don't do that.
I'm-- oh, no.
I'm on the *wrong Earth.*
Oh, no.
Wrong Earth?
Oh, no.
You're-- you're from that other Earth.
Where Peter Parker is still alive.
Who's Peter Parker?
Uh, um. Nobody.
(Don't read my mind again, please.)
That mutant.
[redacted]
An alternate Earth.
Now I'm in the wrong time *and* space.
I am *not* having a great year.
Can you get back?

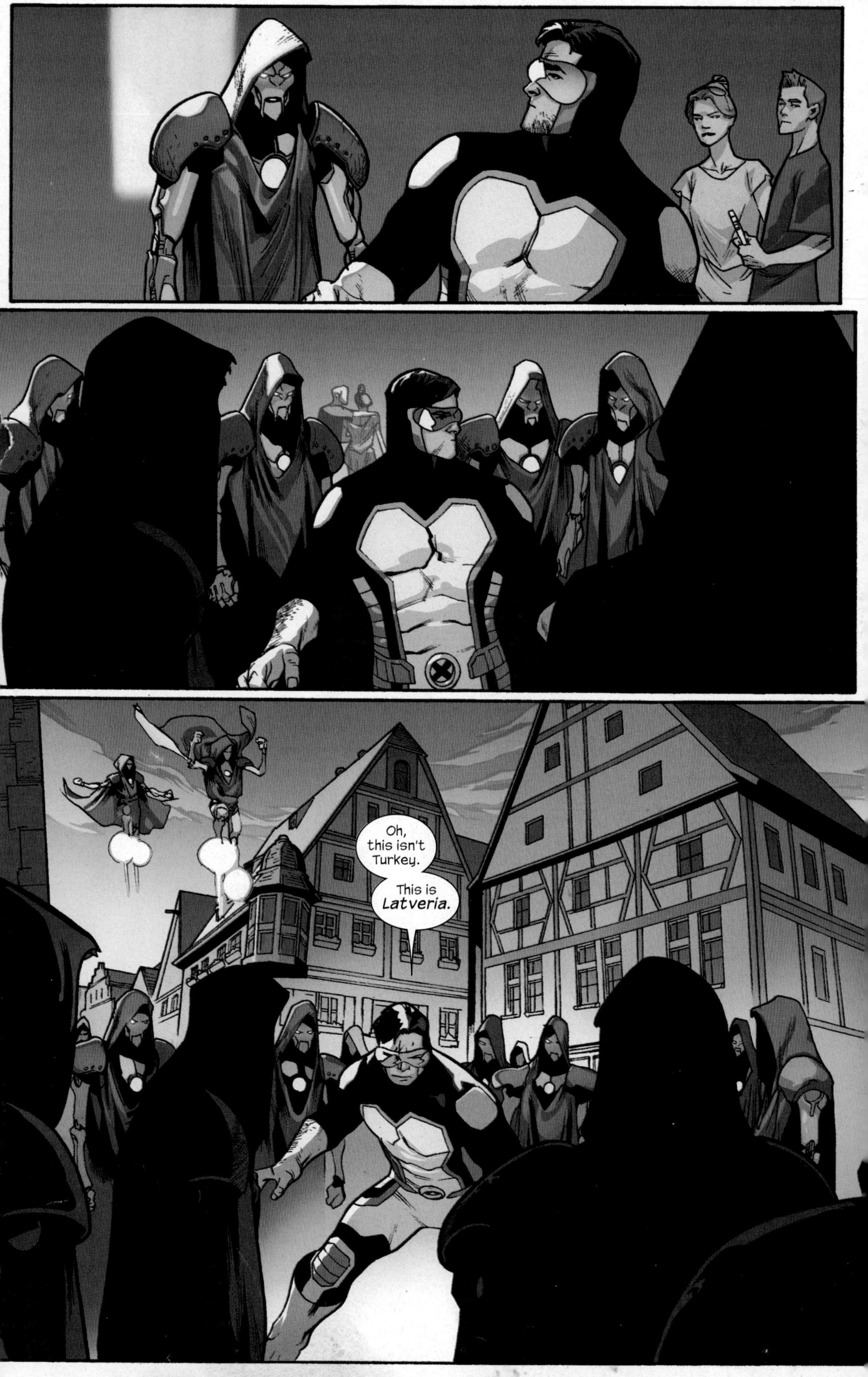
Oh, this isn't Turkey.
This is Latveria.

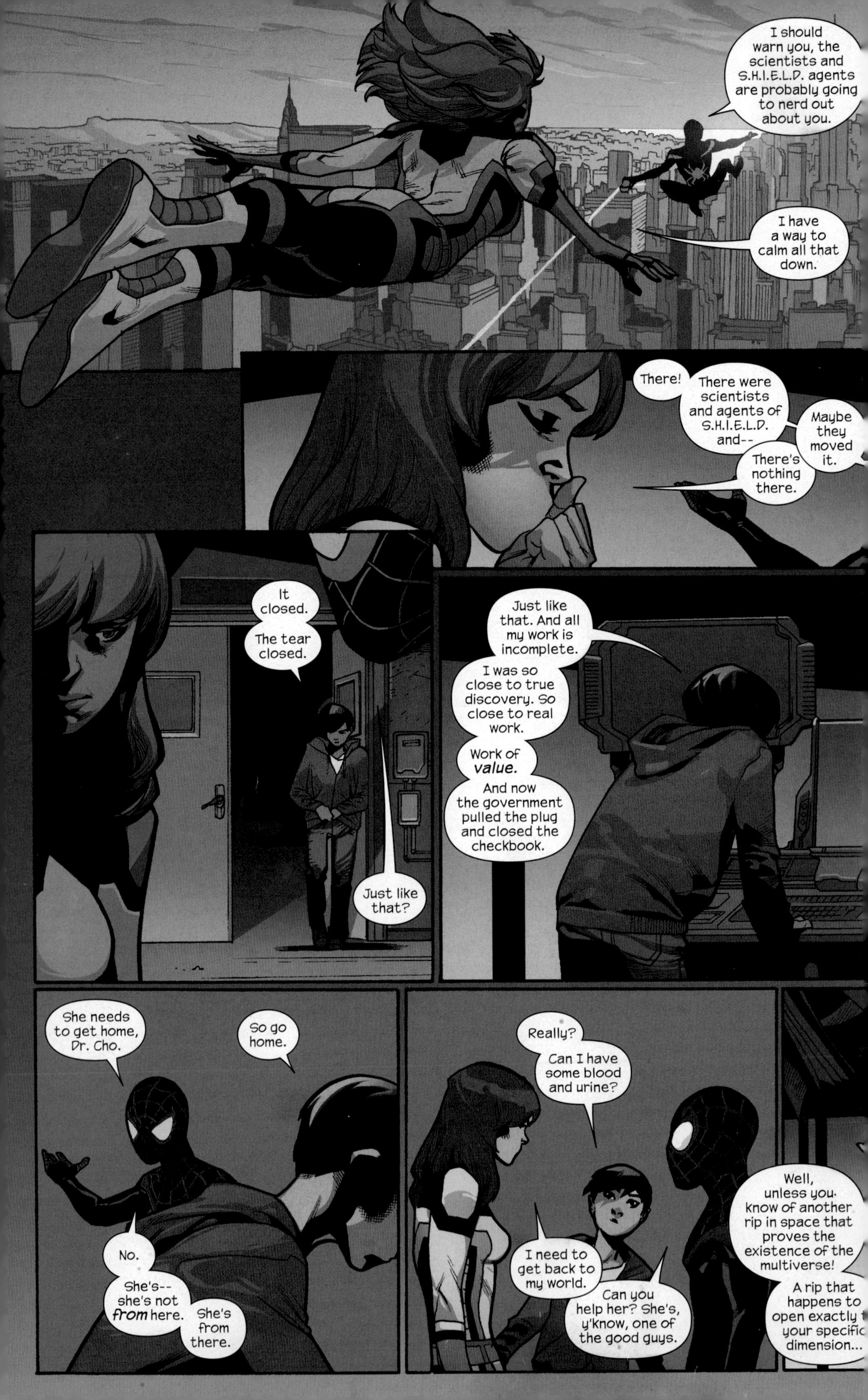
I should warn you, the scientists and S.H.I.E.L.D. agents are probably going to nerd out about you.
I have a way to calm all that down.
There!
There were scientists and agents of S.H.I.E.L.D. and--
There's nothing there.
Maybe they moved it.
It closed.
The tear closed.
Just like that?
Just like that. And all my work is incomplete.
I was so close to true discovery. So close to real work.
Work of *value.*
And now the government pulled the plug and closed the checkbook.
She needs to get home, Dr. Cho.
So go home.
No.
She's--she's not *from* here.
She's from there.
Really?
Can I have some blood and urine?
I need to get back to my world.
Can you help her? She's, y'know, one of the good guys.
Well, unless you know of another rip in space that proves the existence of the multiverse!
A rip that happens to open exactly to your specific dimension...

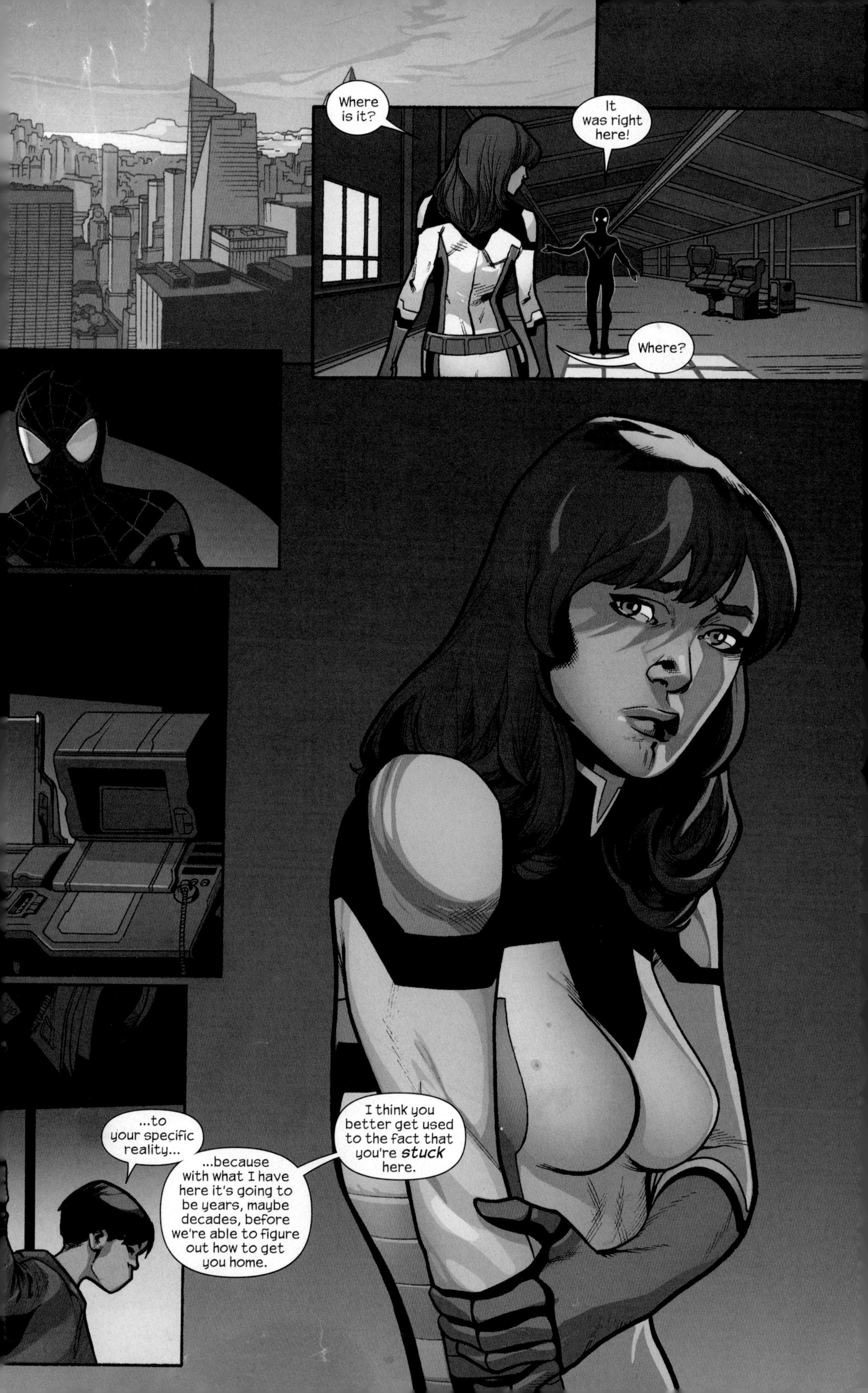
Where is it?
It was right here!
Where?
...to your specific reality...
...because with what I have here it's going to be years, maybe decades, before we're able to figure out how to get you home.
I think you better get used to the fact that you're *stuck* here.

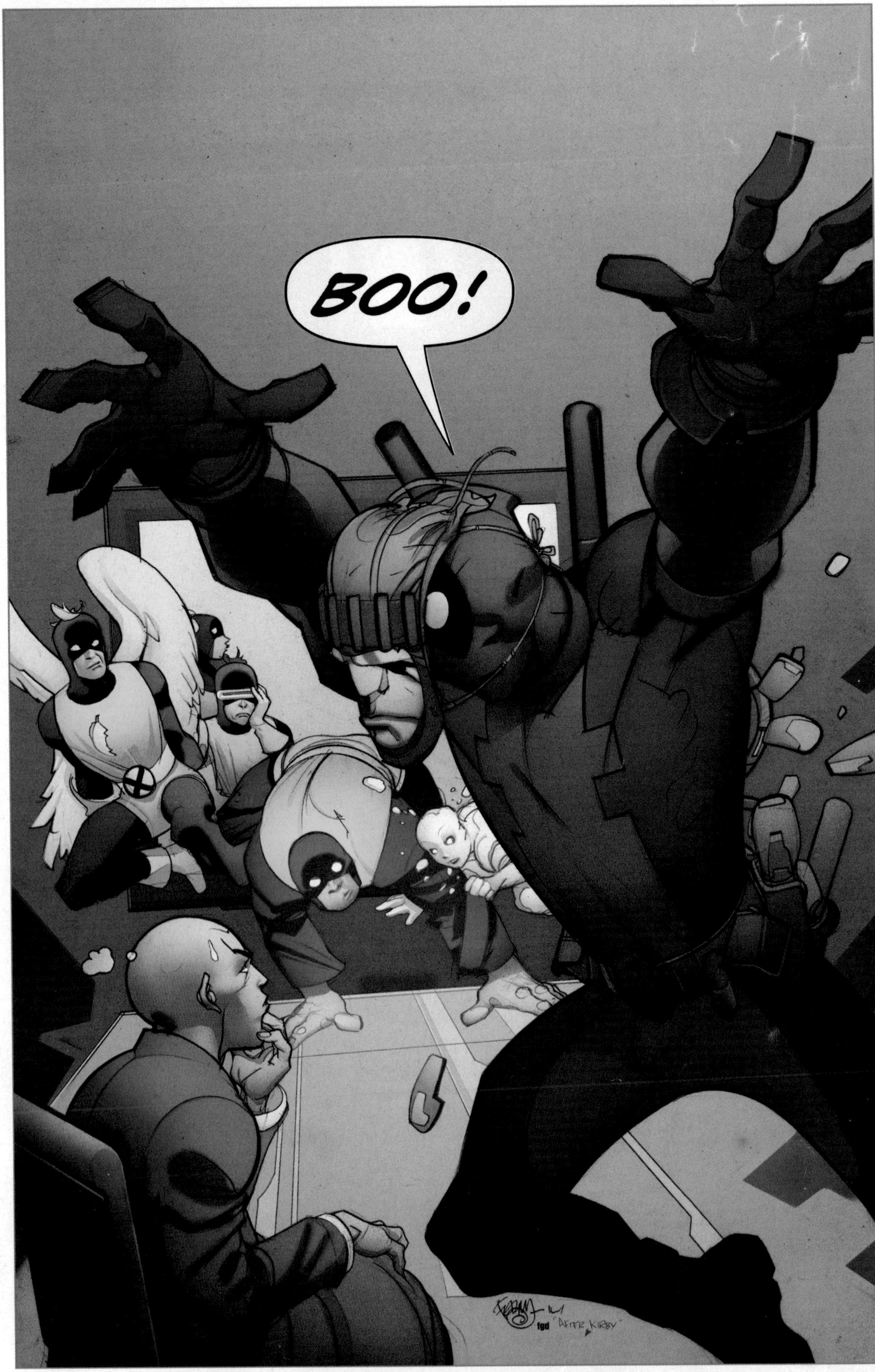
BOO!

ALL-NEW X-MEN #33 DEADPOOL 75TH ANNIVERSARY VARIANT
BY PASQUAL FERRY & FRANK D'ARMATA

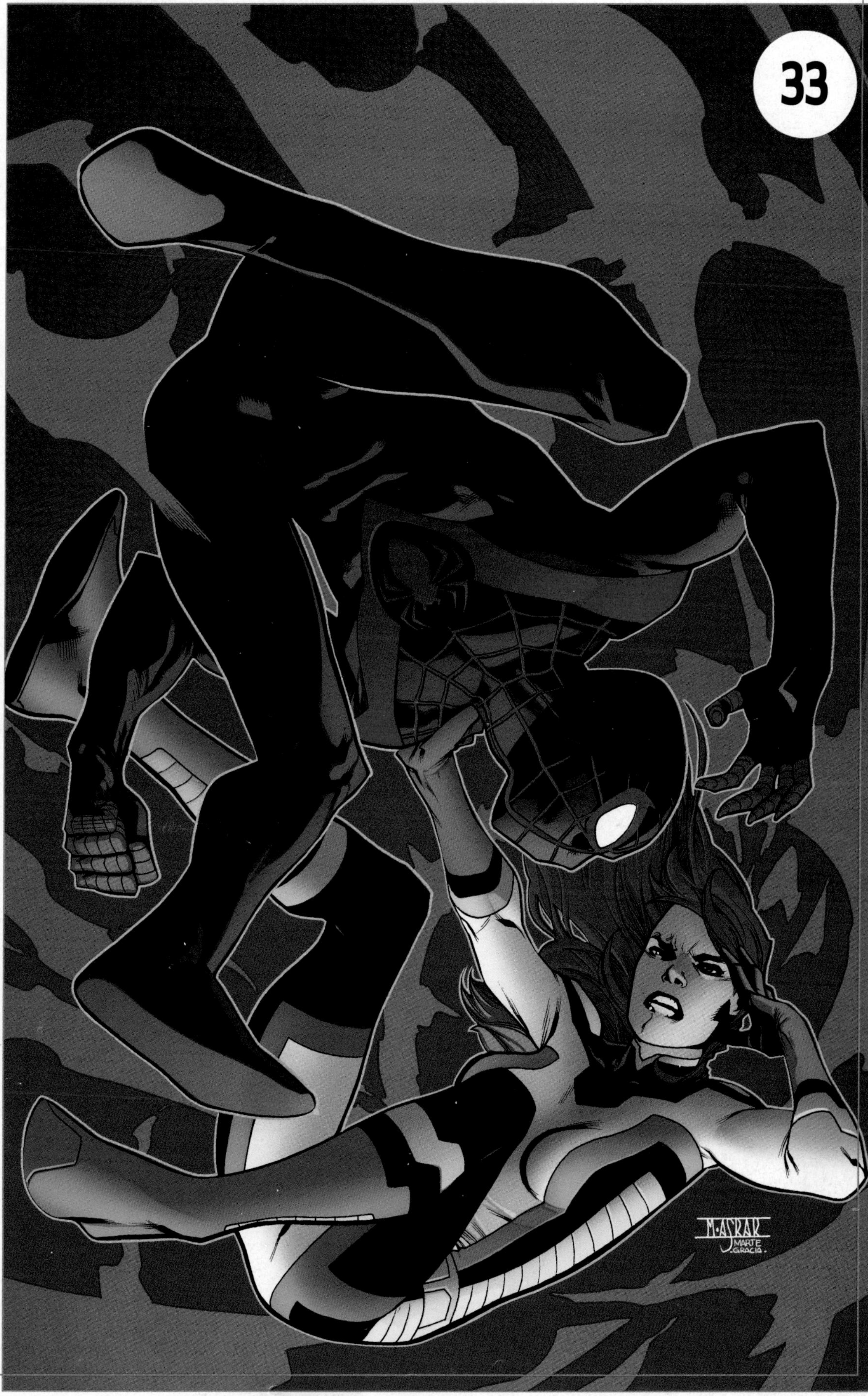
33
M. ASRAR
MARTE GRACIA

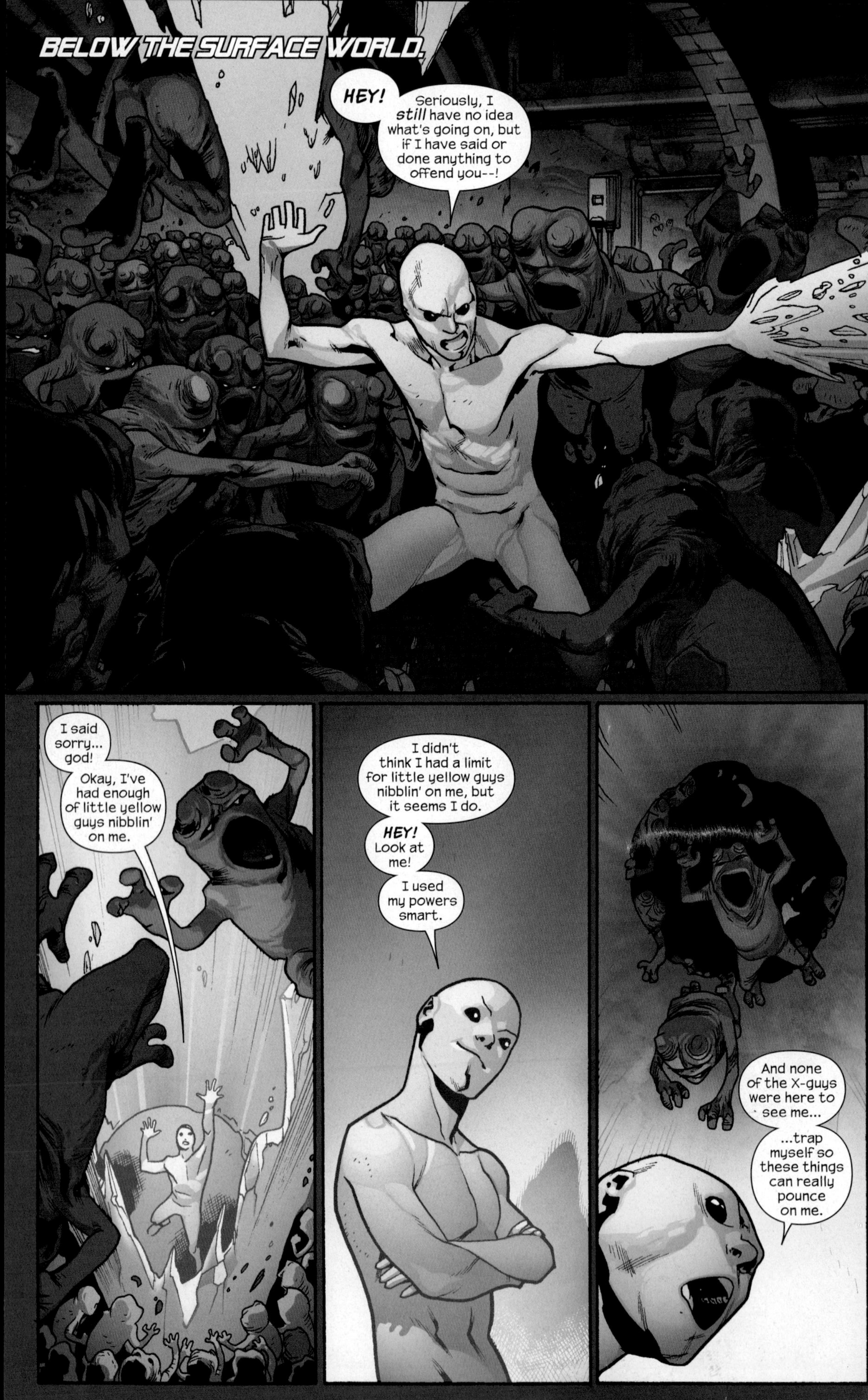
BELOW THE SURFACE WORLD.
HEY!
Seriously, I *still* have no idea what's going on, but if I have said or done anything to offend you--!
I said sorry... god!
Okay, I've had enough of little yellow guys nibblin' on me.
I didn't think I had a limit for little yellow guys nibblin' on me, but it seems I do.
HEY! Look at me!
I used my powers smart.
And none of the X-guys were here to see me...
...trap myself so these things can really pounce on me.

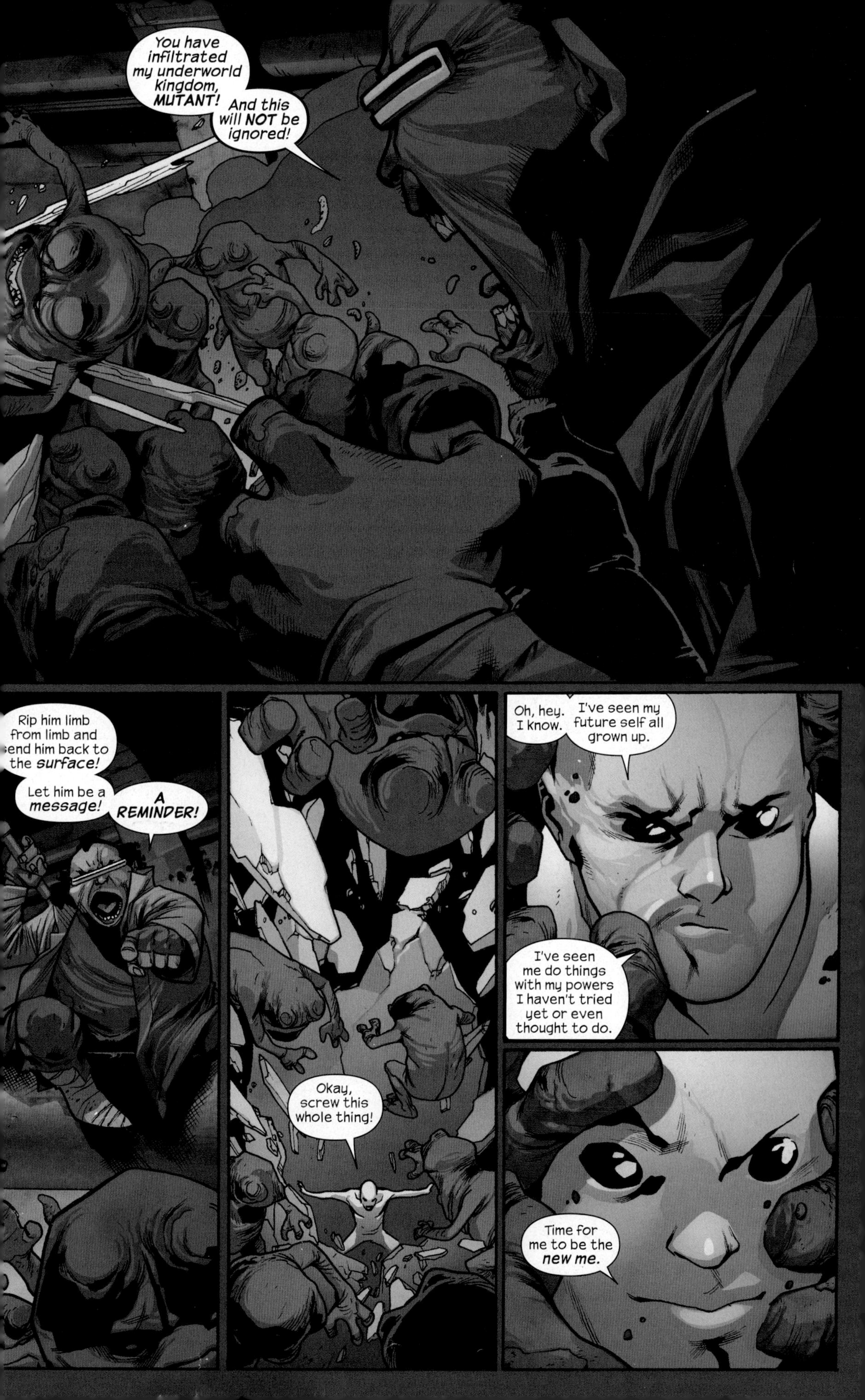
You have infiltrated my underworld kingdom, MUTANT!
And this will NOT be ignored!
Rip him limb from limb and send him back to the surface!
Let him be a message!
A REMINDER!
Okay, screw this whole thing!
Oh, hey. I know.
I've seen my future self all grown up.
I've seen me do things with my powers I haven't tried yet or even thought to do.
Time for me to be the new me.

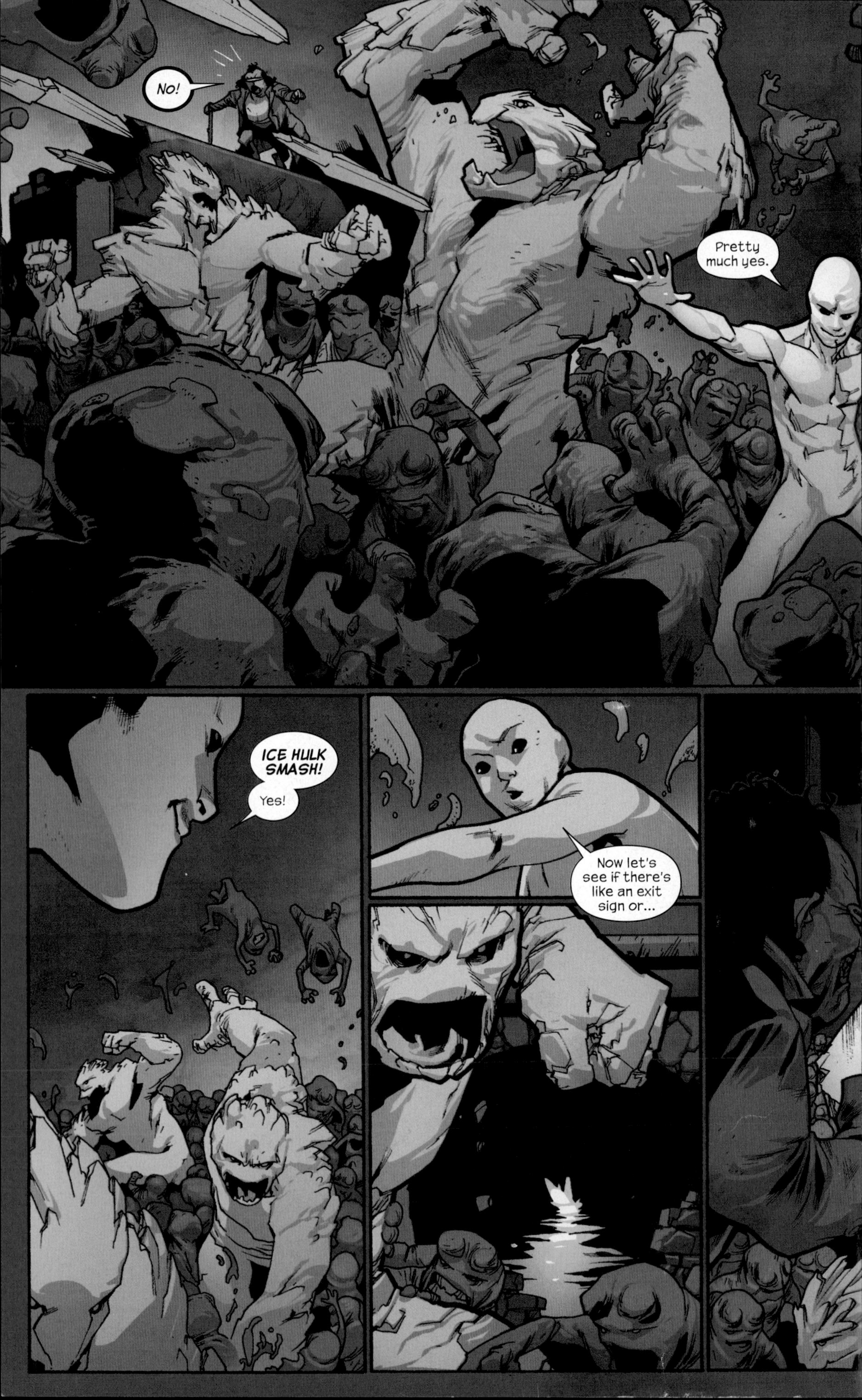
No!
Pretty much yes.
ICE HULK SMASH!
Yes!
Now let's see if there's like an exit sign or...

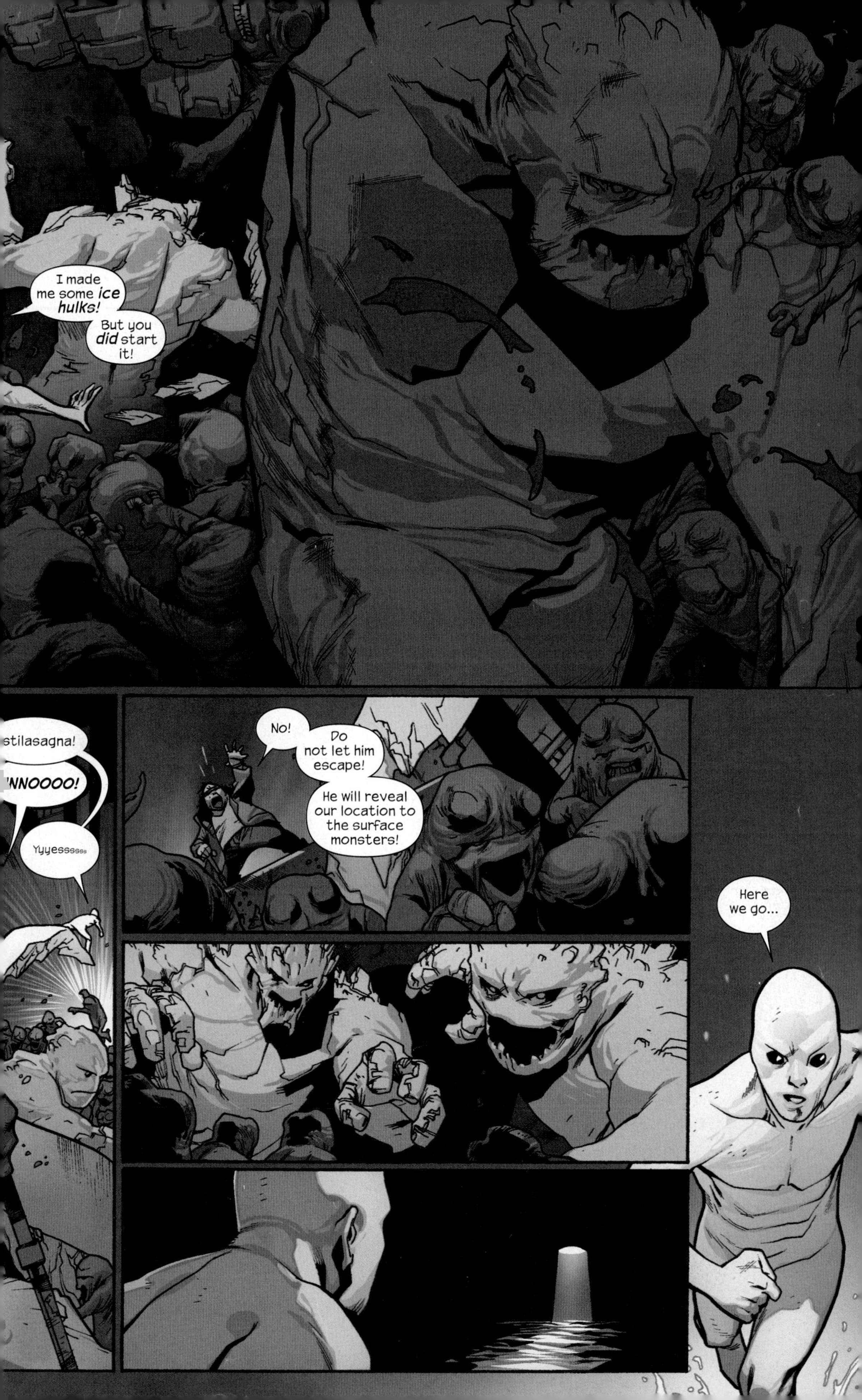
I made me some ice hulks!
But you did start it!
stilasagna!
NNOOOO!
Yyyesssss
No!
Do not let him escape!
He will reveal our location to the surface monsters!
Here we go...

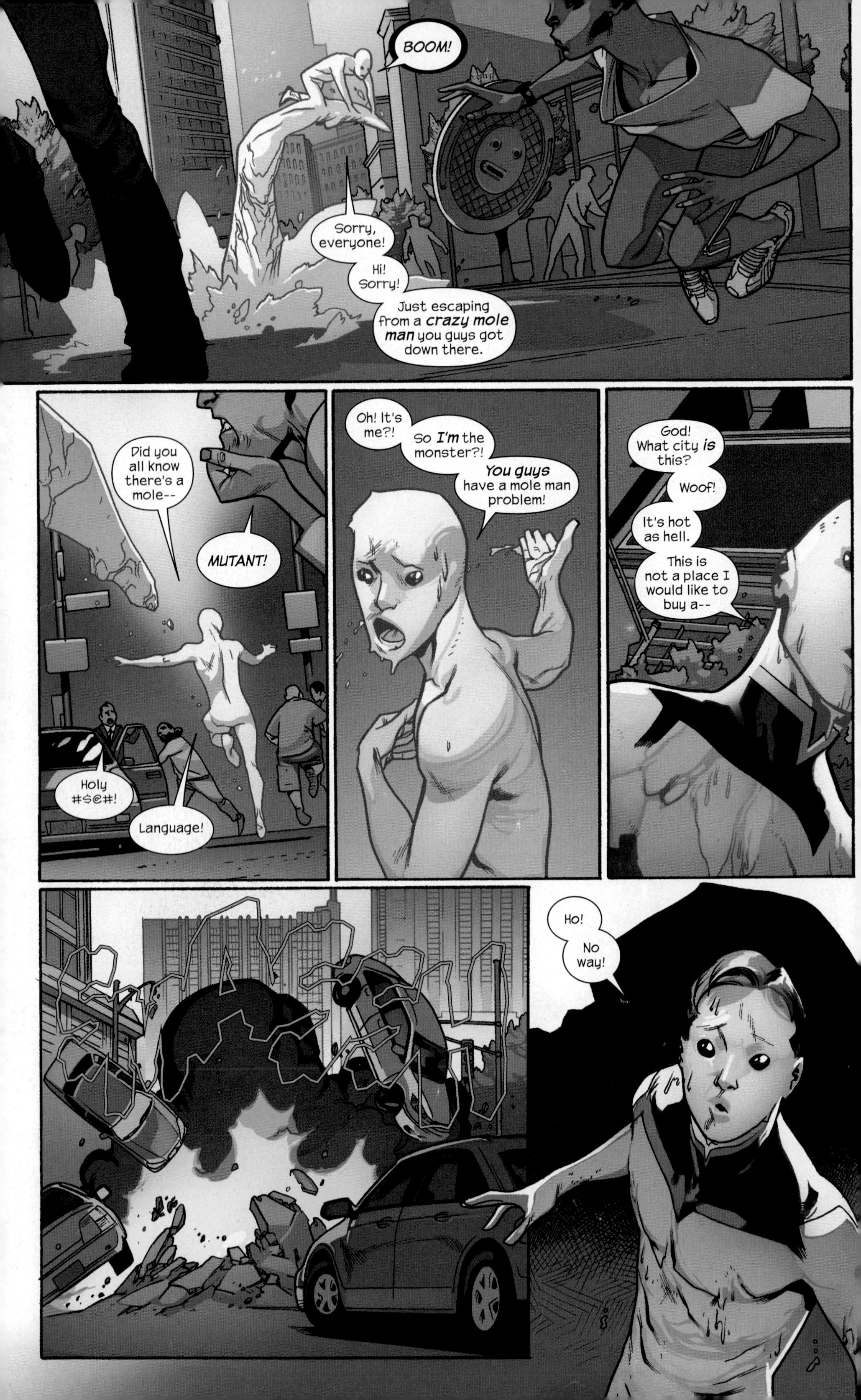
BOOM!
Sorry, everyone!
Hi! Sorry!
Just escaping from a crazy mole man you guys got down there.
Did you all know there's a mole--
MUTANT!
Holy #$@#!
Language!
Oh! It's me?!
So I'm the monster?!
You guys have a mole man problem!
God! What city is this?
Woof!
It's hot as hell.
This is not a place I would like to buy a--
Ho!
No way!

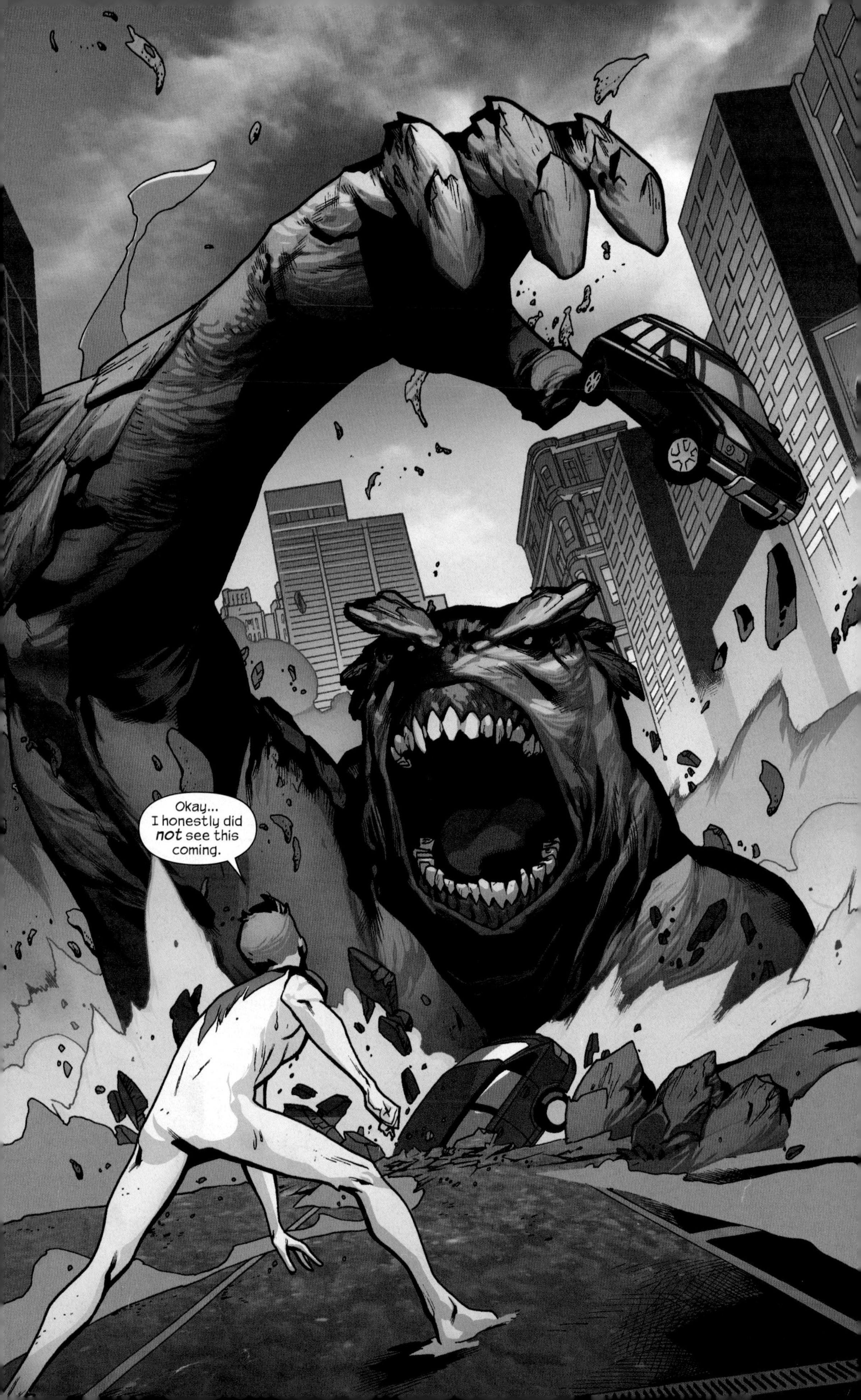
Okay... I honestly did **not** see this coming.

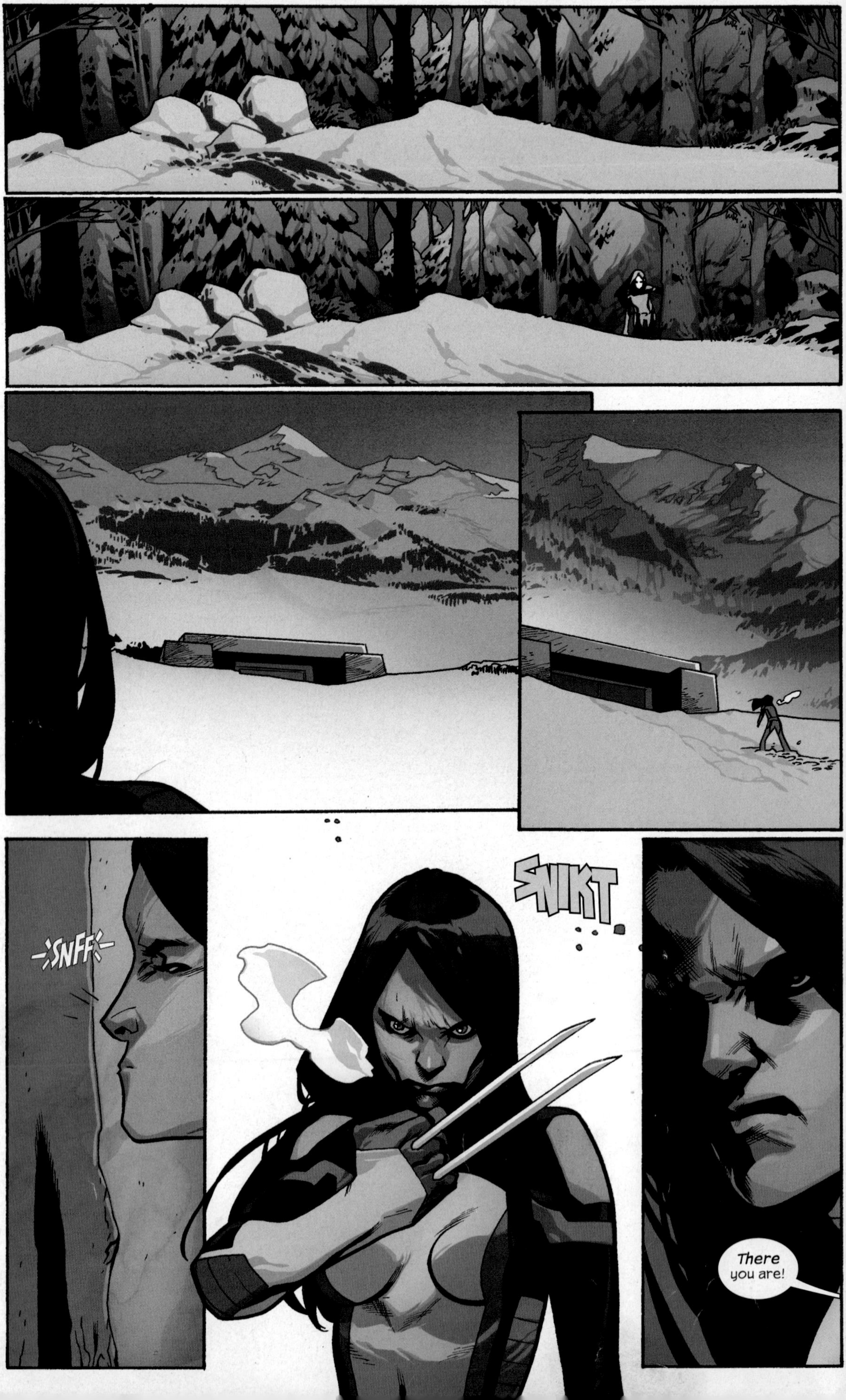
SNFF
SNIKT
There you are!

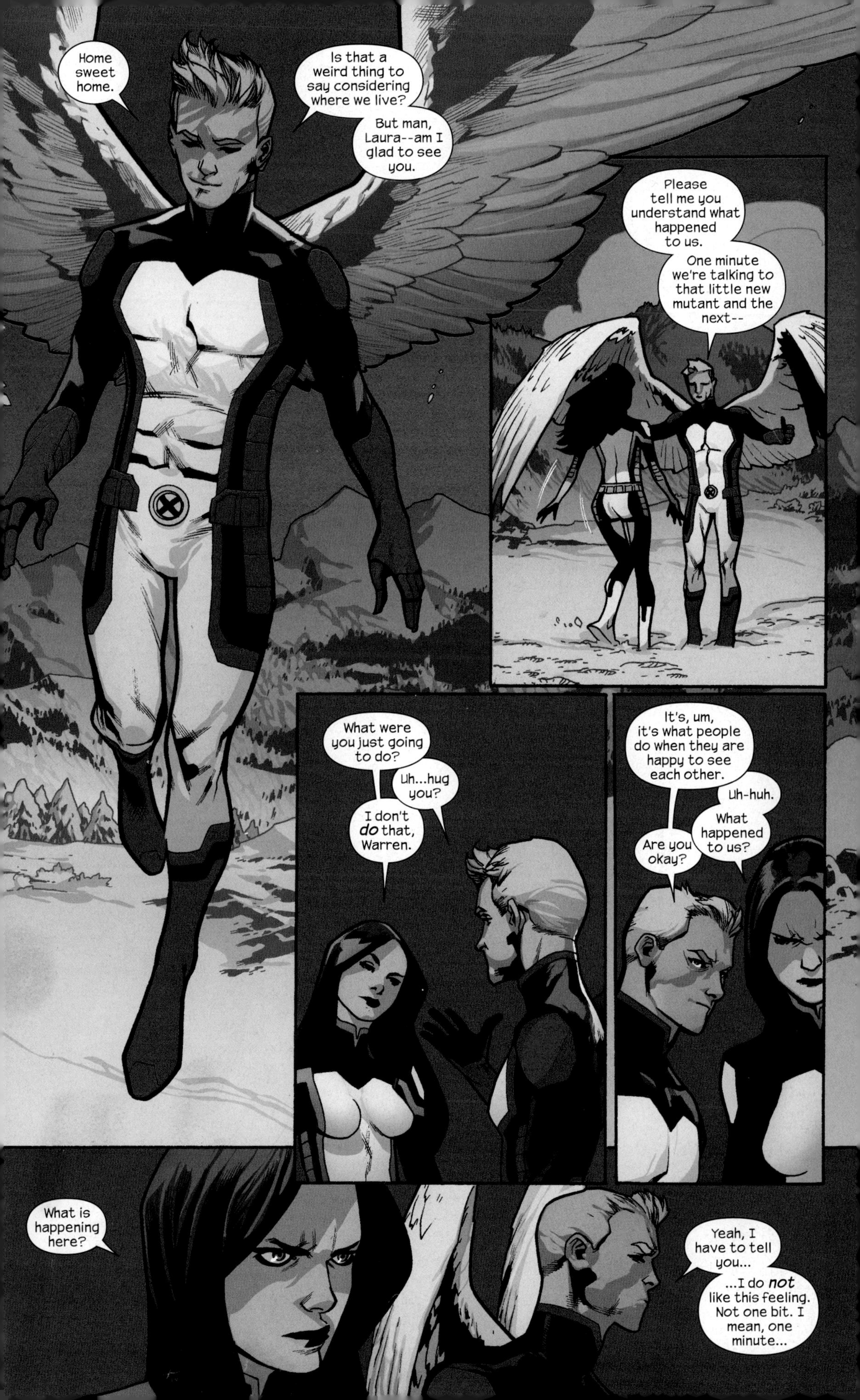
Home sweet home.
Is that a weird thing to say considering where we live?
But man, Laura--am I glad to see you.
Please tell me you understand what happened to us.
One minute we're talking to that little new mutant and the next--
What were you just going to do?
Uh...hug you?
I don't *do* that, Warren.
It's, um, it's what people do when they are happy to see each other.
Uh-huh.
What happened to us?
Are you okay?
What is happening here?
Yeah, I have to tell you...
...I do *not* like this feeling. Not one bit. I mean, one minute...

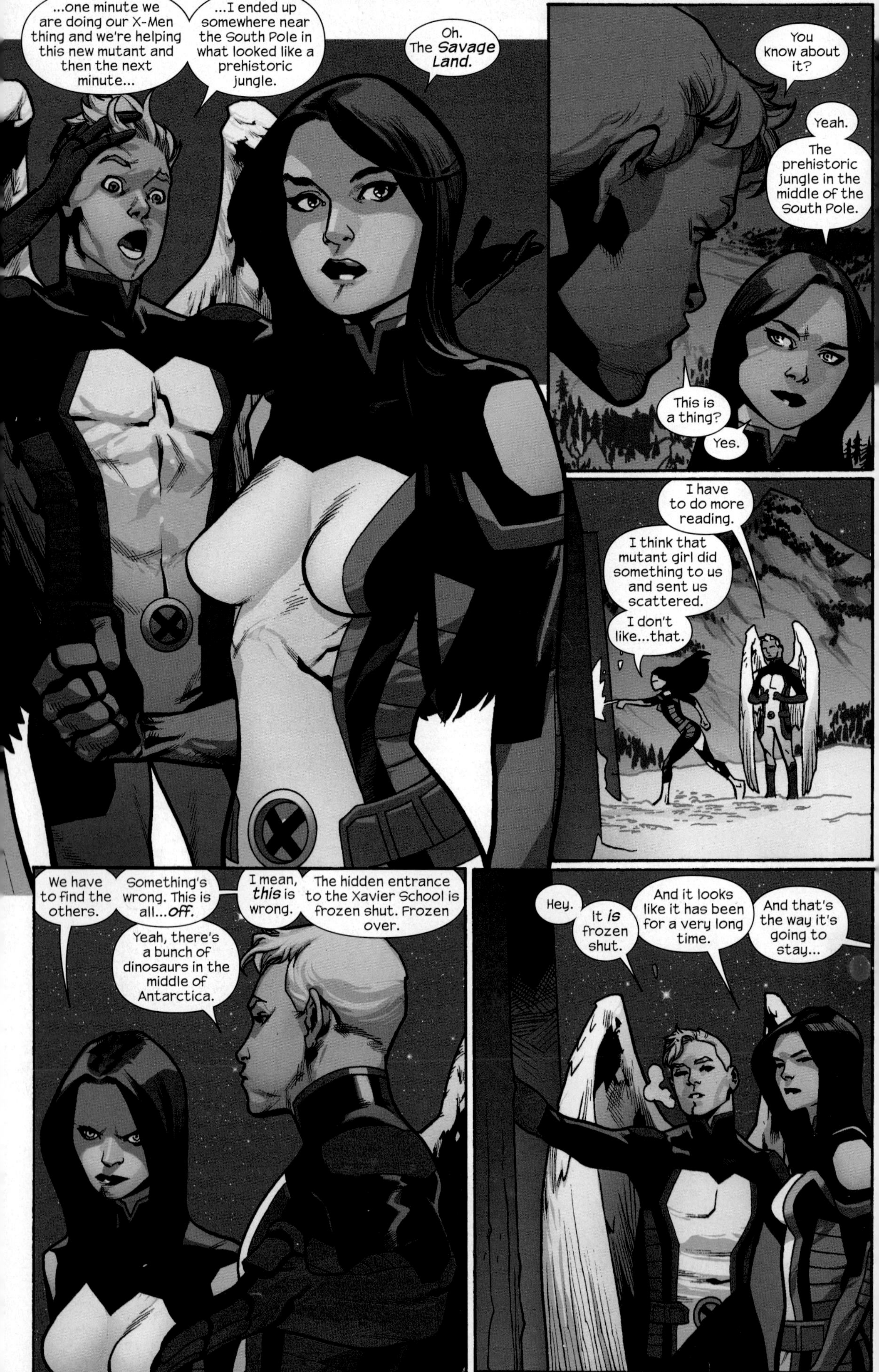
...one minute we are doing our X-Men thing and we're helping this new mutant and then the next minute...
...I ended up somewhere near the South Pole in what looked like a prehistoric jungle.
Oh. The *Savage Land.*
You know about it?
Yeah.
The prehistoric jungle in the middle of the South Pole.
This is a thing?
Yes.
I have to do more reading.
I think that mutant girl did something to us and sent us scattered.
I don't like...that.
We have to find the others.
Something's wrong. This is all...*off.*
Yeah, there's a bunch of dinosaurs in the middle of Antarctica.
I mean, *this* is wrong.
The hidden entrance to the Xavier School is frozen shut. Frozen over.
Hey.
It *is* frozen shut.
And it looks like it has been for a very long time.
And that's the way it's going to stay...

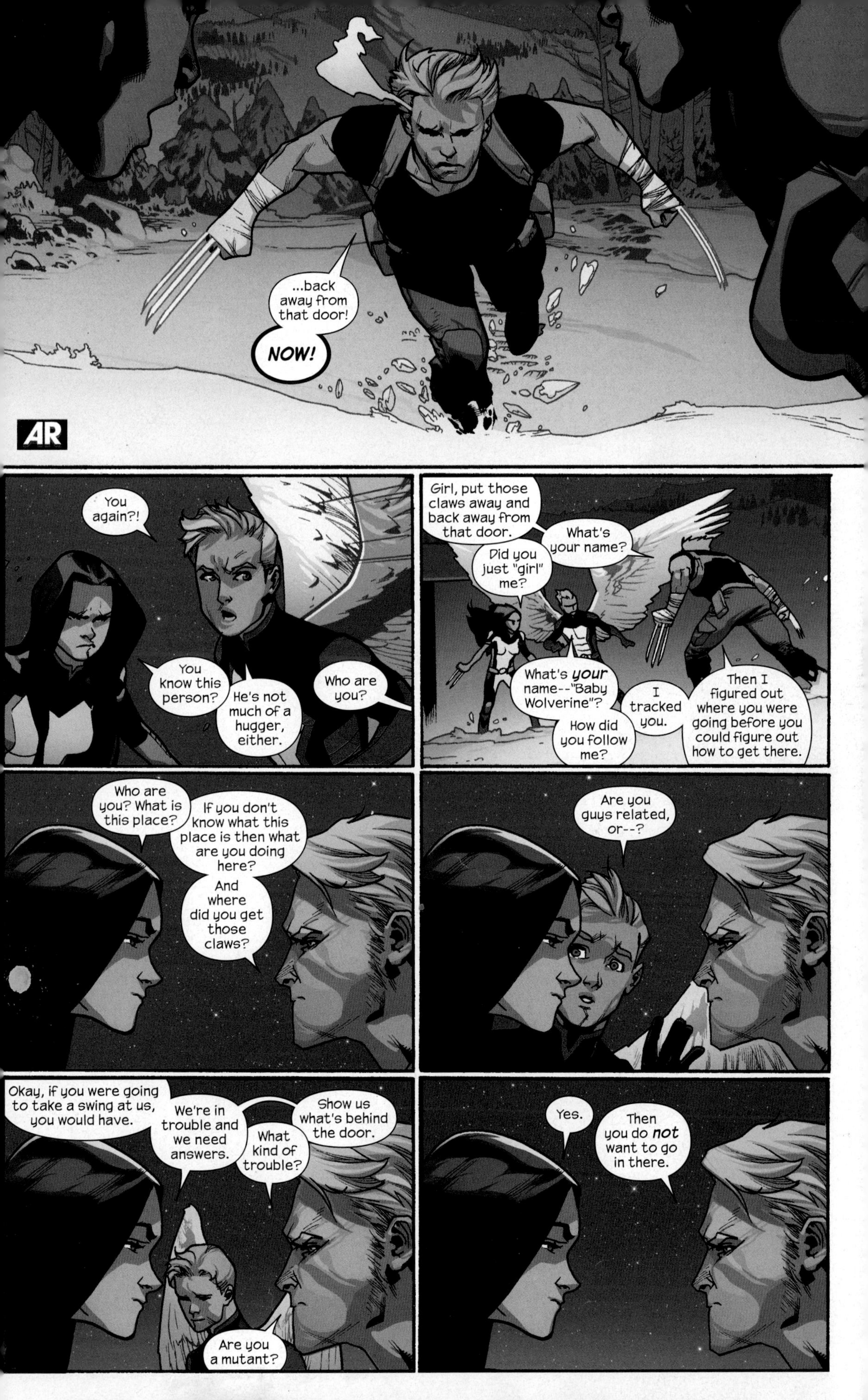

...back away from that door!
NOW!
AR
You again?!
You know this person?
He's not much of a hugger, either.
Who are you?
Girl, put those claws away and back away from that door.
What's your name?
Did you just "girl" me?
What's **your** name--"Baby Wolverine"?
How did you follow me?
I tracked you.
Then I figured out where you were going before you could figure out how to get there.
Who are you? What is this place?
If you don't know what this place is then what are you doing here?
And where did you get those claws?
Are you guys related, or--?
Okay, if you were going to take a swing at us, you would have.
We're in trouble and we need answers.
Show us what's behind the door.
What kind of trouble?
Are you a mutant?
Yes.
Then you do **not** want to go in there.

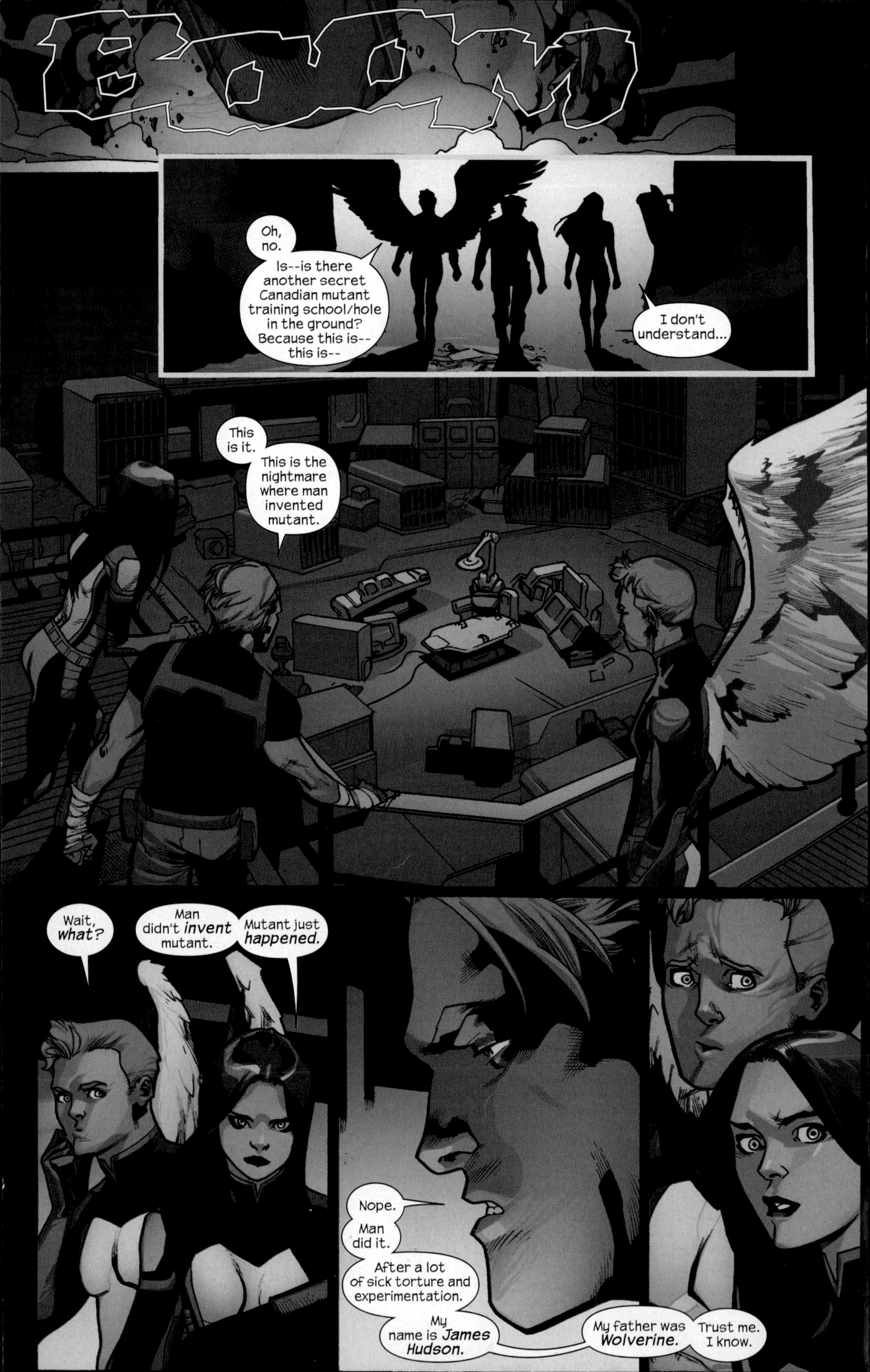
BOOM
Oh, no.
Is--is there another secret Canadian mutant training school/hole in the ground? Because this is-- this is--
I don't understand...
This is it.
This is the nightmare where man invented mutant.
Wait, *what*?
Man didn't *invent* mutant.
Mutant just *happened.*
Nope.
Man did it.
After a lot of sick torture and experimentation.
My name is *James Hudson.*
My father was *Wolverine.*
Trust me. I know.

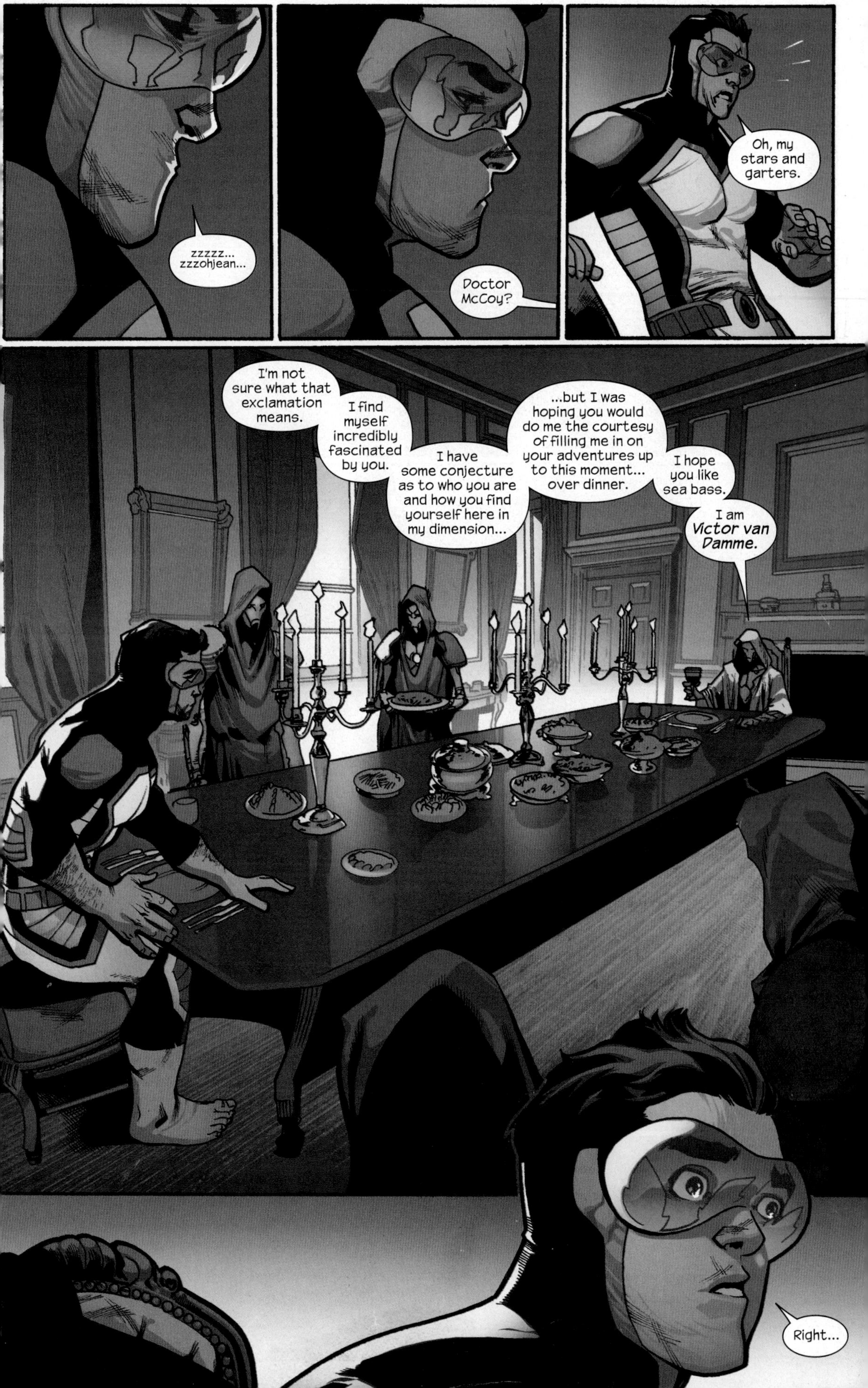
zzzzz...
zzzohjean...
Doctor McCoy?
Oh, my stars and garters.
I'm not sure what that exclamation means.
I find myself incredibly fascinated by you.
I have some conjecture as to who you are and how you find yourself here in my dimension...
...but I was hoping you would do me the courtesy of filling me in on your adventures up to this moment... over dinner.
I hope you like sea bass.
I am *Victor van Damme.*
Right...

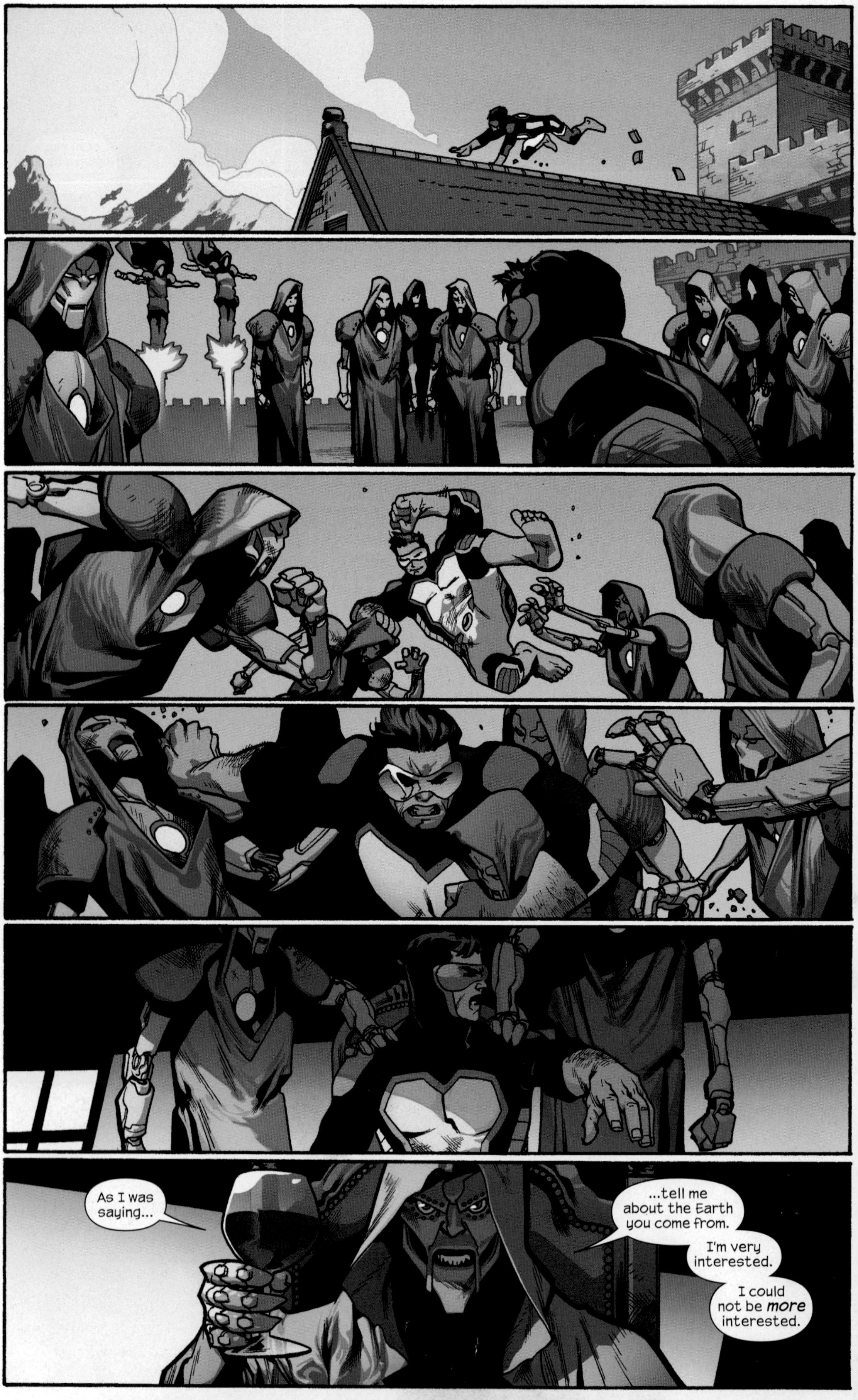
As I was saying...
...tell me about the Earth you come from.
I'm very interested.
I could not be *more* interested.

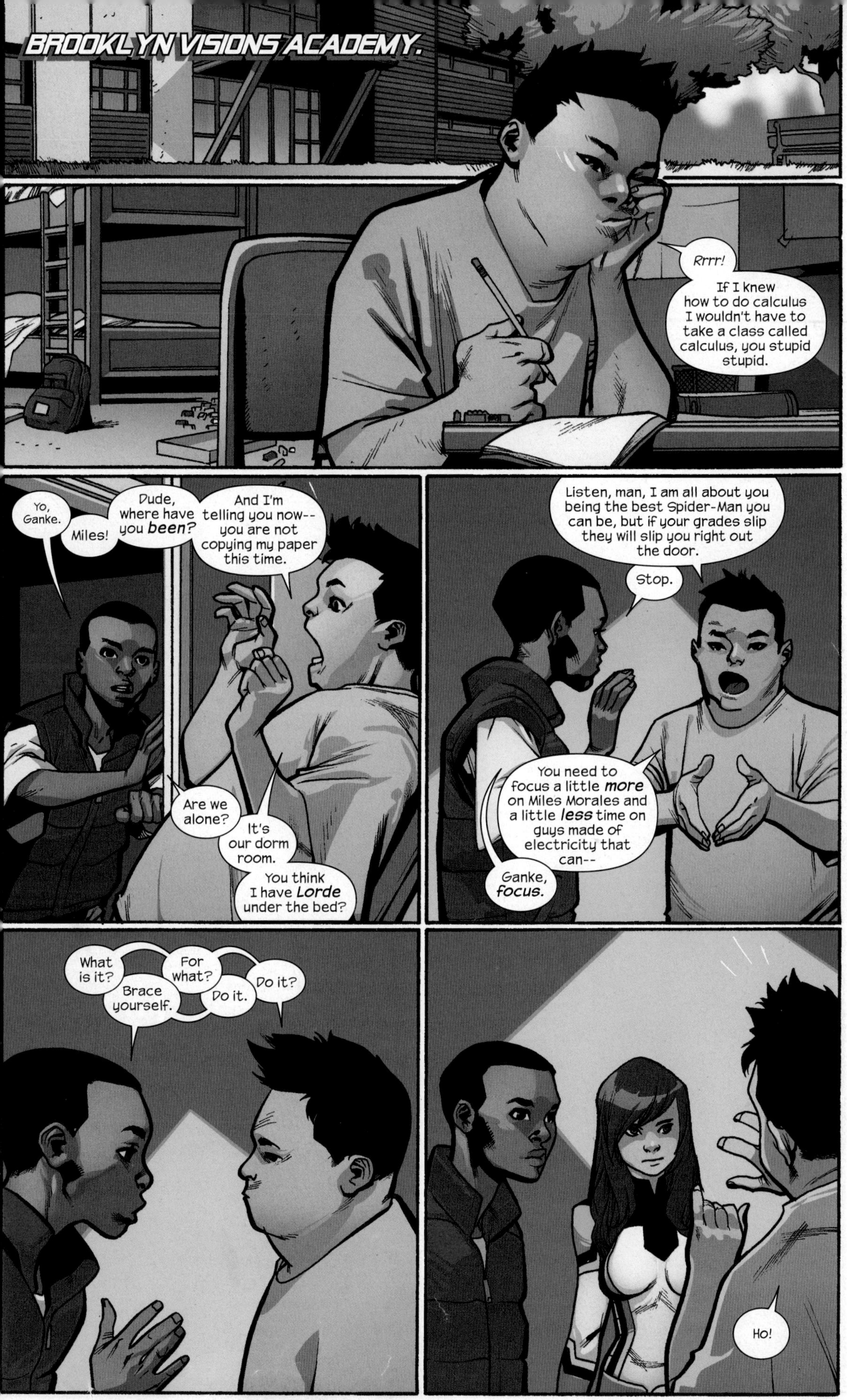
BROOKLYN VISIONS ACADEMY.
Rrrr!
If I knew how to do calculus I wouldn't have to take a class called calculus, you stupid stupid.
Yo, Ganke.
Miles!
Dude, where have you *been*?
And I'm telling you now-- you are not copying my paper this time.
Are we alone?
It's our dorm room.
You think I have *Lorde* under the bed?
Listen, man, I am all about you being the best Spider-Man you can be, but if your grades slip they will slip you right out the door.
Stop.
You need to focus a little *more* on Miles Morales and a little *less* time on guys made of electricity that can--
Ganke, *focus.*
What is it?
Brace yourself.
For what?
Do it.
Do it?
Ho!

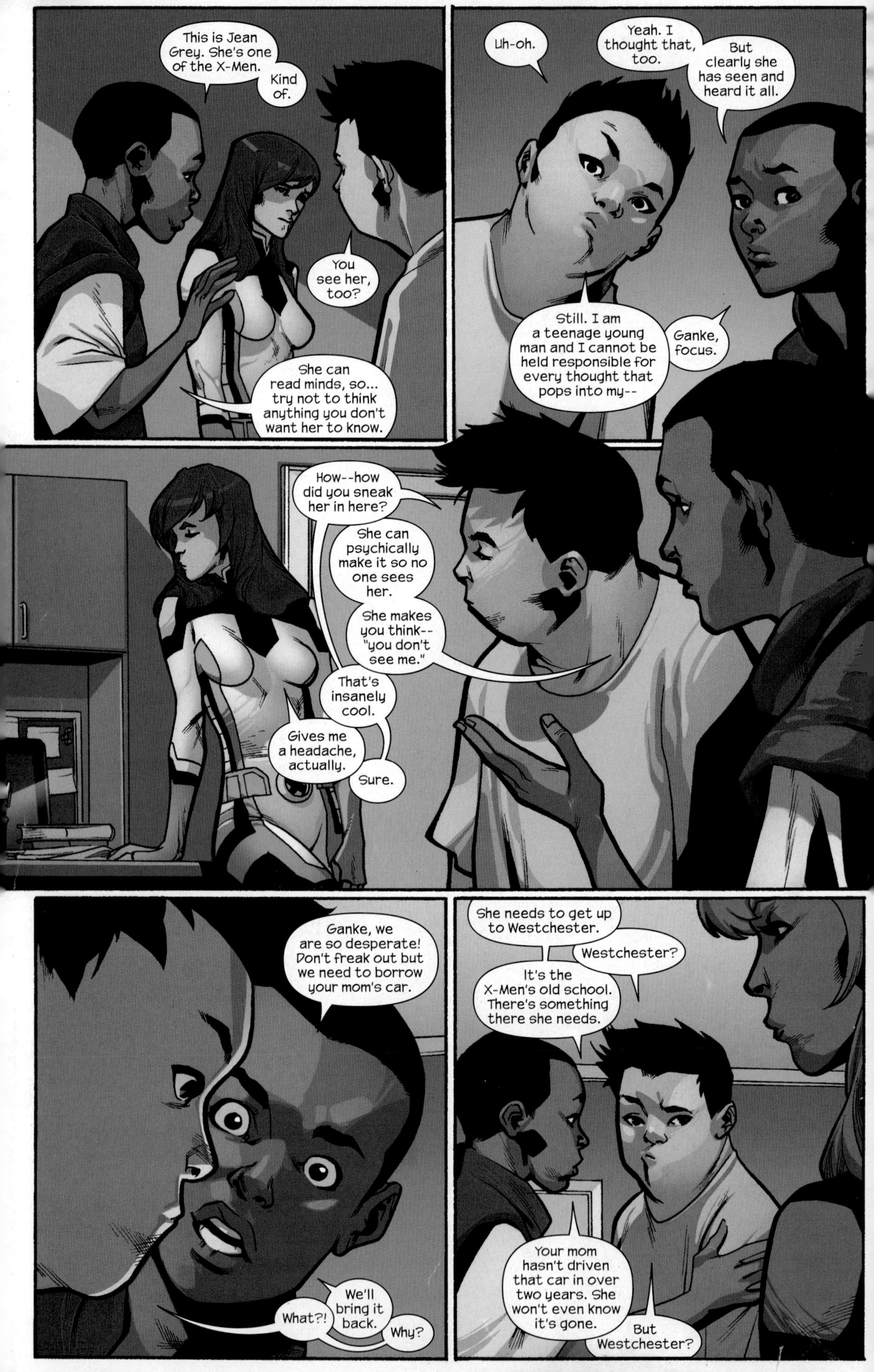
This is Jean Grey. She's one of the X-Men.
Kind of.
You see her, too?
She can read minds, so... try not to think anything you don't want her to know.
Uh-oh.
Yeah. I thought that, too.
But clearly she has seen and heard it all.
Still. I am a teenage young man and I cannot be held responsible for every thought that pops into my--
Ganke, focus.
How--how did you sneak her in here?
She can psychically make it so no one sees her.
She makes you think-- "you don't see me."
That's insanely cool.
Gives me a headache, actually.
Sure.
Ganke, we are so desperate! Don't freak out but we need to borrow your mom's car.
What?!
We'll bring it back.
Why?
She needs to get up to Westchester.
Westchester?
It's the X-Men's old school. There's something there she needs.
Your mom hasn't driven that car in over two years. She won't even know it's gone.
But Westchester?

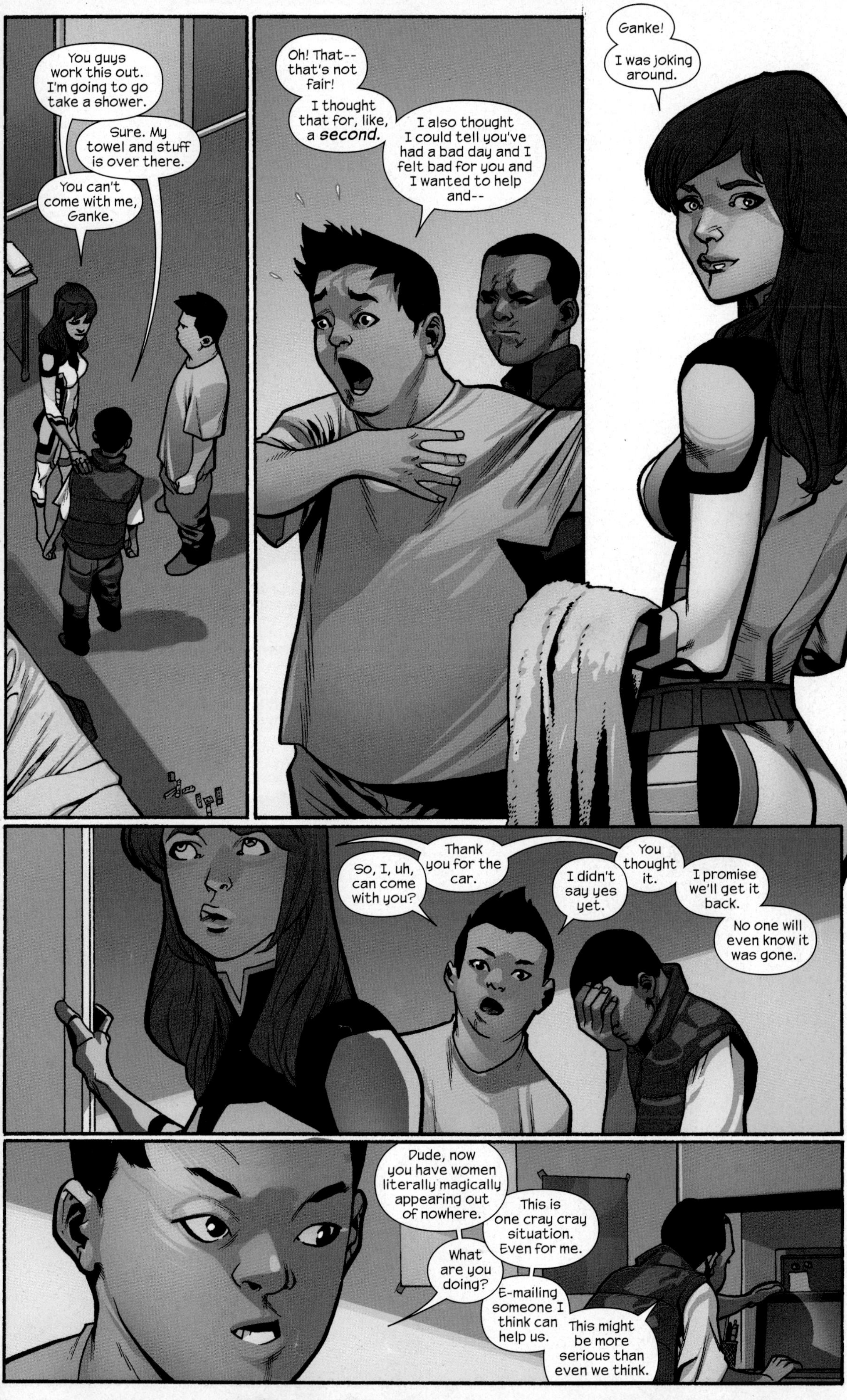

You guys work this out. I'm going to go take a shower.
Sure. My towel and stuff is over there.
You can't come with me, Ganke.
Oh! That-- that's not fair!
I thought that for, like, a **second.**
I also thought I could tell you've had a bad day and I felt bad for you and I wanted to help and--
Ganke!
I was joking around.
So, I, uh, can come with you?
Thank you for the car.
I didn't say yes yet.
You thought it.
I promise we'll get it back.
No one will even know it was gone.
Dude, now you have women literally magically appearing out of nowhere.
This is one cray cray situation. Even for me.
What are you doing?
E-mailing someone I think can help us.
This might be more serious than even we think.

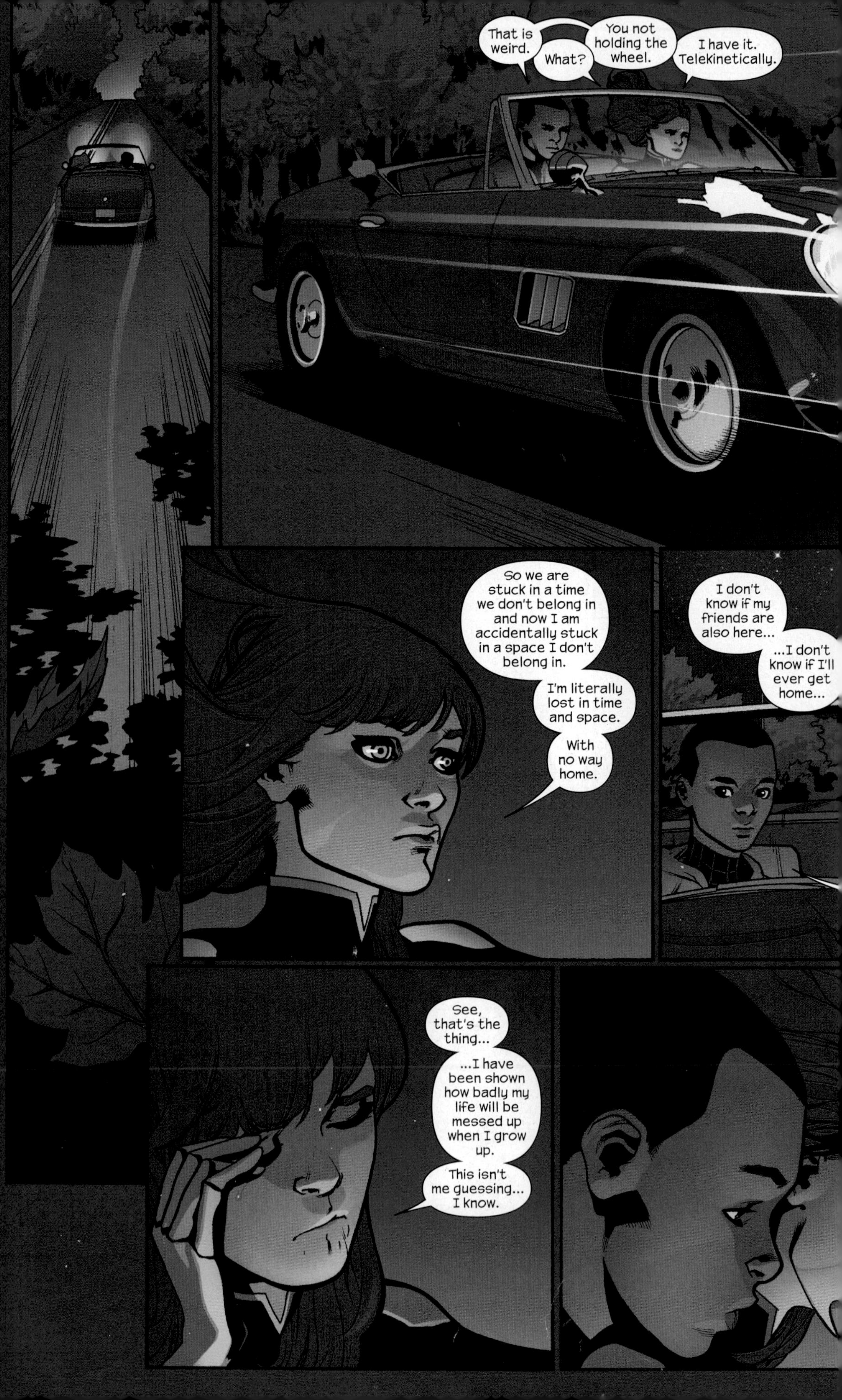
That is weird.
What?
You not holding the wheel.
I have it. Telekinetically.
So we are stuck in a time we don't belong in and now I am accidentally stuck in a space I don't belong in.
I'm literally lost in time and space.
With no way home.
I don't know if my friends are also here...
...I don't know if I'll ever get home...
See, that's the thing...
...I have been shown how badly my life will be messed up when I grow up.
This isn't me guessing... I know.

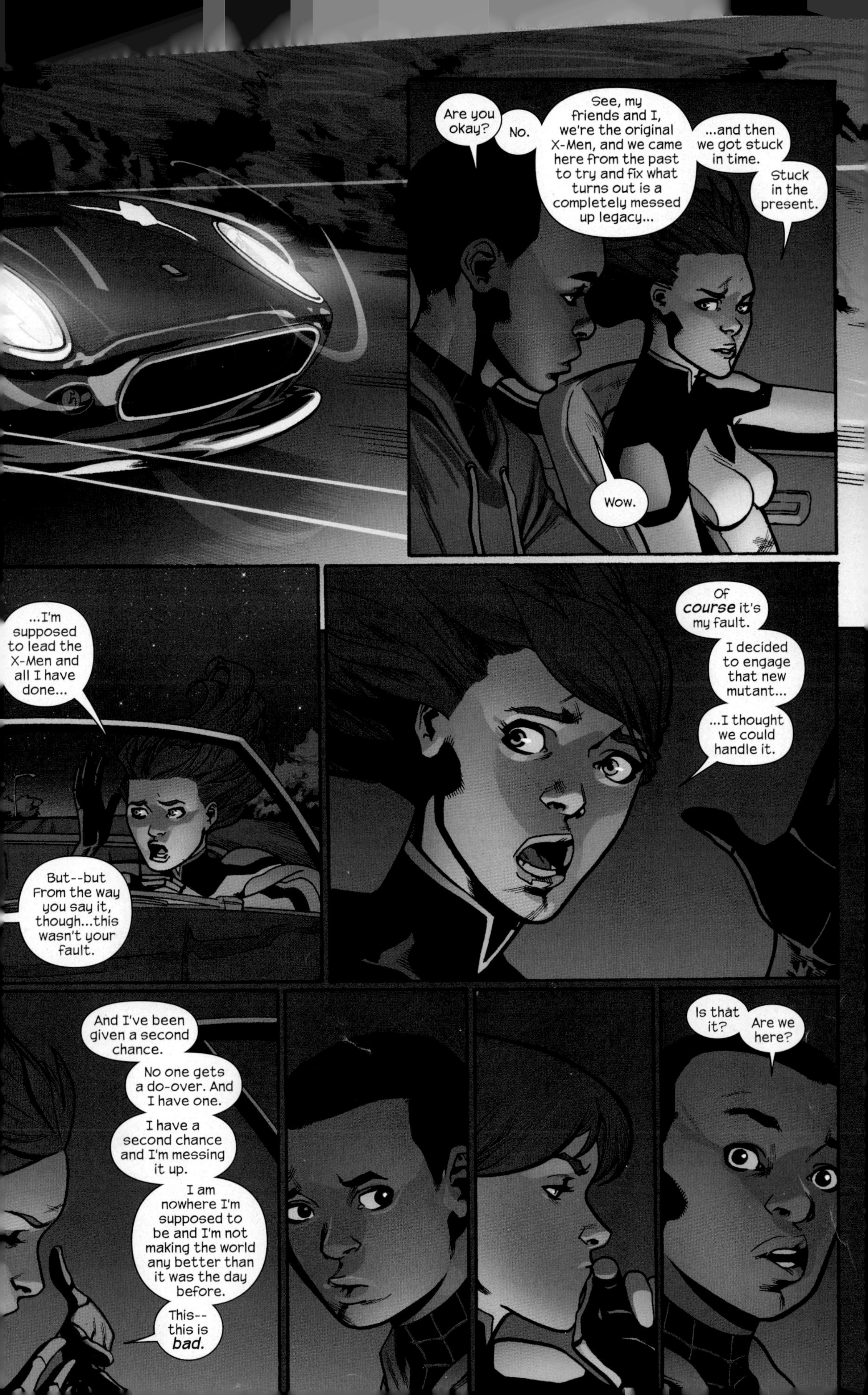
Are you okay?
No.
See, my friends and I, we're the original X-Men, and we came here from the past to try and fix what turns out is a completely messed up legacy...
...and then we got stuck in time.
Stuck in the present.
Wow.
...I'm supposed to lead the X-Men and all I have done...
But--but from the way you say it, though...this wasn't your fault.
Of *course* it's my fault.
I decided to engage that new mutant...
...I thought we could handle it.
And I've been given a second chance.
No one gets a do-over. And I have one.
I have a second chance and I'm messing it up.
I am nowhere I'm supposed to be and I'm not making the world any better than it was the day before.
This--this is *bad.*
Is that it?
Are we here?

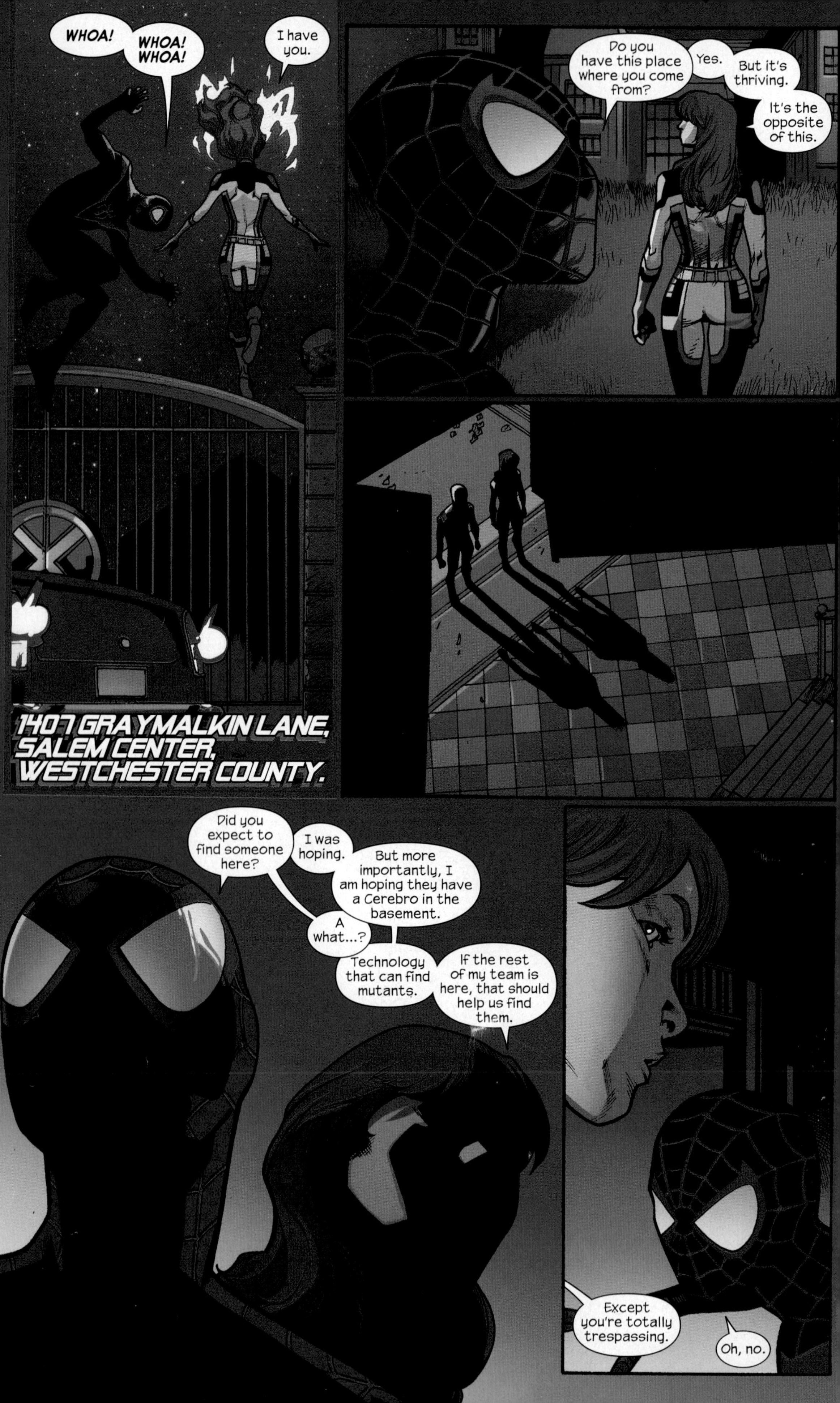
WHOA!
WHOA! WHOA!
I have you.
1407 GRAYMALKIN LANE, SALEM CENTER, WESTCHESTER COUNTY.
Do you have this place where you come from?
Yes.
But it's thriving.
It's the opposite of this.
Did you expect to find someone here?
I was hoping.
But more importantly, I am hoping they have a Cerebro in the basement.
A what...?
Technology that can find mutants.
If the rest of my team is here, that should help us find them.
Except you're totally trespassing.
Oh, no.

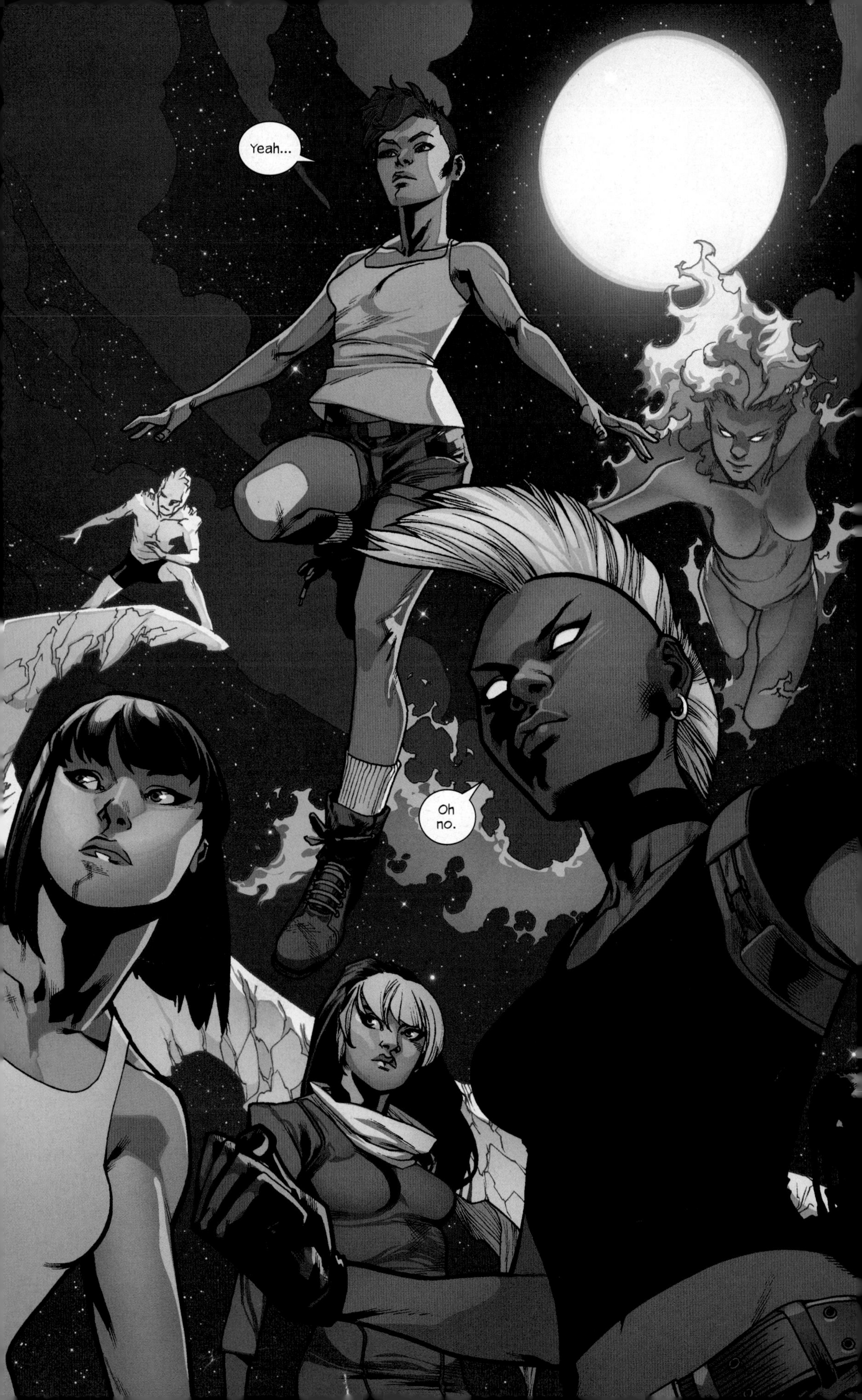
Yeah...
Oh no.

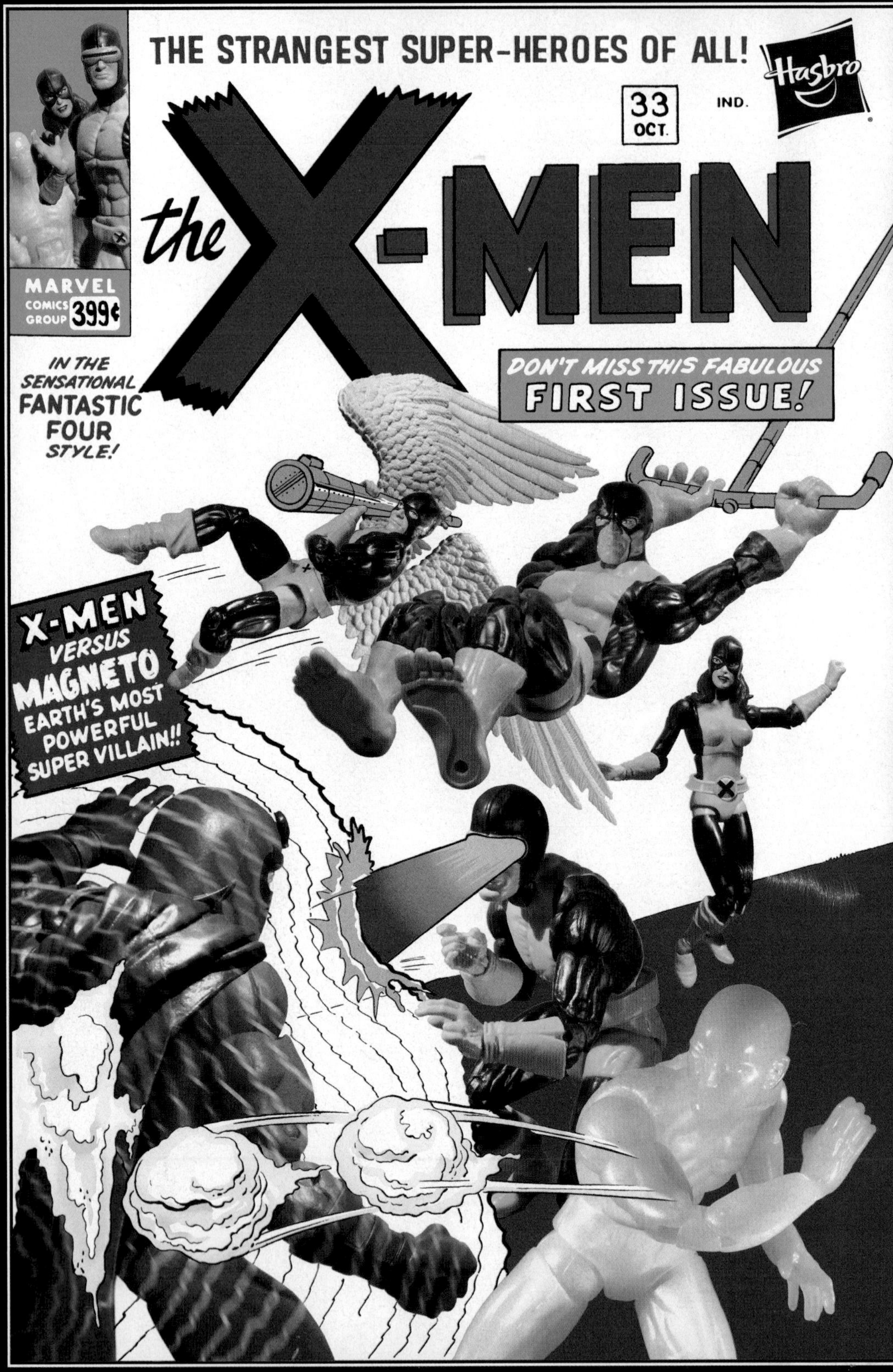

THE STRANGEST SUPER-HEROES OF ALL!
Hasbro
33
OCT.
IND.
MARVEL
COMICS GROUP
399¢
the X-MEN
IN THE SENSATIONAL FANTASTIC FOUR STYLE!
DON'T MISS THIS FABULOUS FIRST ISSUE!
X-MEN VERSUS MAGNETO EARTH'S MOST POWERFUL SUPER VILLAIN!!

ALL-NEW X-MEN #33 HASBRO VARIANT

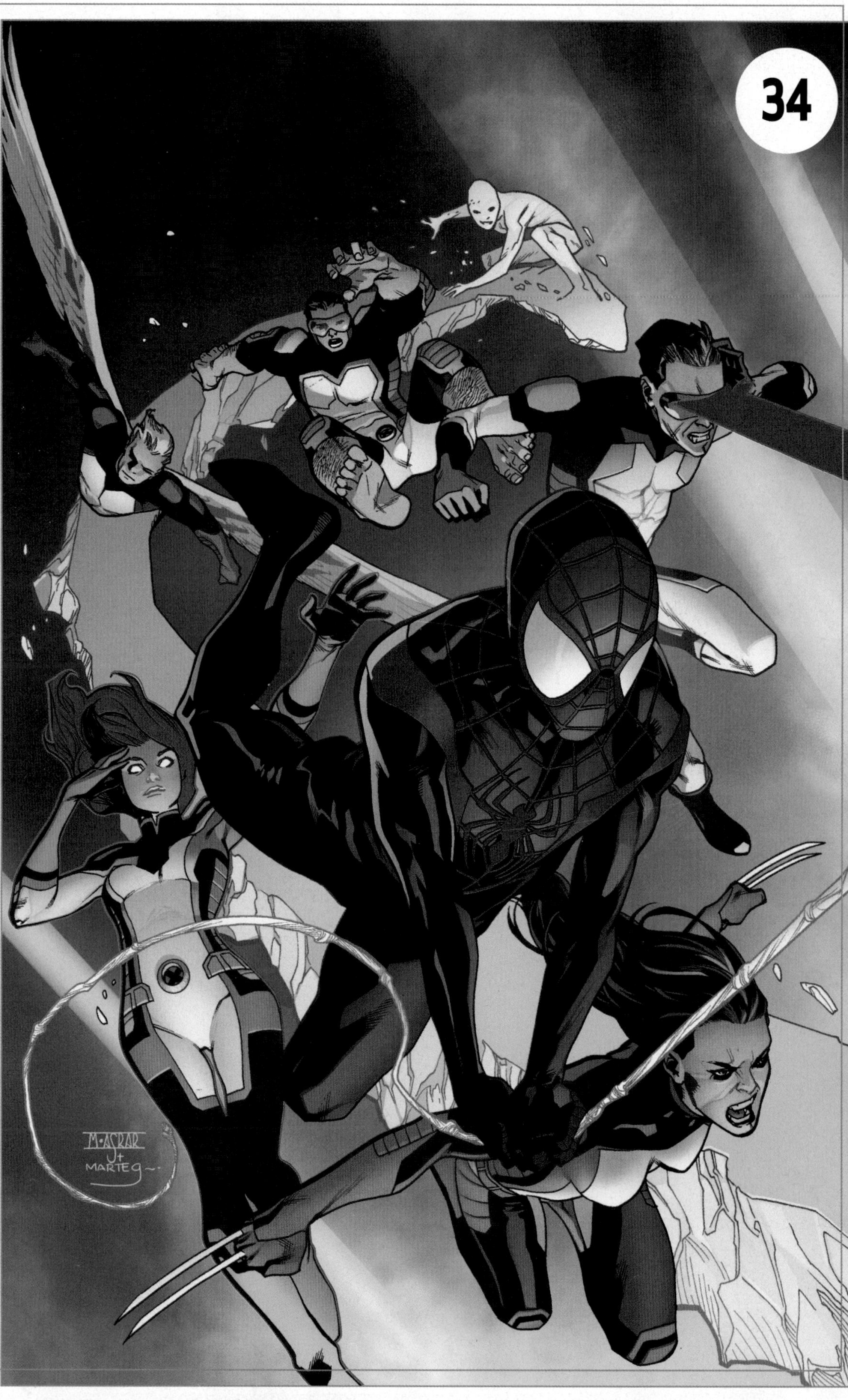
34
M.ASRAR
J+
MARTEG

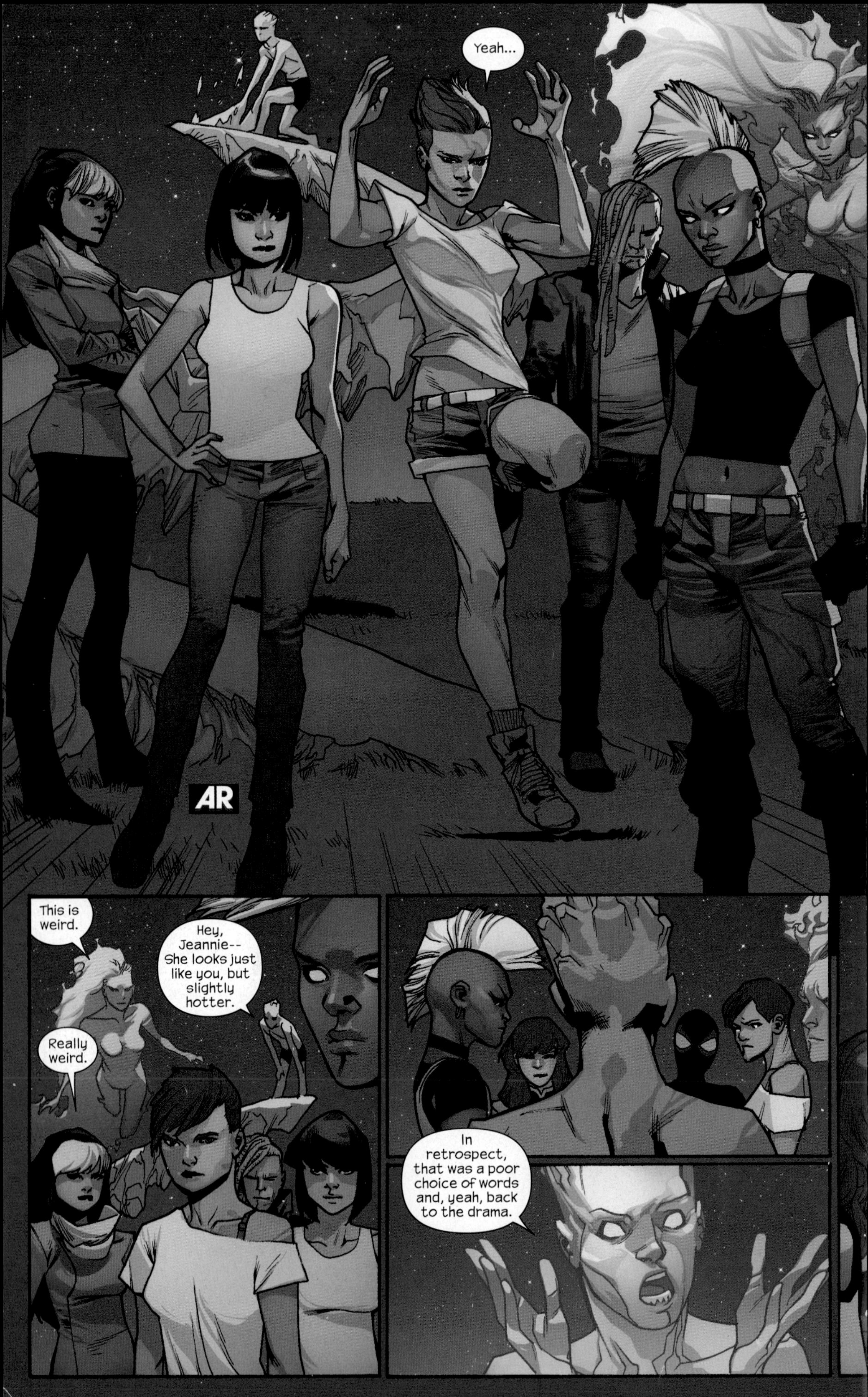
Yeah...
This is weird.
Hey, Jeannie-- She looks just like you, but slightly hotter.
Really weird.
In retrospect, that was a poor choice of words and, yeah, back to the drama.

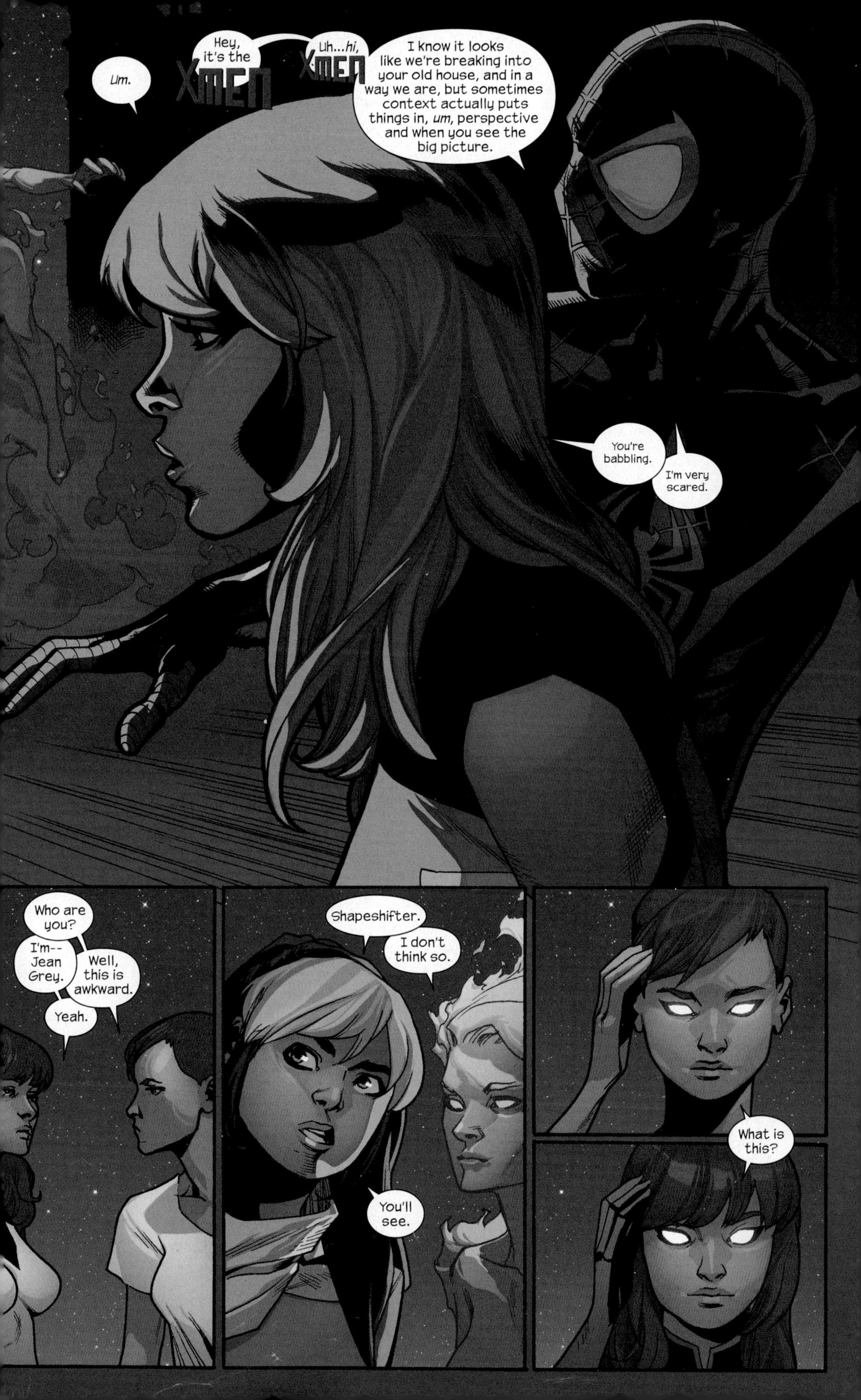
Um.
Hey, it's the X-MEN
Uh...hi, X-MEN
I know it looks like we're breaking into your old house, and in a way we are, but sometimes context actually puts things in, um, perspective and when you see the big picture.
You're babbling.
I'm very scared.
Who are you?
I'm-- Jean Grey.
Well, this is awkward.
Yeah.
Shapeshifter.
I don't think so.
You'll see.
What is this?

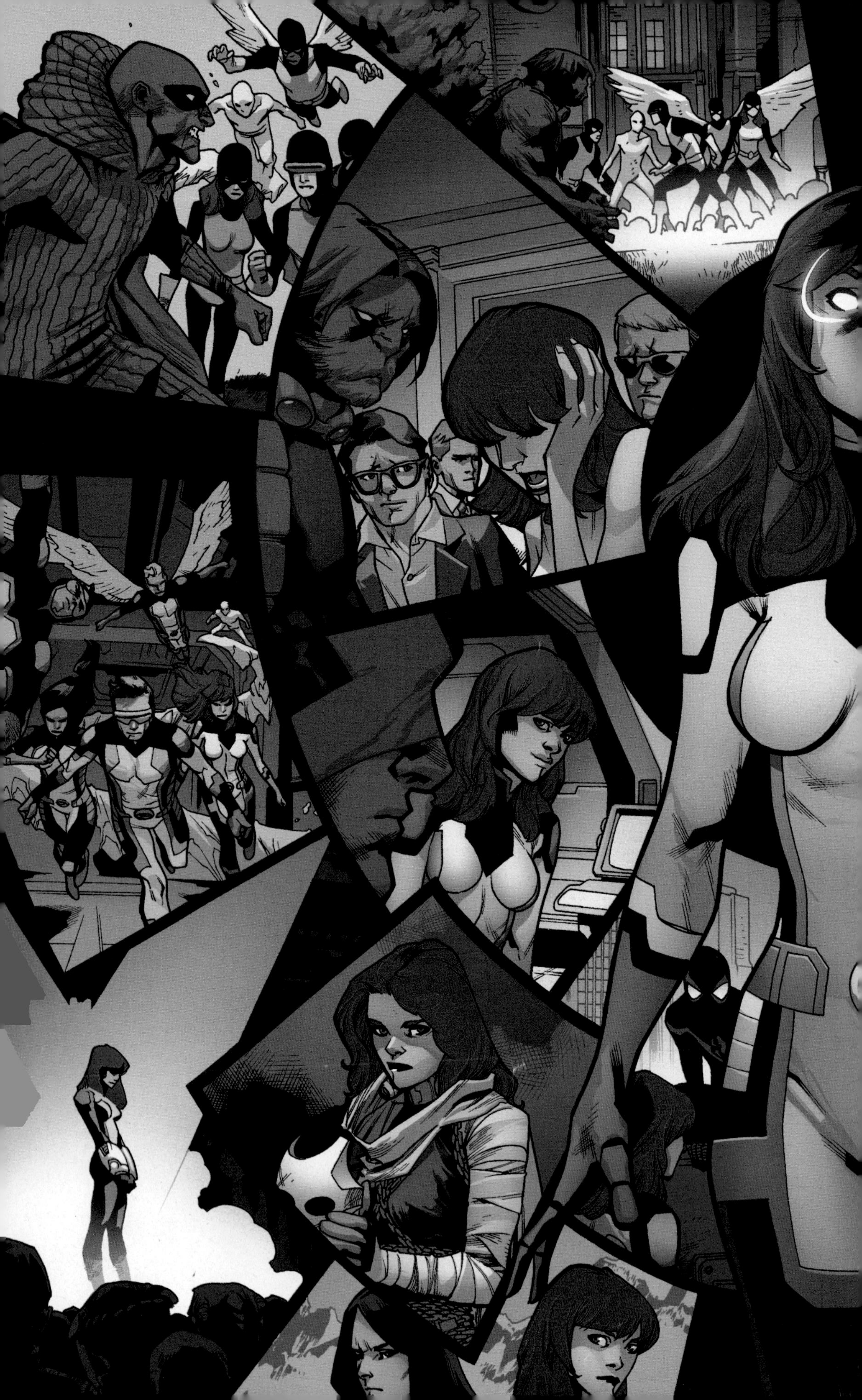

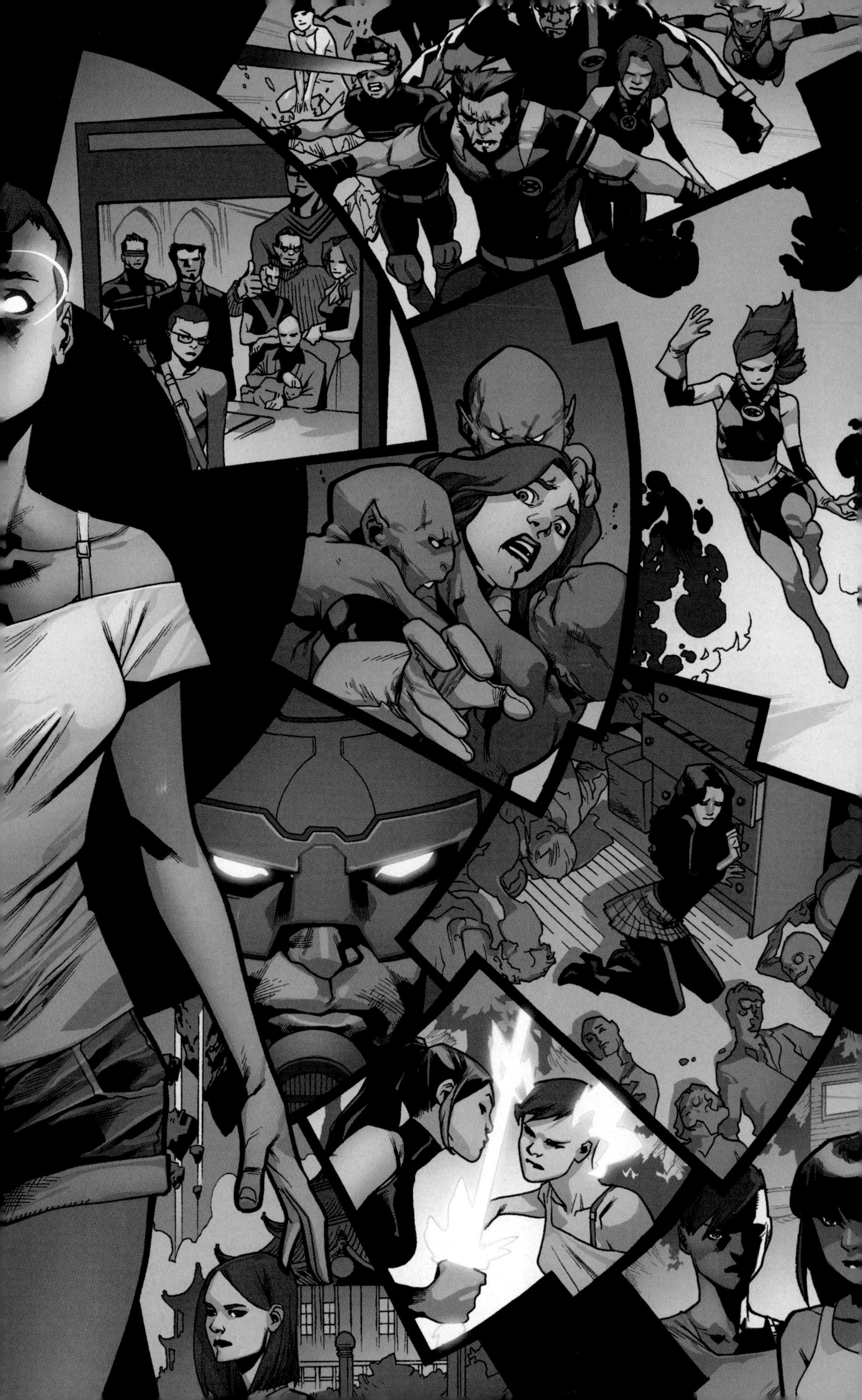

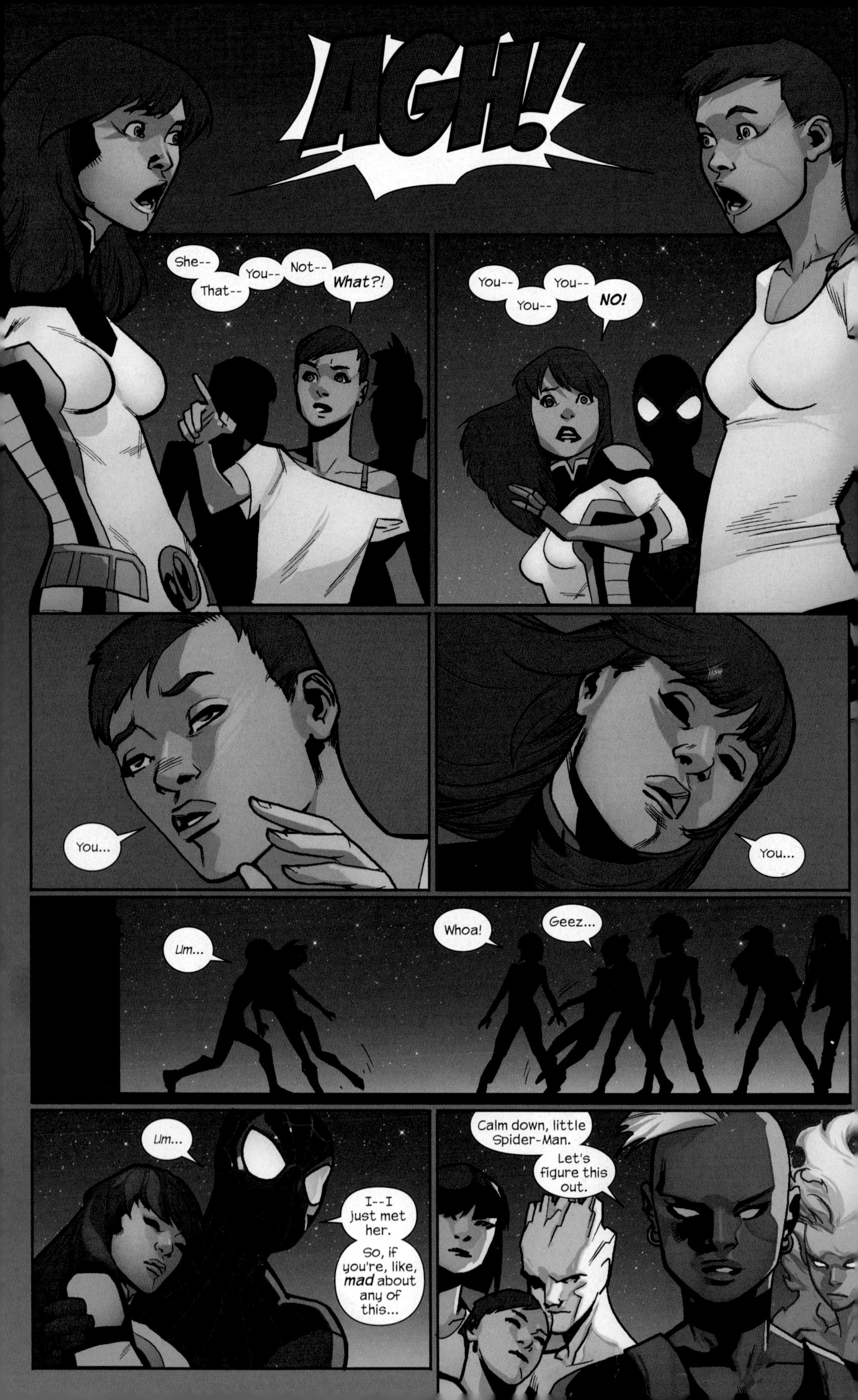
AGH!
She--
That--
You--
Not--
What?!
You--
You--
You--
NO!
You...
You...
Um...
Whoa!
Geez...
Um...
I--I just met her.
So, if you're, like, mad about any of this...
Calm down, little Spider-Man.
Let's figure this out.

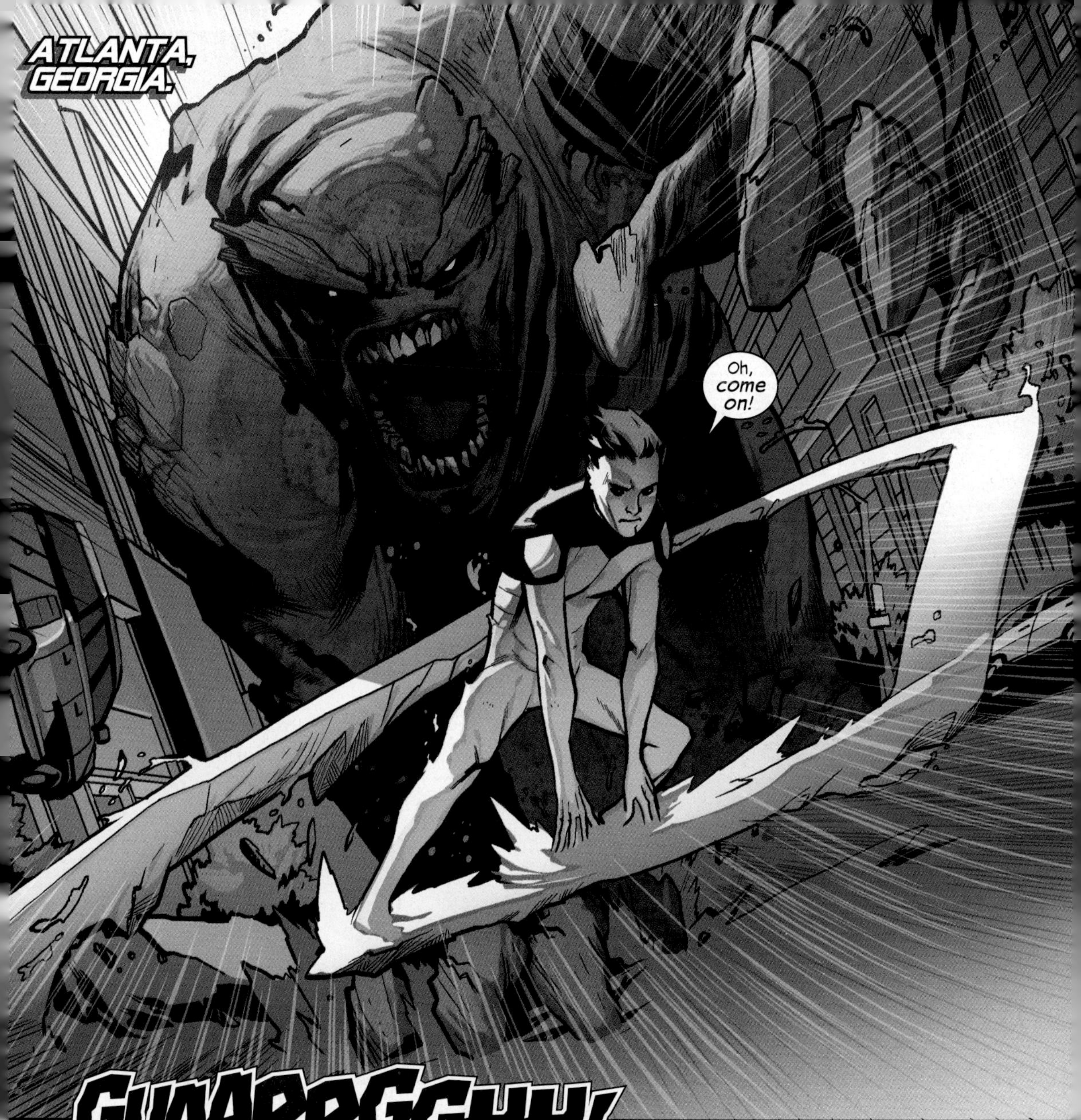
ATLANTA, GEORGIA.
Oh, come on!
GUAARRGGHHH!

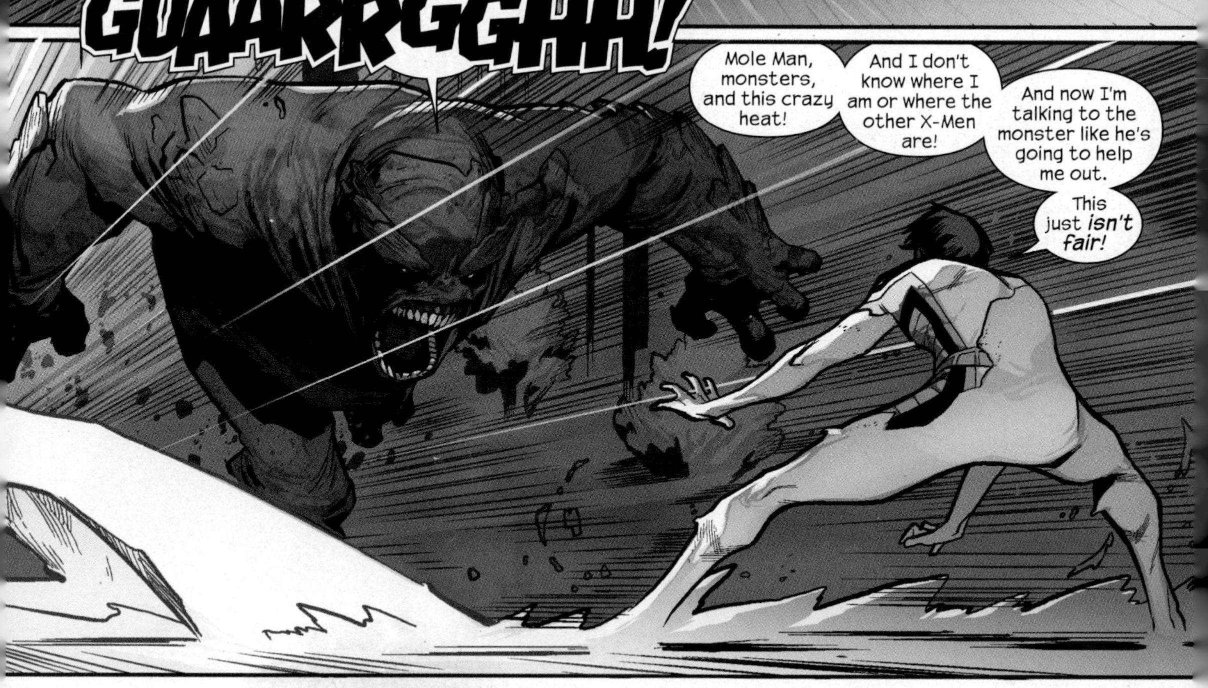
Mole Man, monsters, and this crazy heat!
And I don't know where I am or where the other X-Men are!
And now I'm talking to the monster like he's going to help me out.
This just isn't fair!

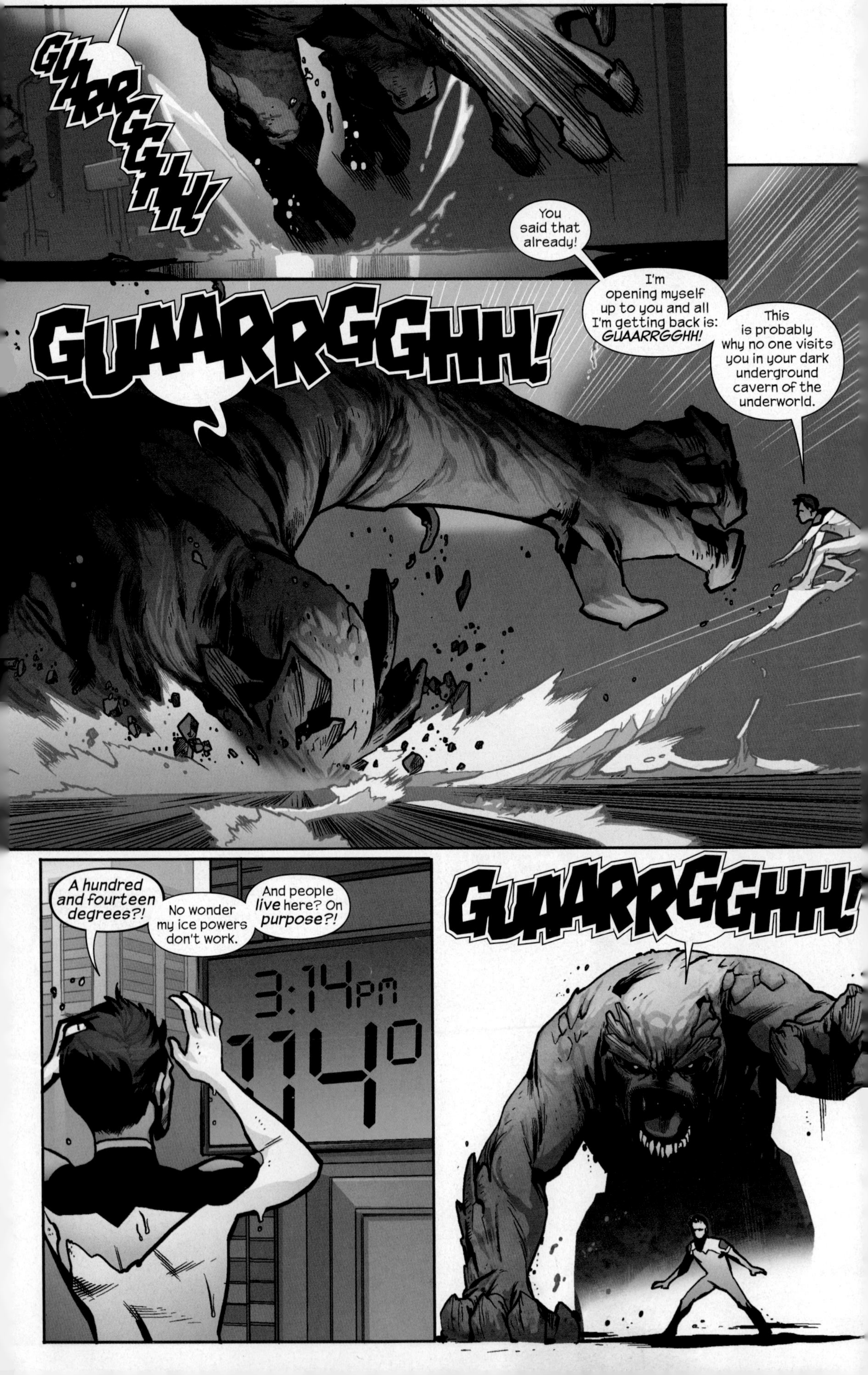
GUAARRGGHH!
You said that already!
GUAARRGGHH!
I'm opening myself up to you and all I'm getting back is: GUAARRGGHH!
This is probably why no one visits you in your dark underground cavern of the underworld.
A hundred and fourteen degrees?!
No wonder my ice powers don't work.
And people live here? On purpose?!
3:14PM
114°
GUAARRGGHH!

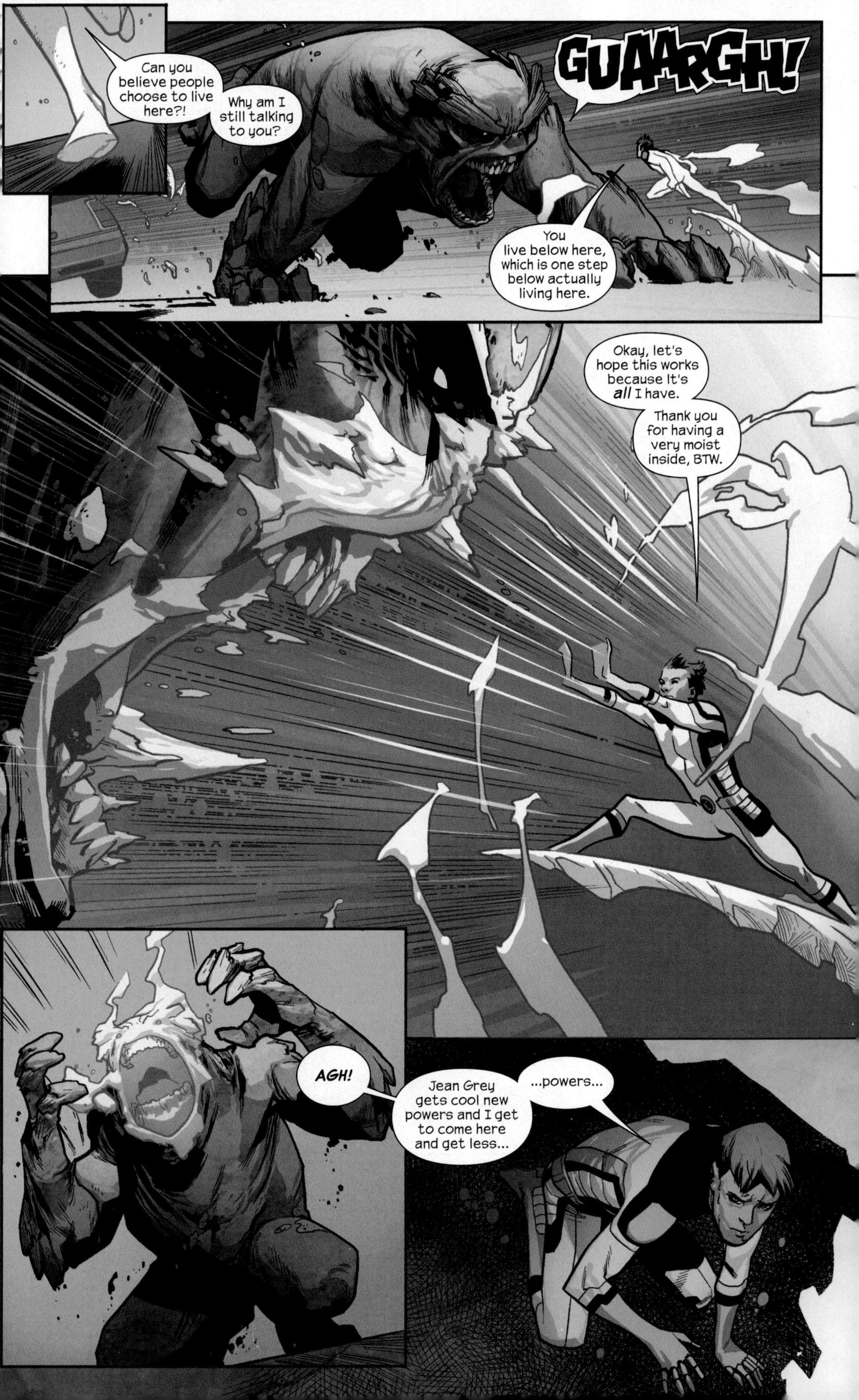
Can you believe people choose to live here?!
Why am I still talking to you?
GUAARGH!
You live below here, which is one step below actually living here.
Okay, let's hope this works because It's *all* I have.
Thank you for having a very moist inside, BTW.
AGH!
Jean Grey gets cool new powers and I get to come here and get less...
...powers...

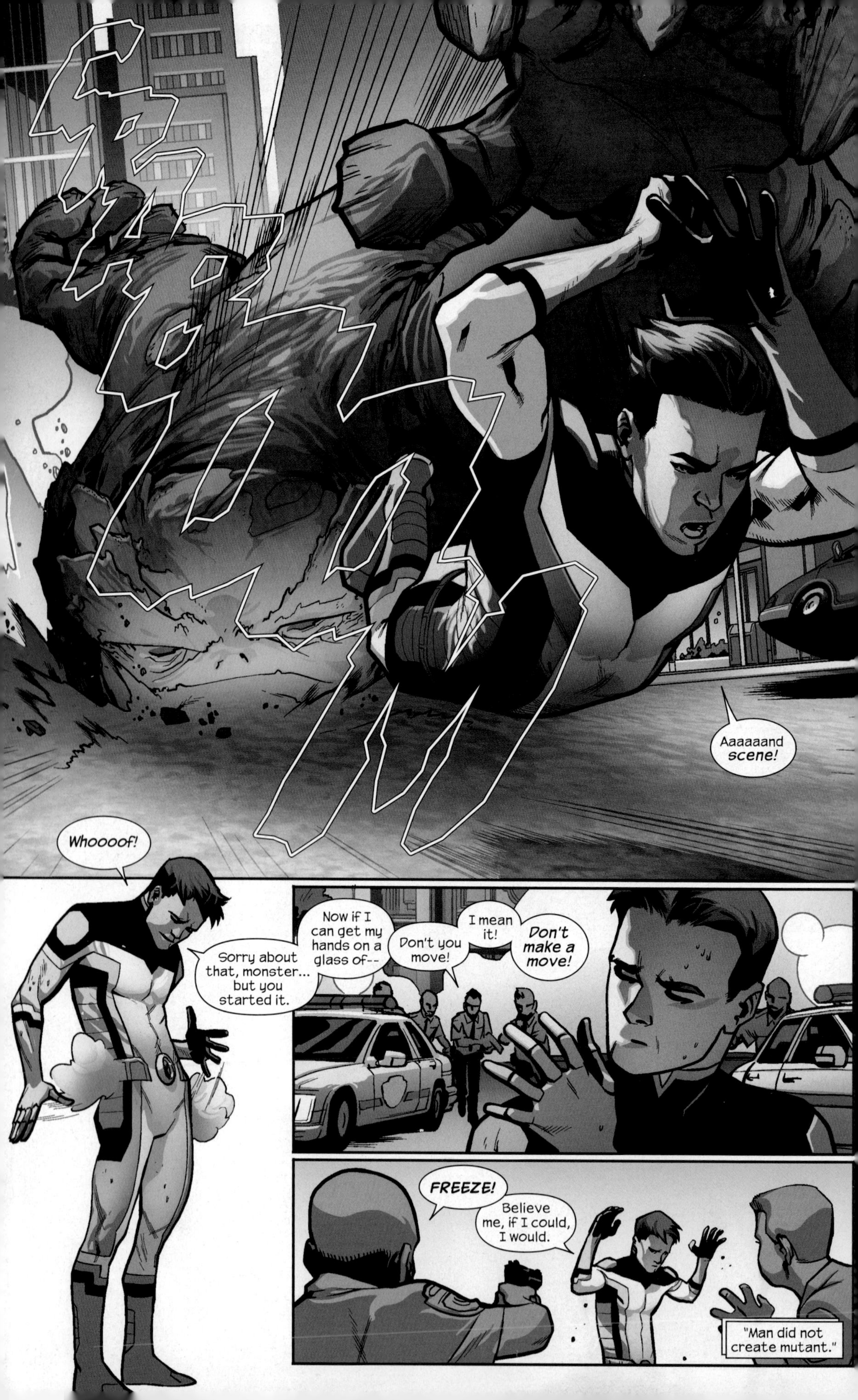
Aaaaaand scene!
Whoooof!
Sorry about that, monster... but you started it.
Now if I can get my hands on a glass of--
Don't you move!
I mean it!
Don't make a move!
FREEZE!
Believe me, if I could, I would.
"Man did not create mutant."

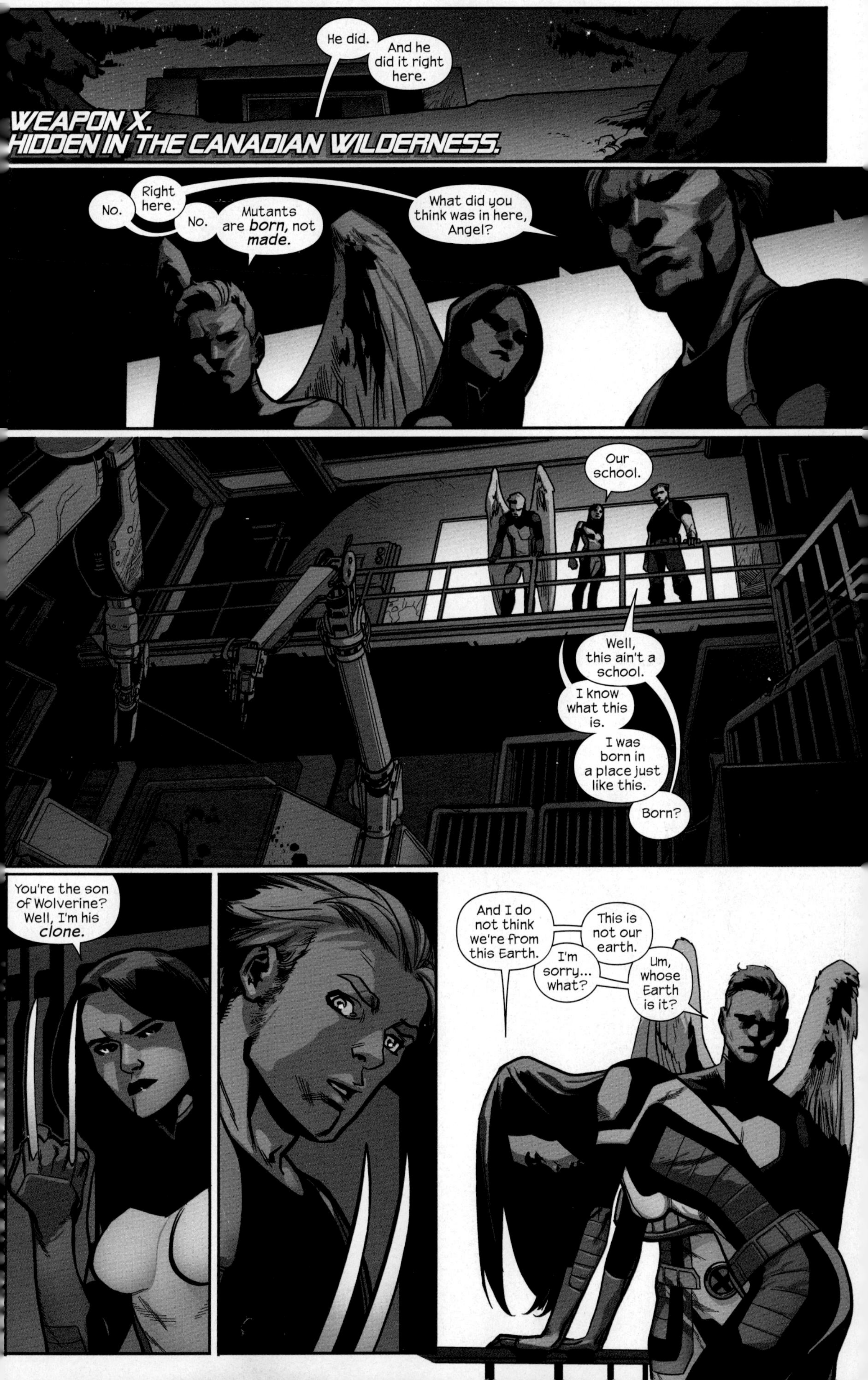
He did.
And he did it right here.
WEAPON X.
HIDDEN IN THE CANADIAN WILDERNESS.
What did you think was in here, Angel?
Right here.
No.
No.
Mutants are *born*, not *made.*
Our school.
Well, this ain't a school.
I know what this is.
I was born in a place just like this.
Born?
You're the son of Wolverine? Well, I'm his *clone.*
And I do not think we're from this Earth.
This is not our earth.
I'm sorry... what?
Um, whose Earth is it?

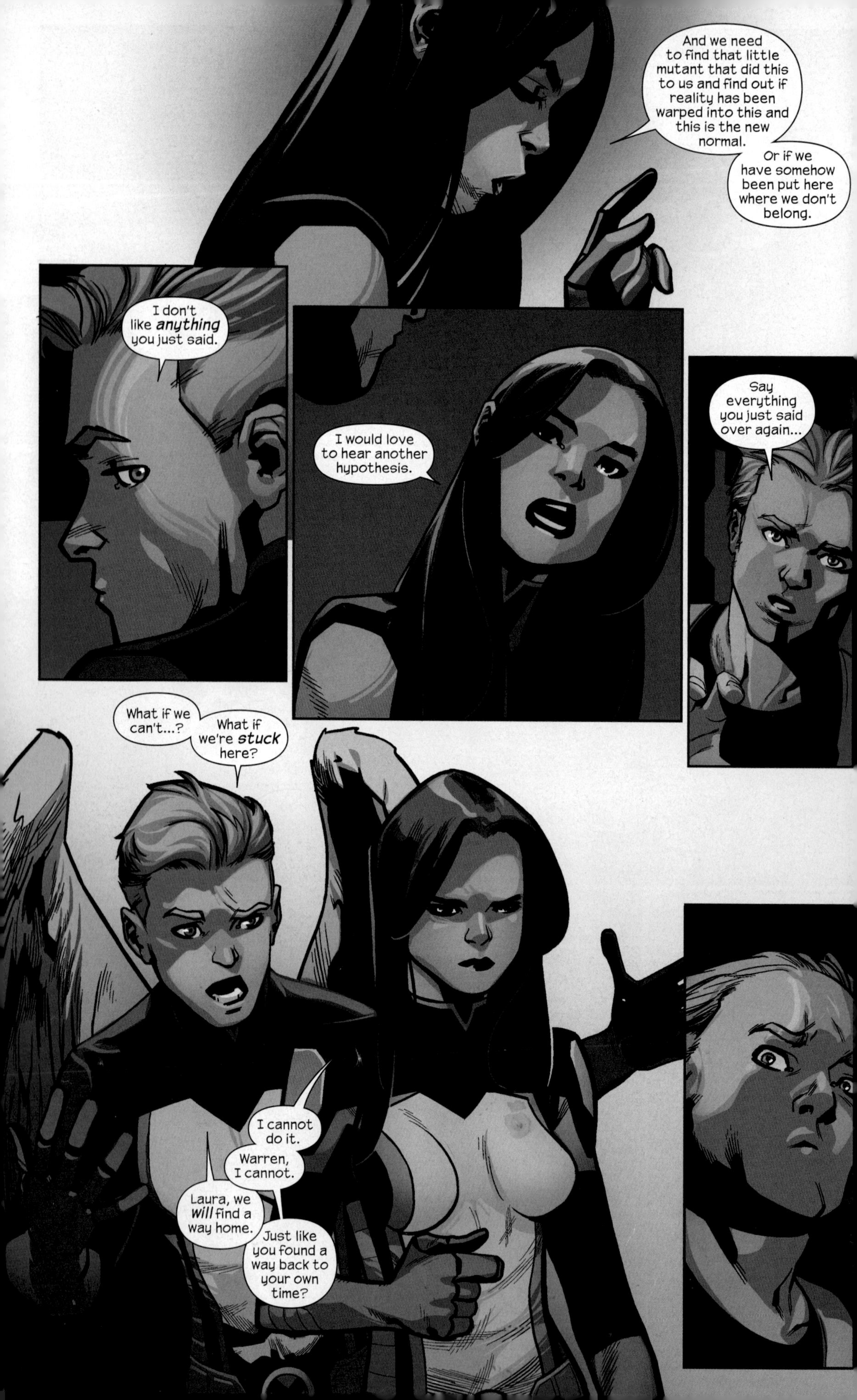
And we need to find that little mutant that did this to us and find out if reality has been warped into this and this is the new normal.
Or if we have somehow been put here where we don't belong.
I don't like anything you just said.
I would love to hear another hypothesis.
Say everything you just said over again...
What if we can't...?
What if we're stuck here?
I cannot do it.
Warren, I cannot.
Laura, we will find a way home.
Just like you found a way back to your own time?

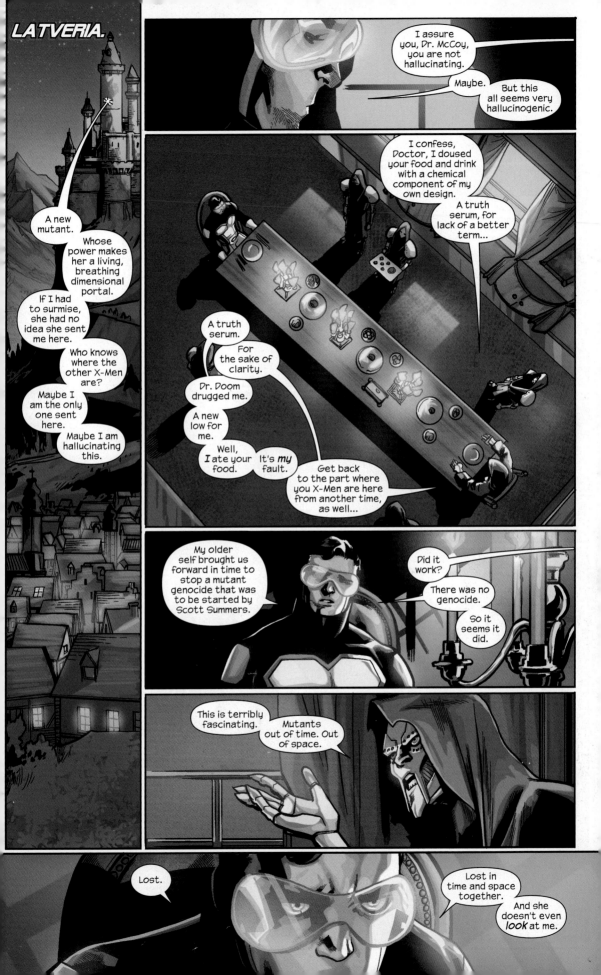

LATVERIA.

I assure you, Dr. McCoy, you are not hallucinating.

Maybe. But this all seems very hallucinogenic.

I confess, Doctor, I doused your food and drink with a chemical component of my own design.

A truth serum, for lack of a better term...

A new mutant.

Whose power makes her a living, breathing dimensional portal.

If I had to surmise, she had no idea she sent me here.

Who knows where the other X-Men are?

Maybe I am the only one sent here.

Maybe I am hallucinating this.

A truth serum.

For the sake of clarity.

Dr. Doom drugged me.

A new low for me.

Well, I ate your food.

It's my fault.

Get back to the part where you X-Men are here from another time, as well...

My older self brought us forward in time to stop a mutant genocide that was to be started by Scott Summers.

Did it work?

There was no genocide.

So it seems it did.

This is terribly fascinating.

Mutants out of time. Out of space.

Lost.

Lost in time and space together.

And she doesn't even look at me.

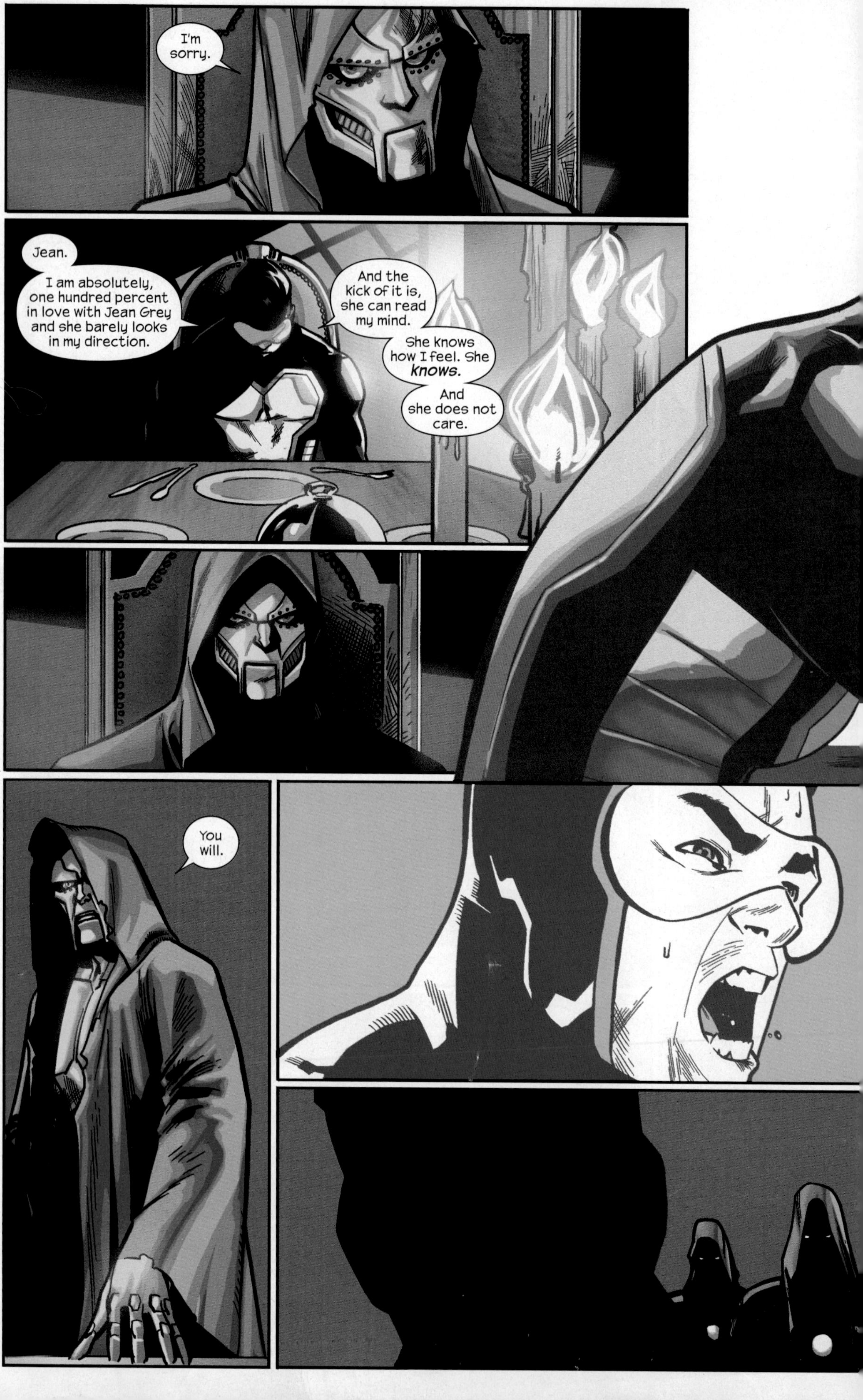
I'm sorry.
Jean.
I am absolutely, one hundred percent in love with Jean Grey and she barely looks in my direction.
And the kick of it is, she can read my mind.
She knows how I feel. She *knows.*
And she does not care.
You will.

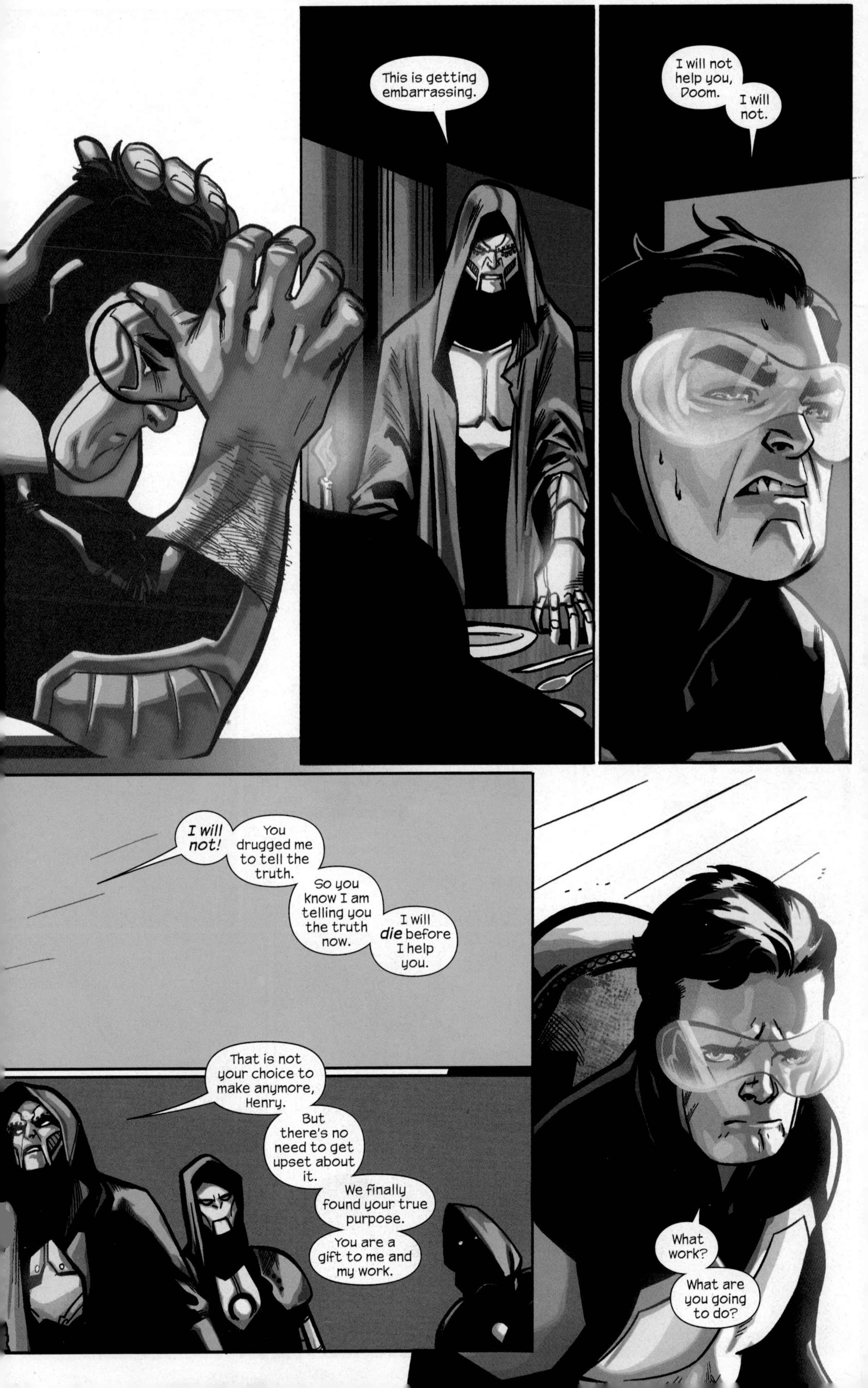
This is getting embarrassing.
I will not help you, Doom.
I will not.
I will not!
You drugged me to tell the truth.
So you know I am telling you the truth now.
I will die before I help you.
That is not your choice to make anymore, Henry.
But there's no need to get upset about it.
We finally found your true purpose.
You are a gift to me and my work.
What work?
What are you going to do?

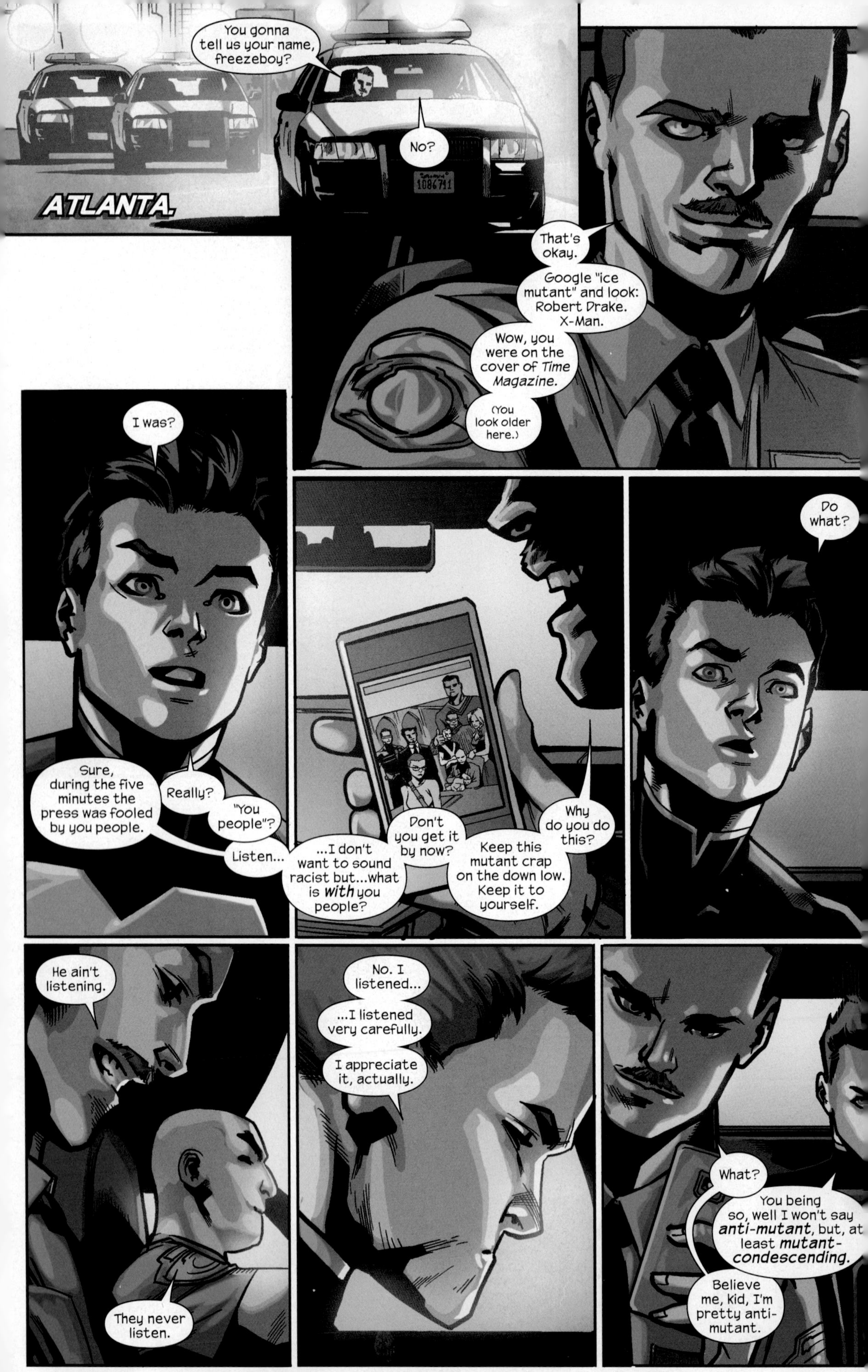
ATLANTA.
You gonna tell us your name, freezeboy?
No?
That's okay.
Google "ice mutant" and look: Robert Drake. X-Man.
Wow, you were on the cover of *Time Magazine*.
(You look older here.)
I was?
Sure, during the five minutes the press was fooled by you people.
Really?
"You people"?
Listen...
...I don't want to sound racist but...what is ***with*** you people?
Don't you get it by now?
Keep this mutant crap on the down low. Keep it to yourself.
Why do you do this?
Do what?
He ain't listening.
They never listen.
No. I listened...
...I listened very carefully.
I appreciate it, actually.
What?
You being so, well I won't say ***anti-mutant***, but, at least ***mutant-condescending***.
Believe me, kid, I'm pretty anti-mutant.

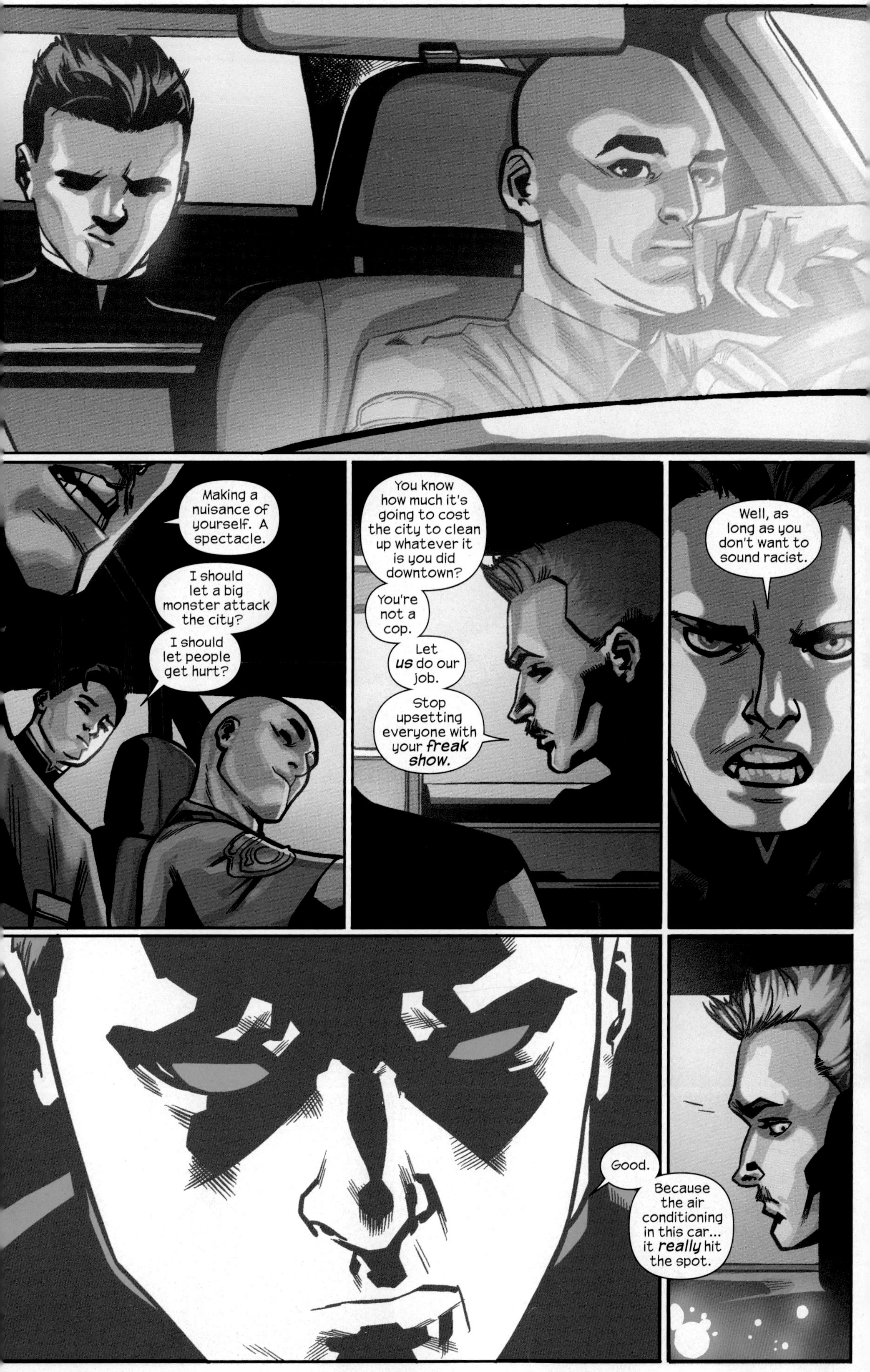
Making a nuisance of yourself. A spectacle.
I should let a big monster attack the city?
I should let people get hurt?
You know how much it's going to cost the city to clean up whatever it is you did downtown?
You're not a cop.
Let us do our job.
Stop upsetting everyone with your freak show.
Well, as long as you don't want to sound racist.
Good.
Because the air conditioning in this car... it really hit the spot.

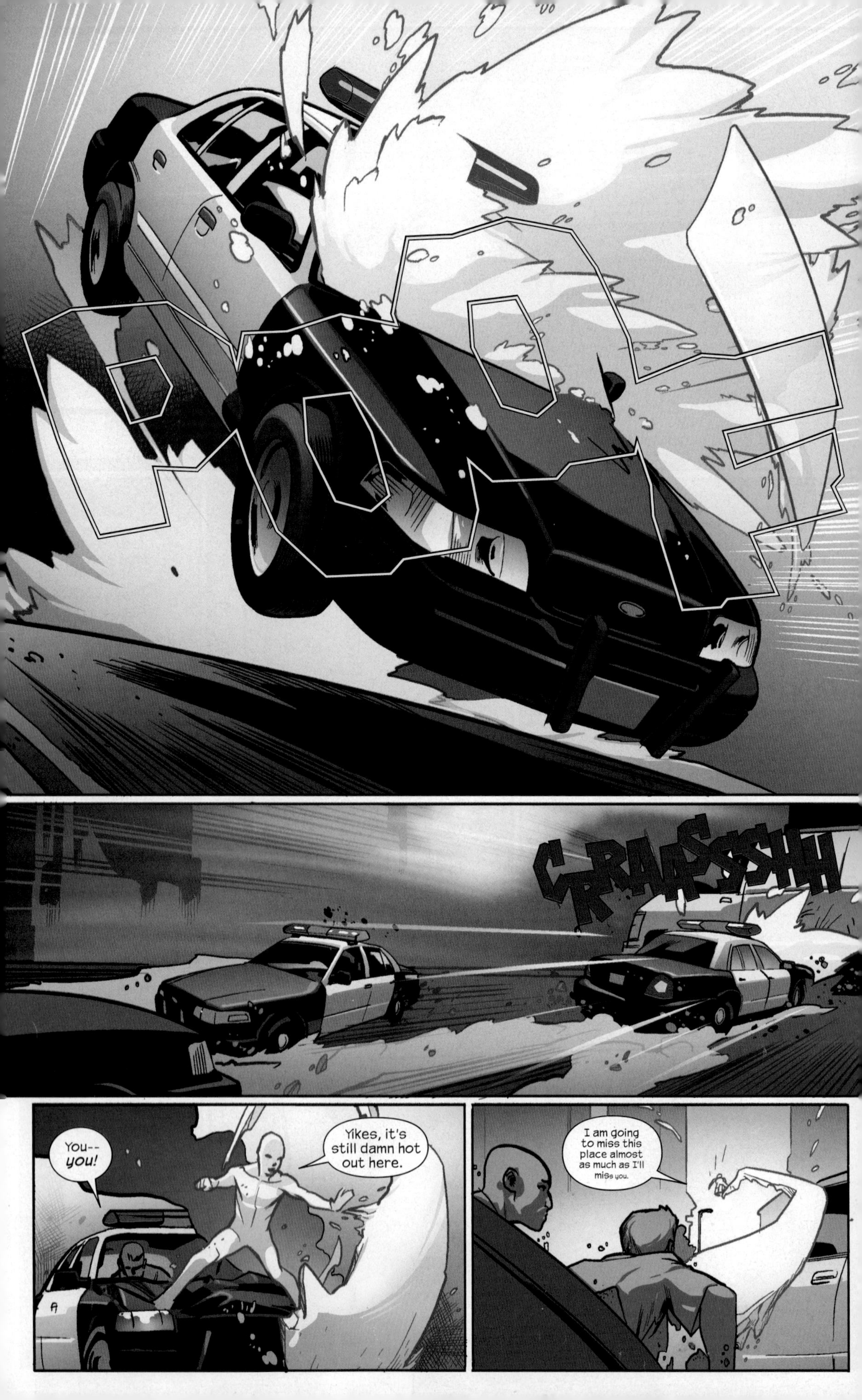
CRRAASSSHH
You-- you!
Yikes, it's still damn hot out here.
I am going to miss this place almost as much as I'll miss you.

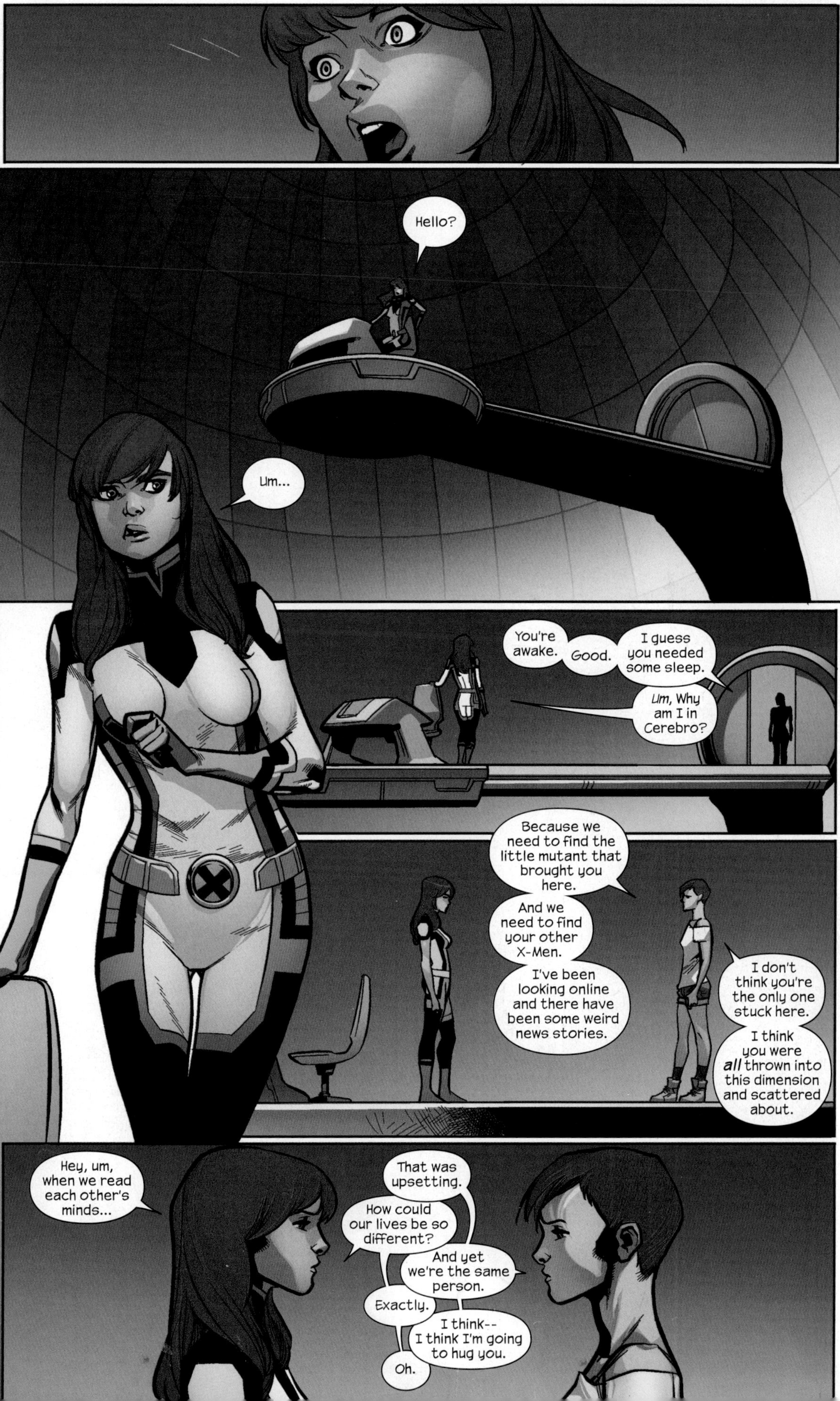
Hello?
Um...
You're awake.
Good.
I guess you needed some sleep.
Um, Why am I in Cerebro?
Because we need to find the little mutant that brought you here.
And we need to find your other X-Men.
I've been looking online and there have been some weird news stories.
I don't think you're the only one stuck here.
I think you were all thrown into this dimension and scattered about.
Hey, um, when we read each other's minds...
That was upsetting.
How could our lives be so different?
And yet we're the same person.
Exactly.
I think-- I think I'm going to hug you.
Oh.

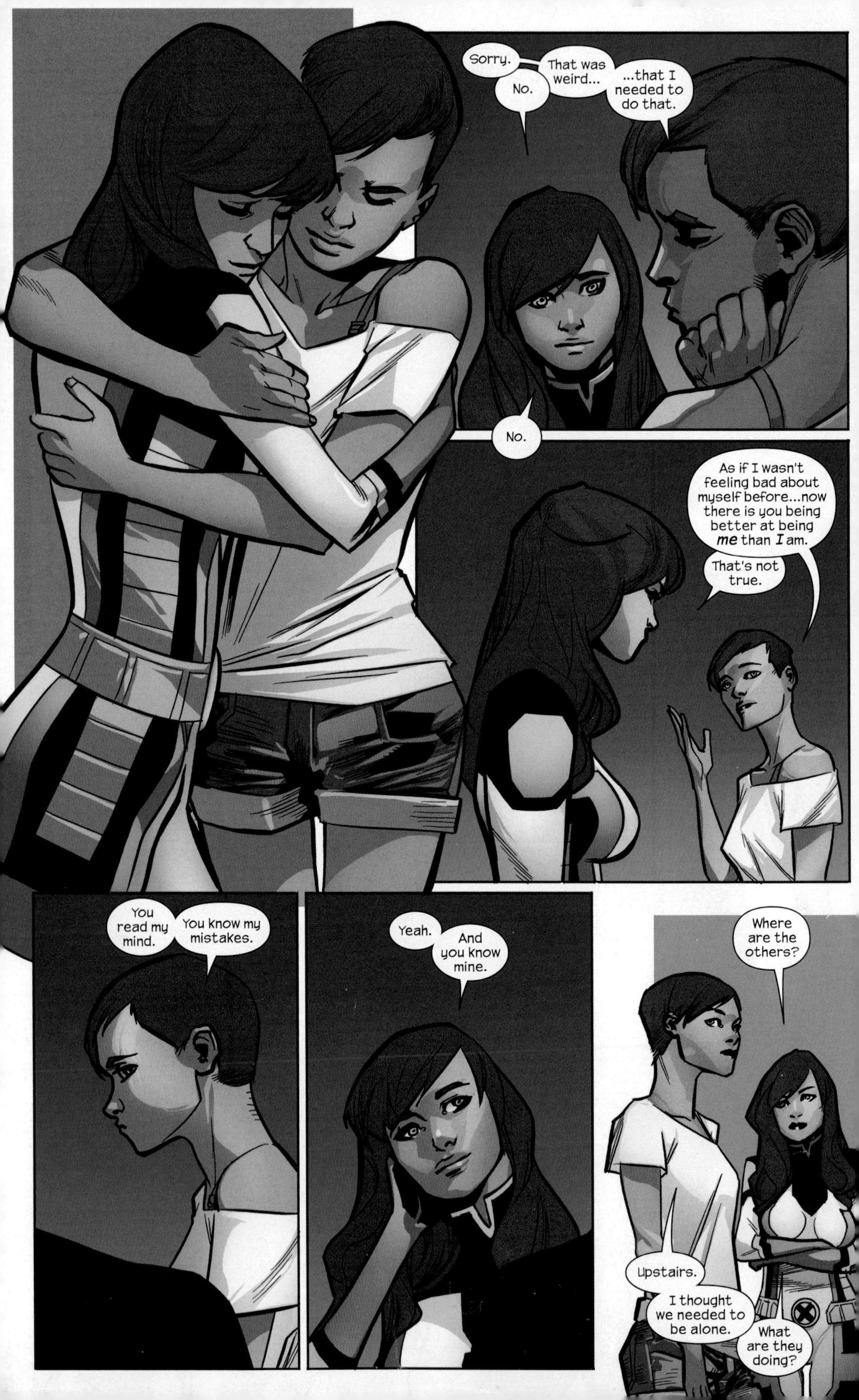
Sorry.
No.
That was weird...
...that I needed to do that.
No.
As if I wasn't feeling bad about myself before...now there is you being better at being *me* than *I* am.
That's not true.
You read my mind.
You know my mistakes.
Yeah.
And you know mine.
Where are the others?
Upstairs.
I thought we needed to be alone.
What are they doing?

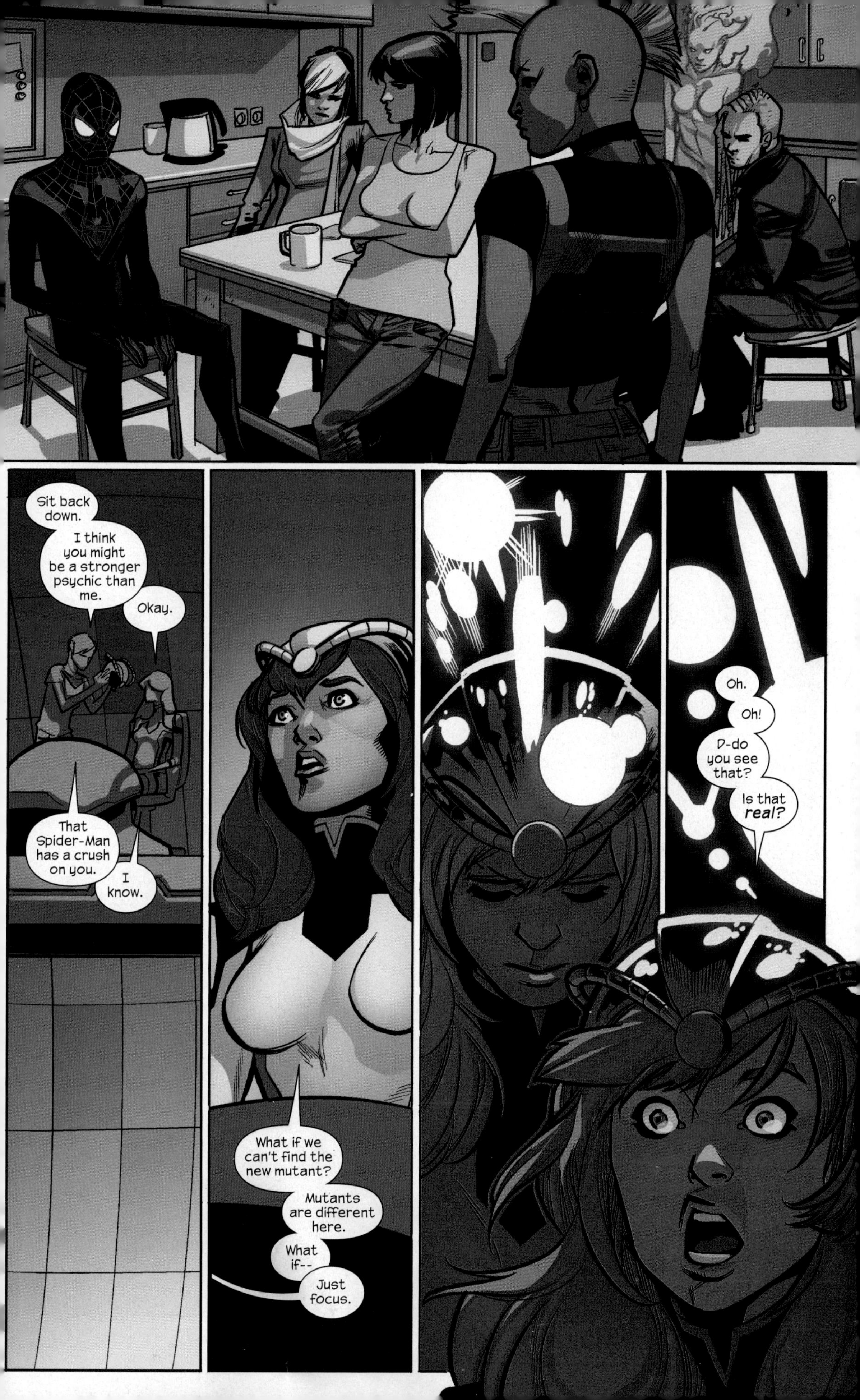
Sit back down.
I think you might be a stronger psychic than me.
Okay.
That Spider-Man has a crush on you.
I know.
What if we can't find the new mutant?
Mutants are different here.
What if--
Just focus.
Oh.
Oh!
D-do you see that?
Is that *real?*

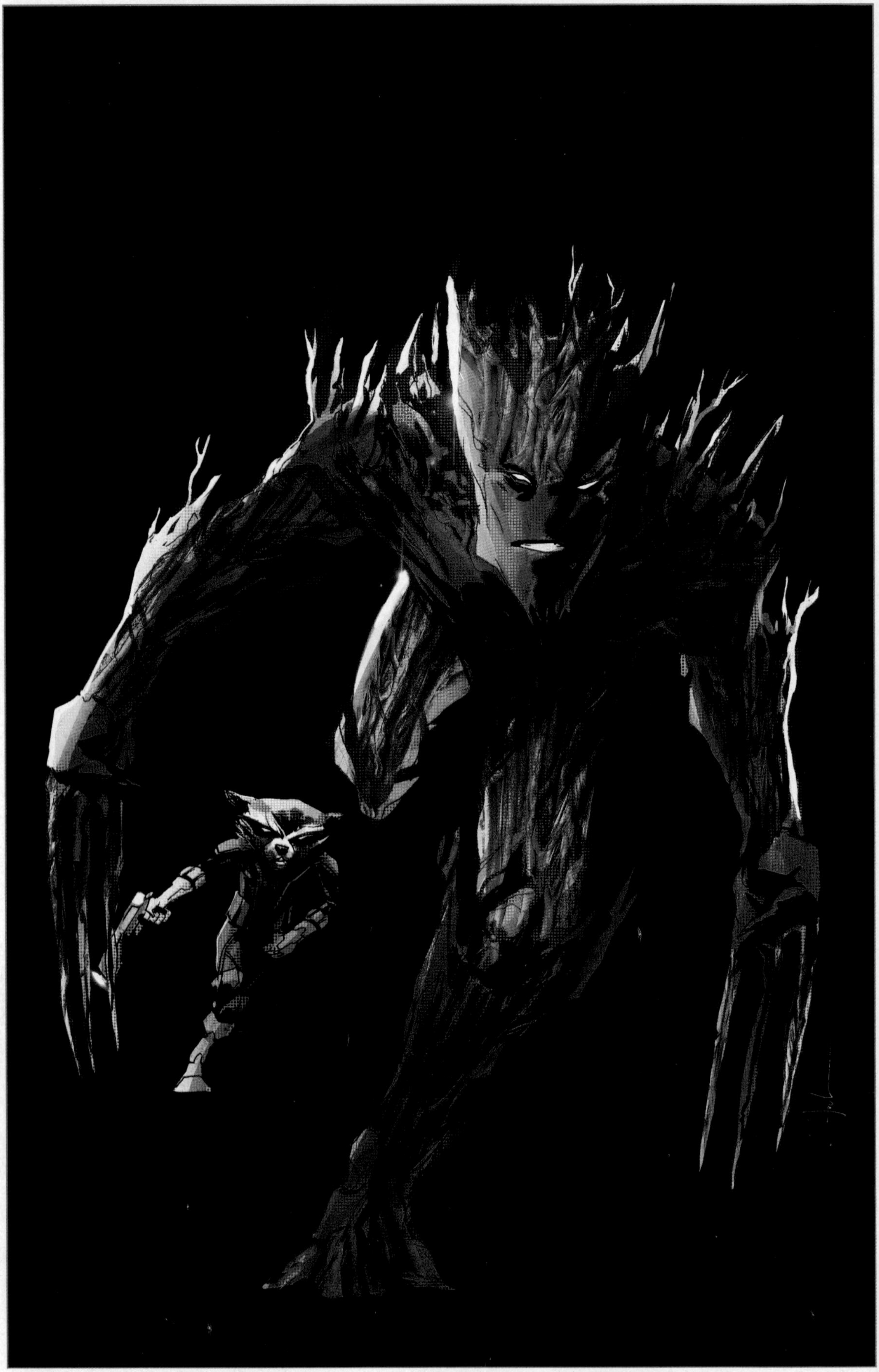

ALL-NEW X-MEN #34 ROCKET RACCOON & GROOT VARIANT
BY JOCK

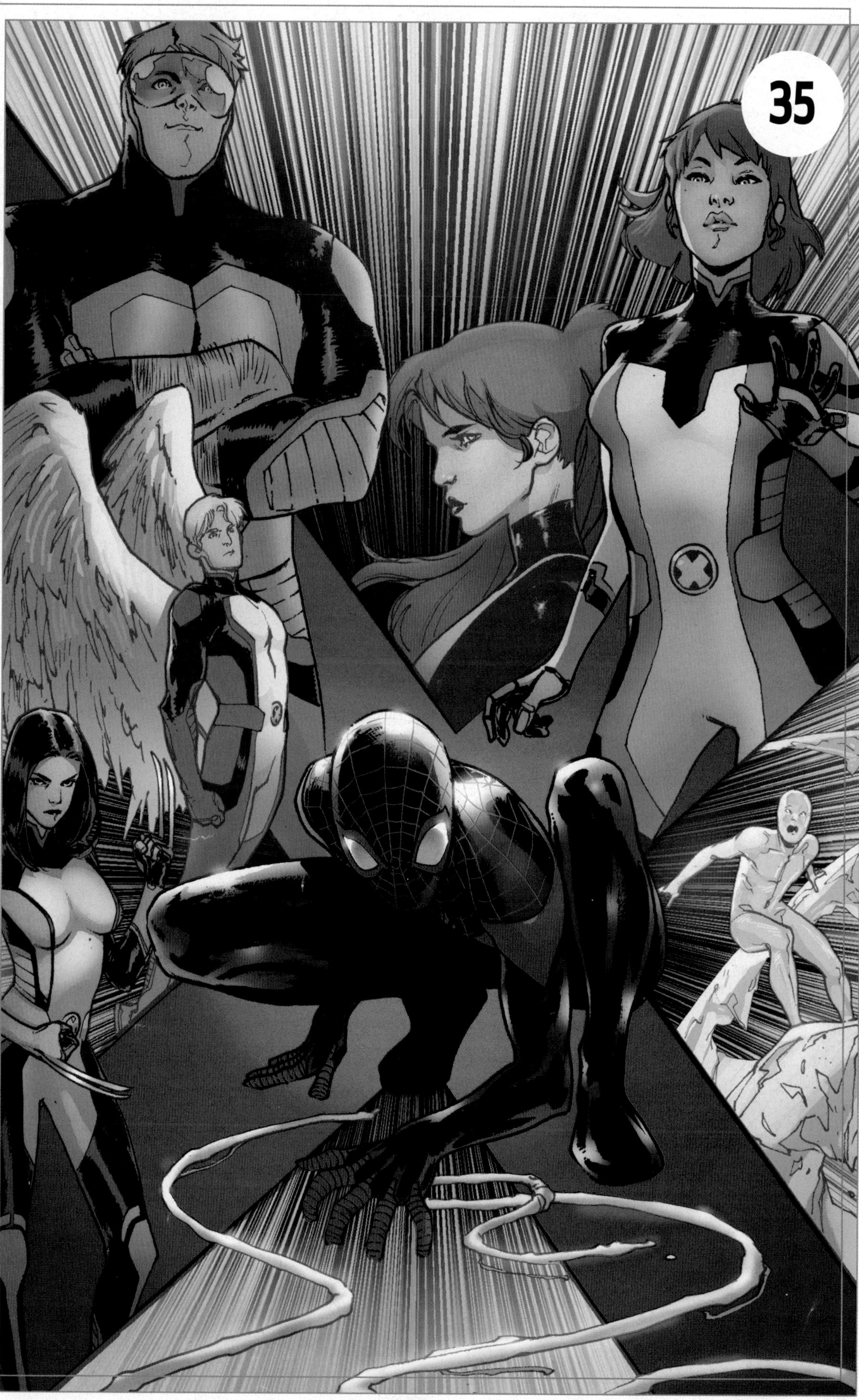
35

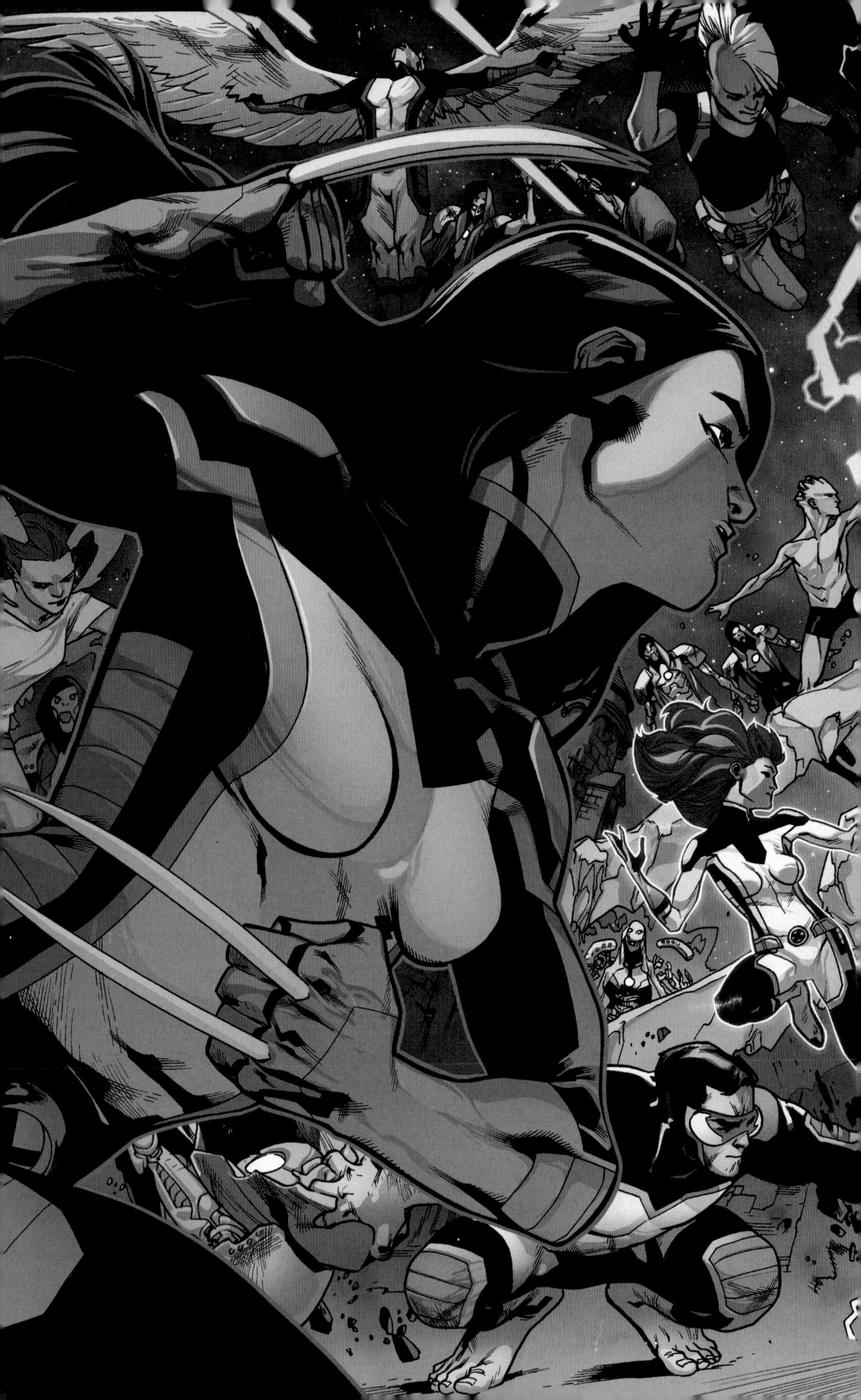

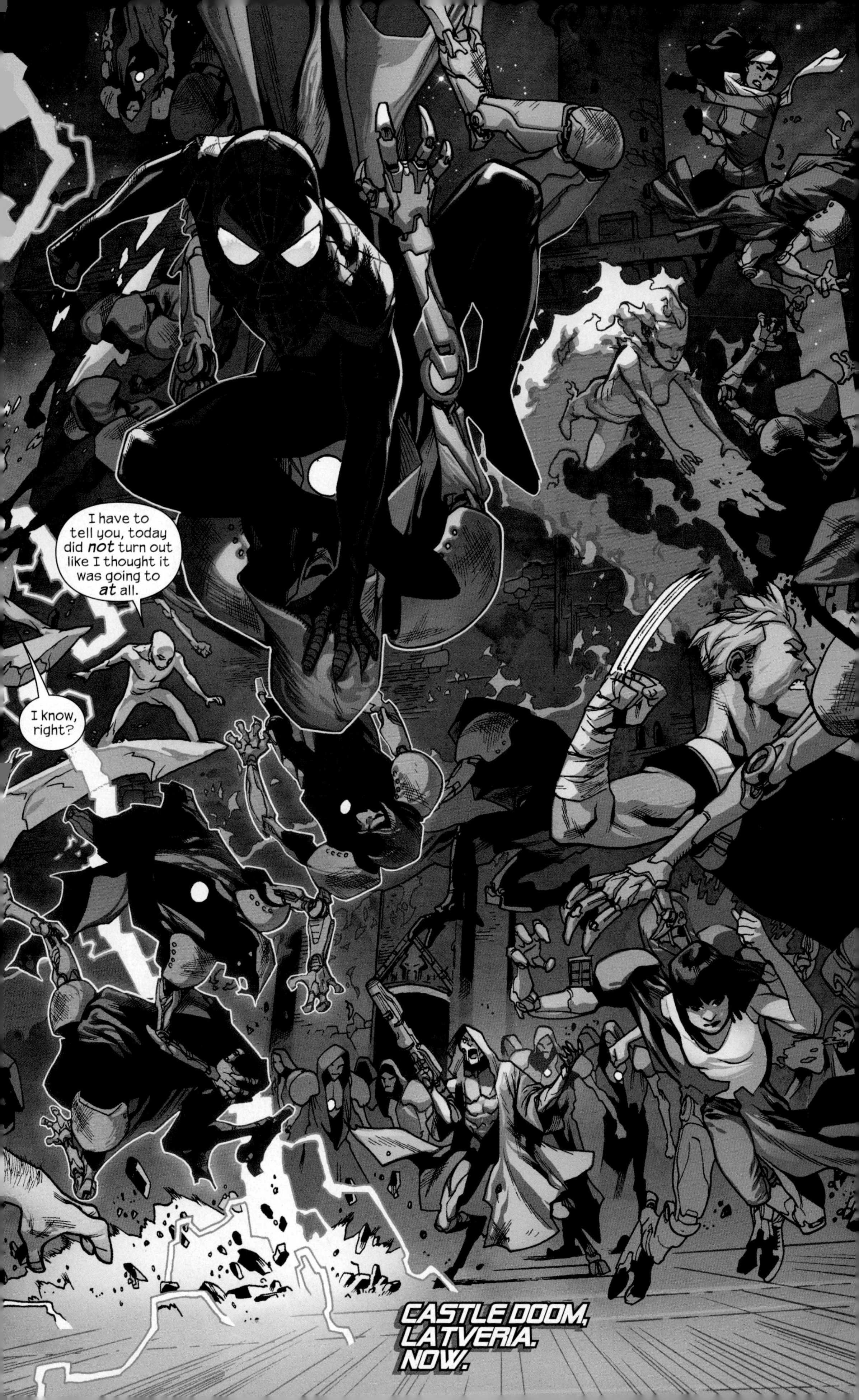
I have to tell you, today did **not** turn out like I thought it was going to **at** all.
I know, right?
CASTLE DOOM, LATVERIA. NOW.

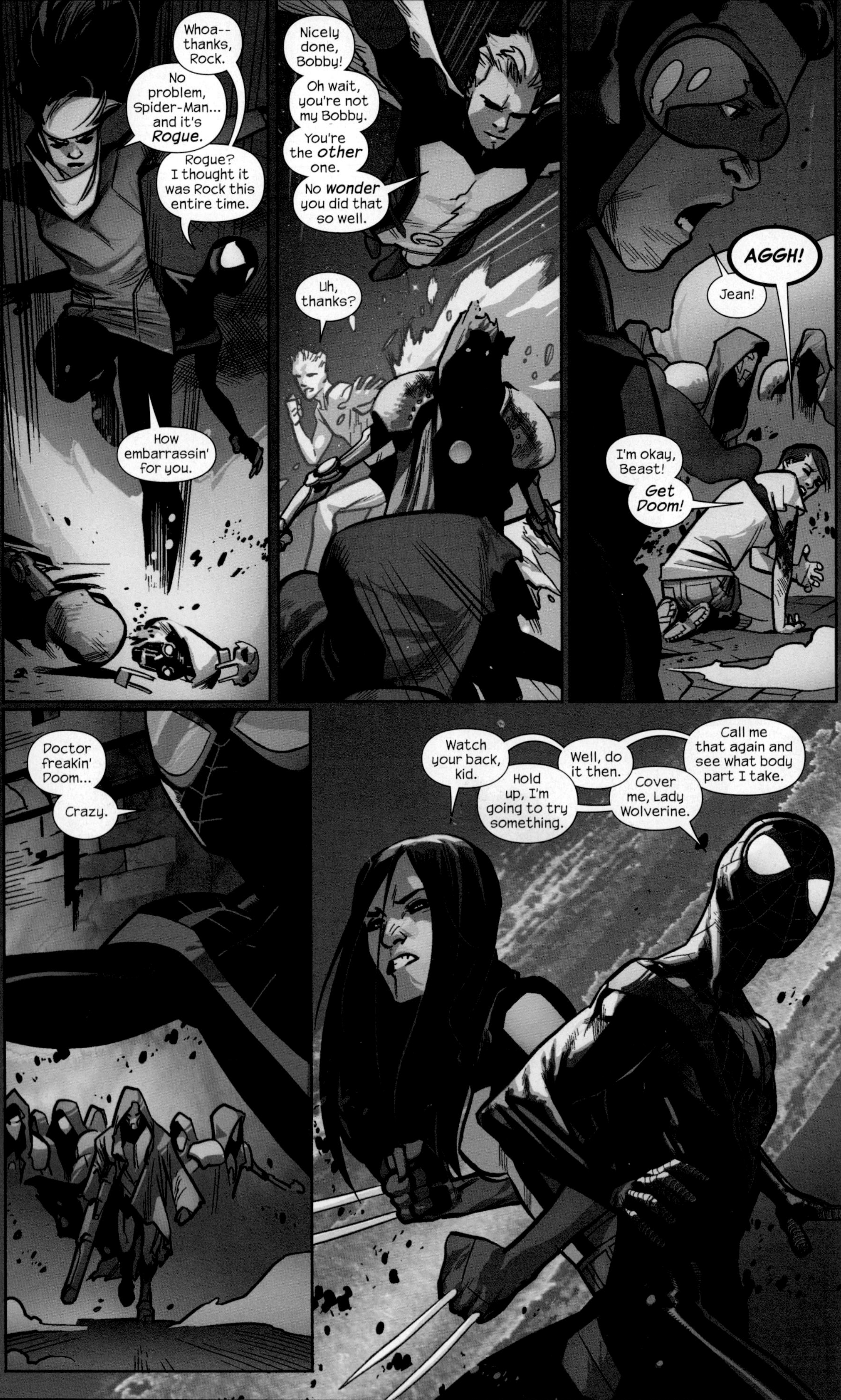
Whoa--thanks, Rock.
No problem, Spider-Man... and it's *Rogue.*
Rogue? I thought it was Rock this entire time.
How embarrassin' for you.
Nicely done, Bobby!
Oh wait, you're not my Bobby.
You're the *other* one.
No *wonder* you did that so well.
Uh, thanks?
AGGH!
Jean!
I'm okay, Beast! *Get Doom!*
Doctor freakin' Doom...
Crazy.
Watch your back, kid.
Hold up, I'm going to try something.
Well, do it then.
Cover me, Lady Wolverine.
Call me that again and see what body part I take.

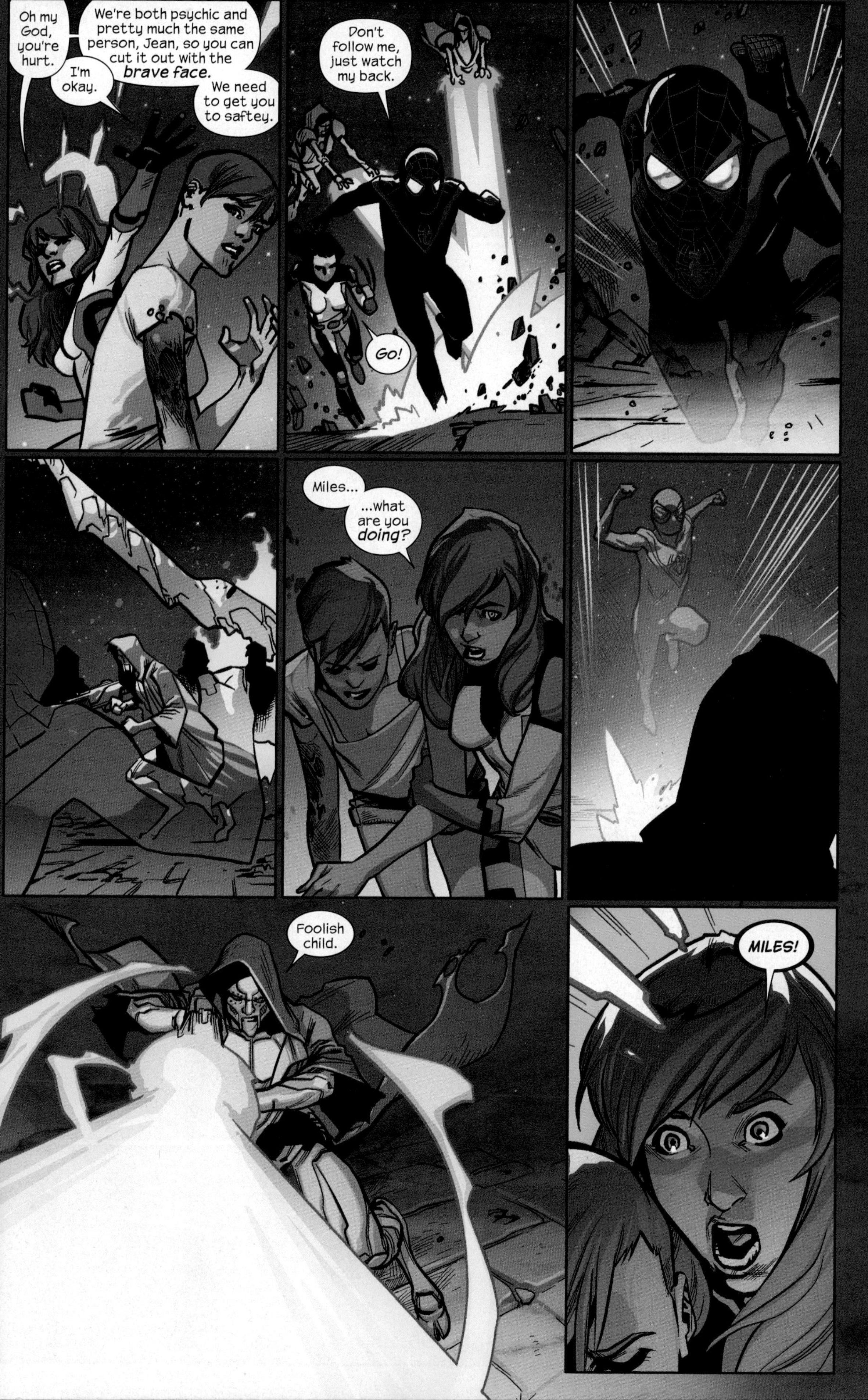
Oh my God, you're hurt.
I'm okay.
We're both psychic and pretty much the same person, Jean, so you can cut it out with the brave face.
We need to get you to saftey.
Don't follow me, just watch my back.
Go!
Miles...
...what are you doing?
Foolish child.
MILES!

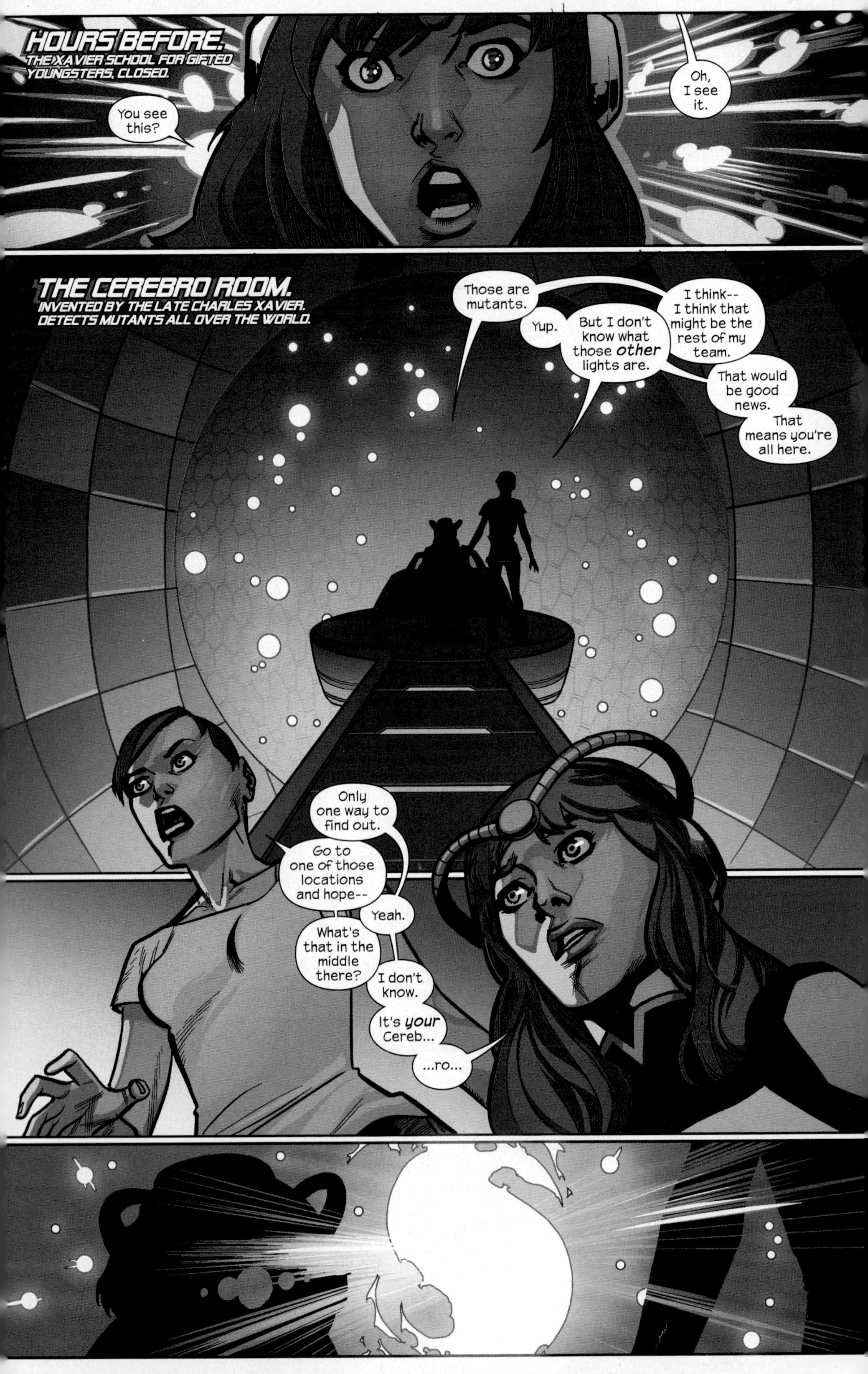
HOURS BEFORE.
THE XAVIER SCHOOL FOR GIFTED YOUNGSTERS, CLOSED.
You see this?
Oh, I see it.
THE CEREBRO ROOM.
INVENTED BY THE LATE CHARLES XAVIER. DETECTS MUTANTS ALL OVER THE WORLD.
Those are mutants.
Yup.
But I don't know what those *other* lights are.
I think-- I think that might be the rest of my team.
That would be good news.
That means you're all here.
Only one way to find out.
Go to one of those locations and hope--
Yeah.
What's that in the middle there?
I don't know.
It's *your* Cereb...
...ro...

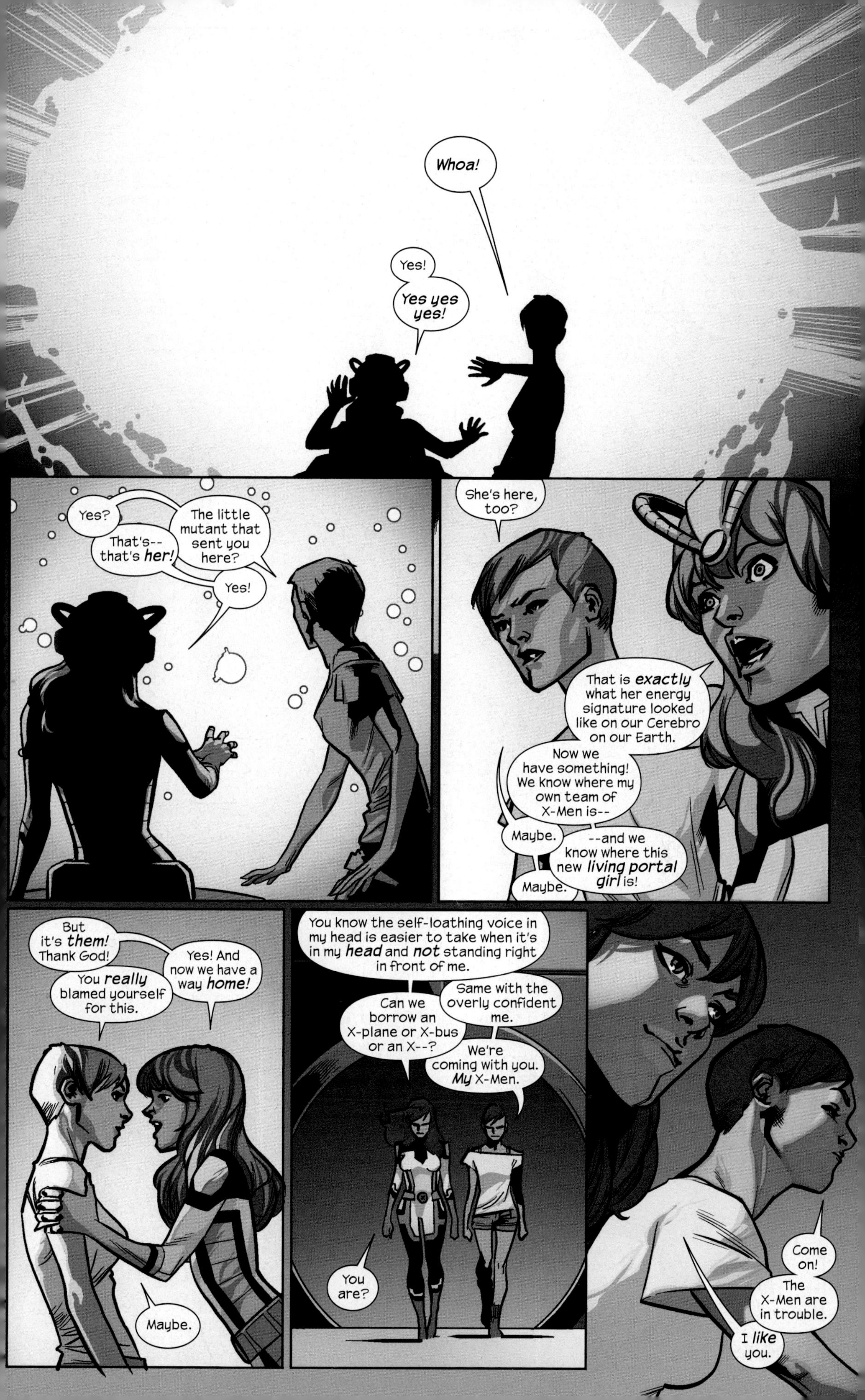
Whoa!
Yes!
Yes yes yes!
Yes?
That's-- that's her!
The little mutant that sent you here?
Yes!
She's here, too?
That is exactly what her energy signature looked like on our Cerebro on our Earth.
Now we have something! We know where my own team of X-Men is--
Maybe.
--and we know where this new living portal girl is!
Maybe.
But it's them! Thank God!
Yes! And now we have a way home!
You really blamed yourself for this.
Maybe.
You know the self-loathing voice in my head is easier to take when it's in my head and not standing right in front of me.
Same with the overly confident me.
Can we borrow an X-plane or X-bus or an X--?
We're coming with you. My X-Men.
You are?
Come on!
The X-Men are in trouble.
I like you.

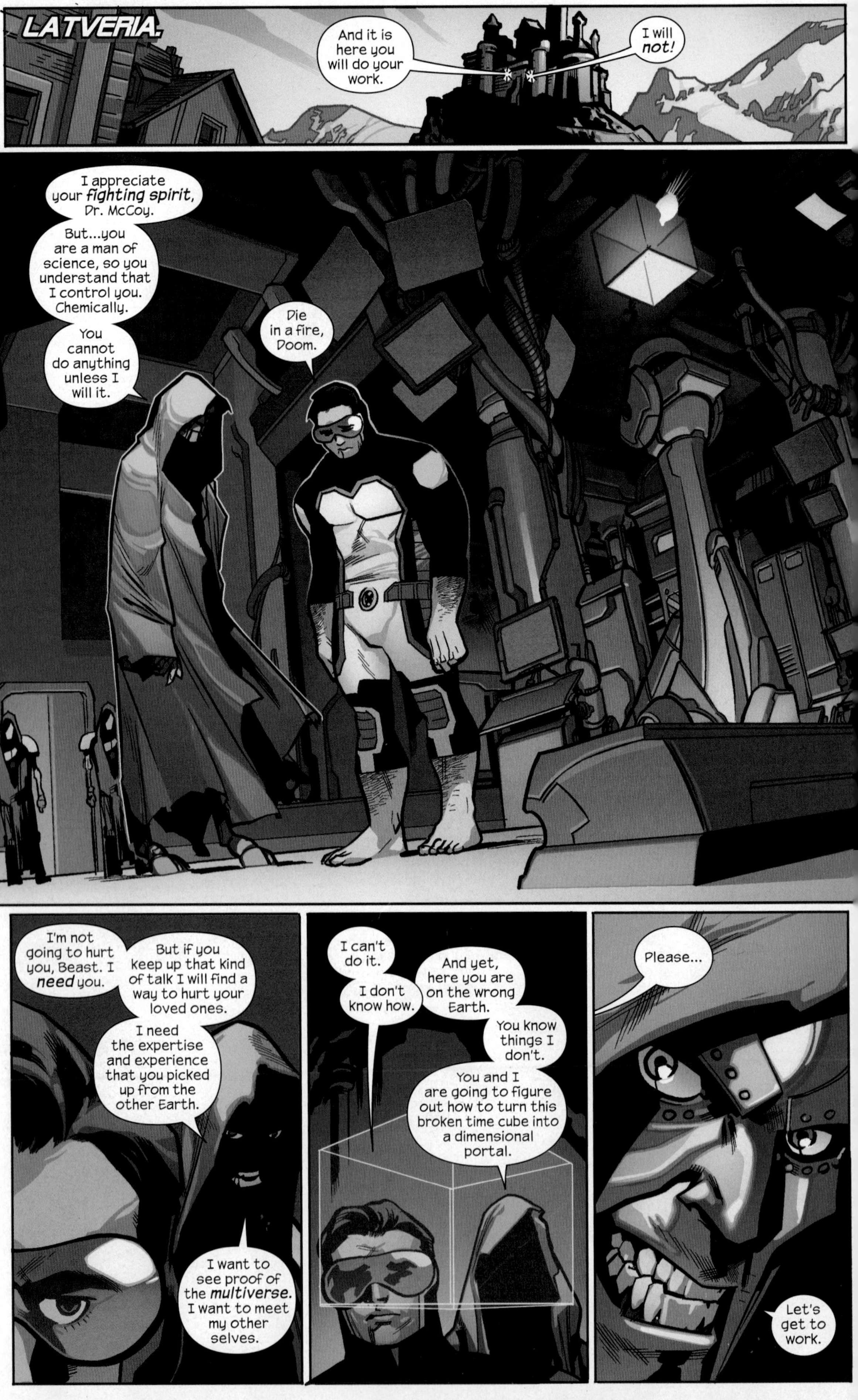
LATVERIA.
And it is here you will do your work.
I will not!
I appreciate your fighting spirit, Dr. McCoy.
But...you are a man of science, so you understand that I control you. Chemically.
You cannot do anything unless I will it.
Die in a fire, Doom.
I'm not going to hurt you, Beast. I need you.
But if you keep up that kind of talk I will find a way to hurt your loved ones.
I need the expertise and experience that you picked up from the other Earth.
I want to see proof of the multiverse. I want to meet my other selves.
I can't do it.
I don't know how.
And yet, here you are on the wrong Earth.
You know things I don't.
You and I are going to figure out how to turn this broken time cube into a dimensional portal.
Please...
Let's get to work.

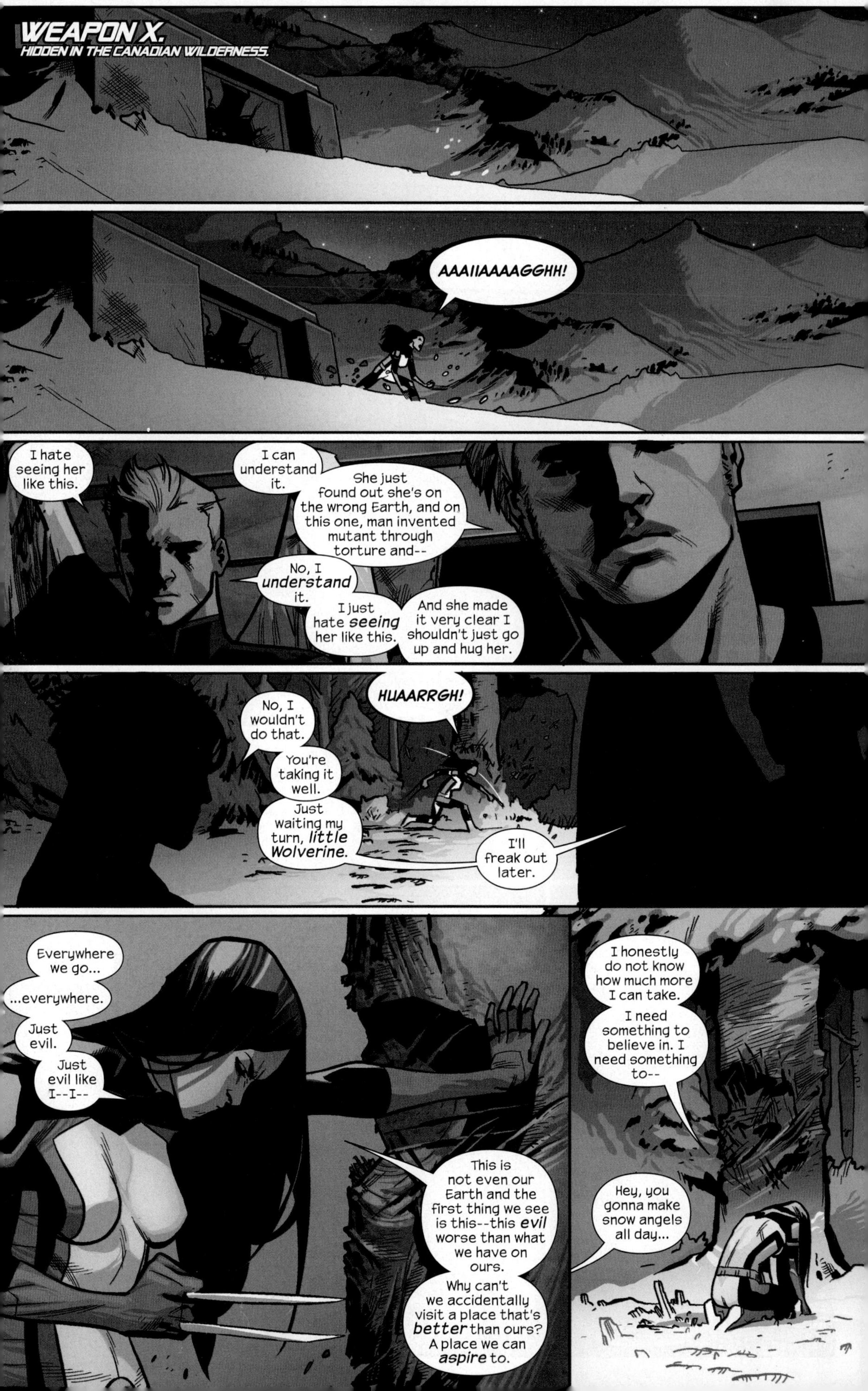
WEAPON X.
HIDDEN IN THE CANADIAN WILDERNESS.
AAAIIAAAAGGHH!
I hate seeing her like this.
I can understand it.
She just found out she's on the wrong Earth, and on this one, man invented mutant through torture and--
No, I understand it.
I just hate seeing her like this.
And she made it very clear I shouldn't just go up and hug her.
No, I wouldn't do that.
HUAARRGH!
You're taking it well.
Just waiting my turn, little Wolverine.
I'll freak out later.
Everywhere we go...
...everywhere.
Just evil.
Just evil like I--I--
This is not even our Earth and the first thing we see is this--this evil worse than what we have on ours.
Why can't we accidentally visit a place that's better than ours? A place we can aspire to.
I honestly do not know how much more I can take.
I need something to believe in. I need something to--
Hey, you gonna make snow angels all day...

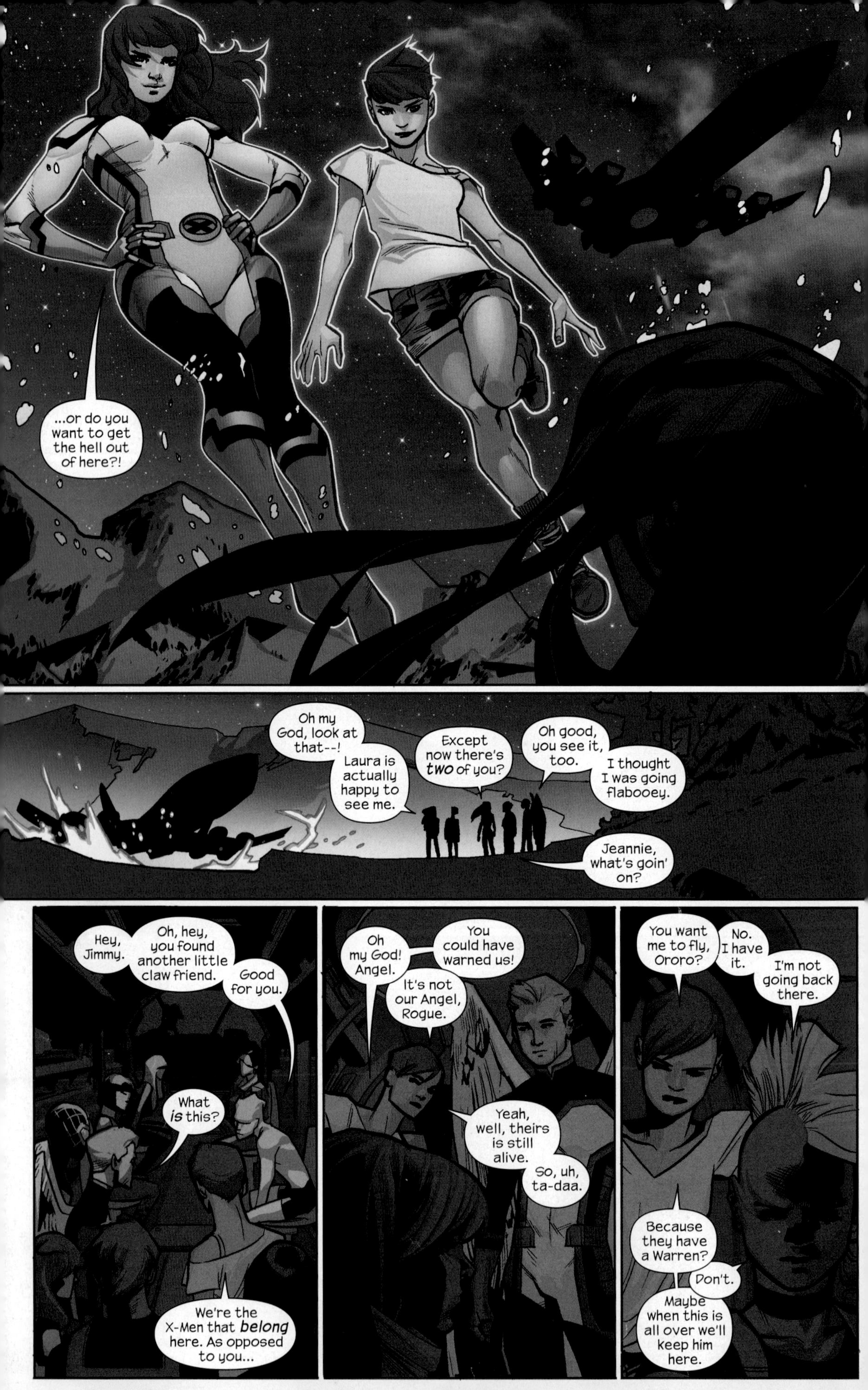
...or do you want to get the hell out of here?!
Oh my God, look at that--!
Laura is actually happy to see me.
Except now there's **two** of you?
Oh good, you see it, too.
I thought I was going flabooey.
Jeannie, what's goin' on?
Hey, Jimmy.
Oh, hey, you found another little claw friend.
Good for you.
What **is** this?
We're the X-Men that **belong** here. As opposed to you...
Oh my God! Angel.
You could have warned us!
It's not our Angel, Rogue.
Yeah, well, theirs is still alive.
So, uh, ta-daa.
You want me to fly, Ororo?
No. I have it.
I'm not going back there.
Because they have a Warren?
Don't.
Maybe when this is all over we'll keep him here.

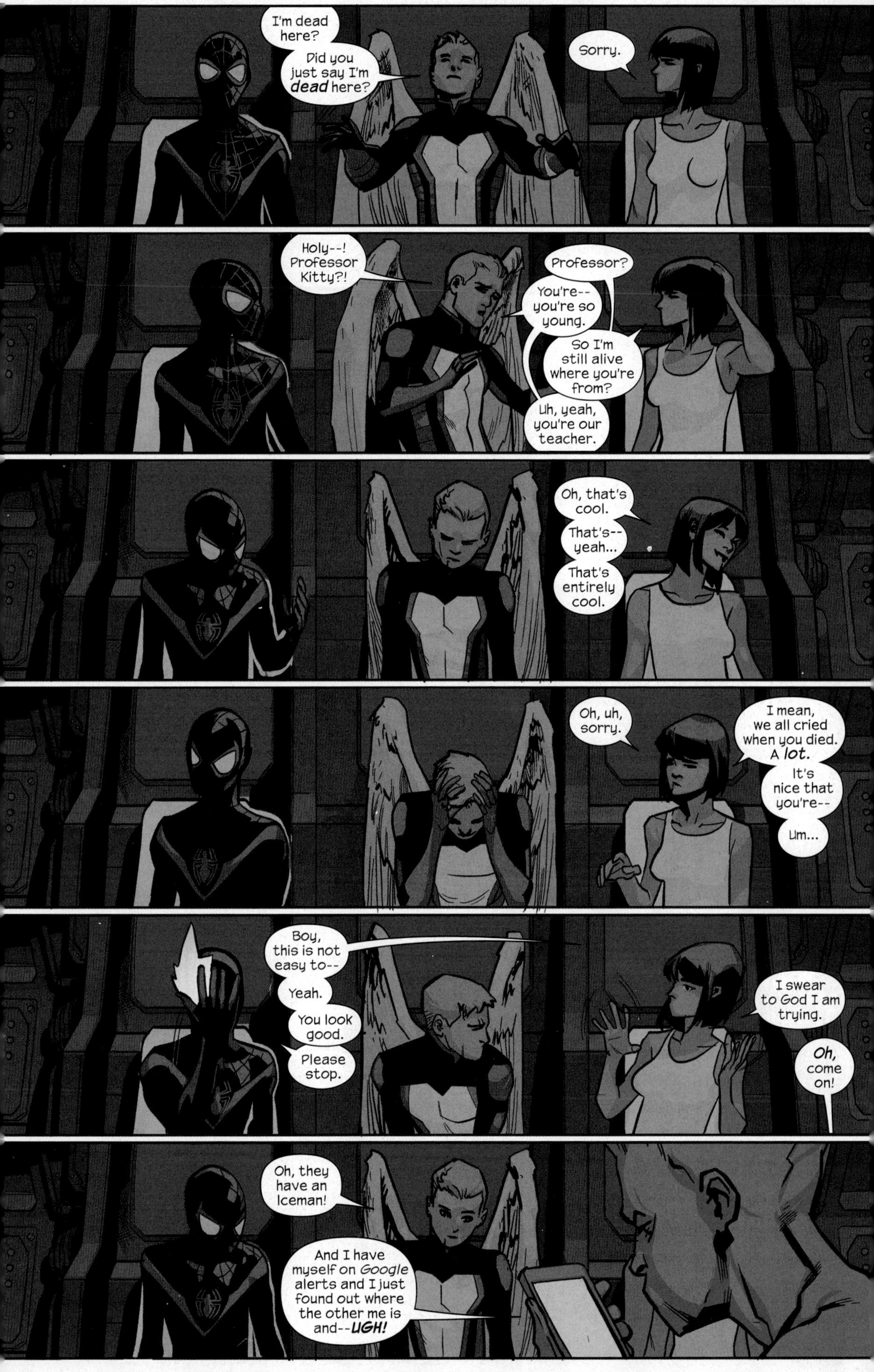
I'm dead here?
Did you just say I'm *dead* here?
Sorry.
Holy--! Professor Kitty?!
Professor?
You're-- you're so young.
So I'm still alive where you're from?
Uh, yeah, you're our teacher.
Oh, that's cool.
That's-- yeah...
That's entirely cool.
Oh, uh, sorry.
I mean, we all cried when you died. A *lot.*
It's nice that you're--
Um...
Boy, this is not easy to--
Yeah.
You look good.
Please stop.
I swear to God I am trying.
Oh, come on!
Oh, they have an Iceman!
And I have myself on *Google* alerts and I just found out where the other me is and--*UGH!*

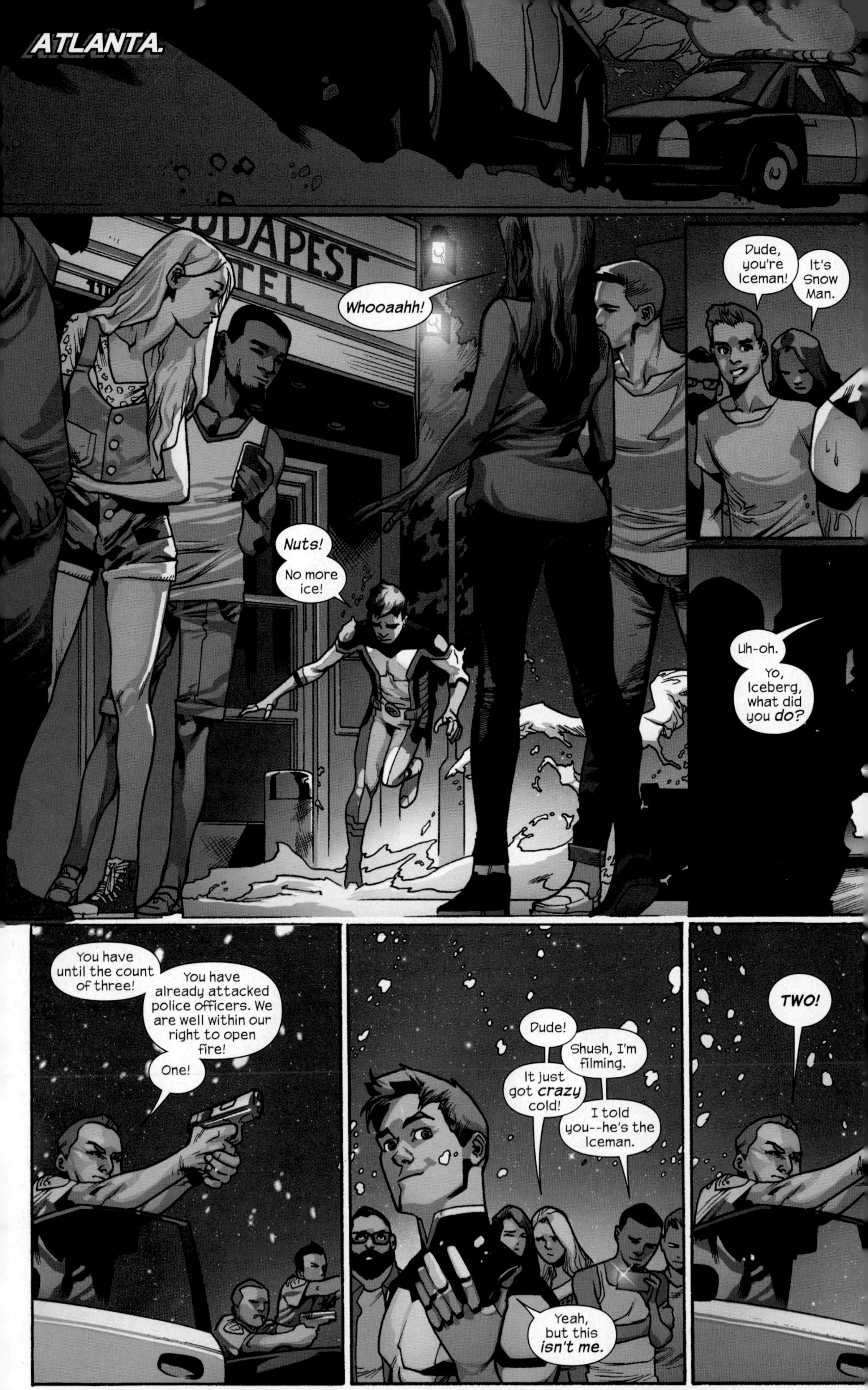
ATLANTA.
BUDAPEST
TEL
Whooaahh!
Dude, you're Iceman!
It's Snow Man.
Nuts!
No more ice!
Uh-oh.
Yo, Iceberg, what did you *do?*
You have until the count of three!
You have already attacked police officers. We are well within our right to open fire!
One!
Dude!
Shush, I'm filming.
It just got *crazy* cold!
I told you--he's the Iceman.
Yeah, but this *isn't me.*
TWO!

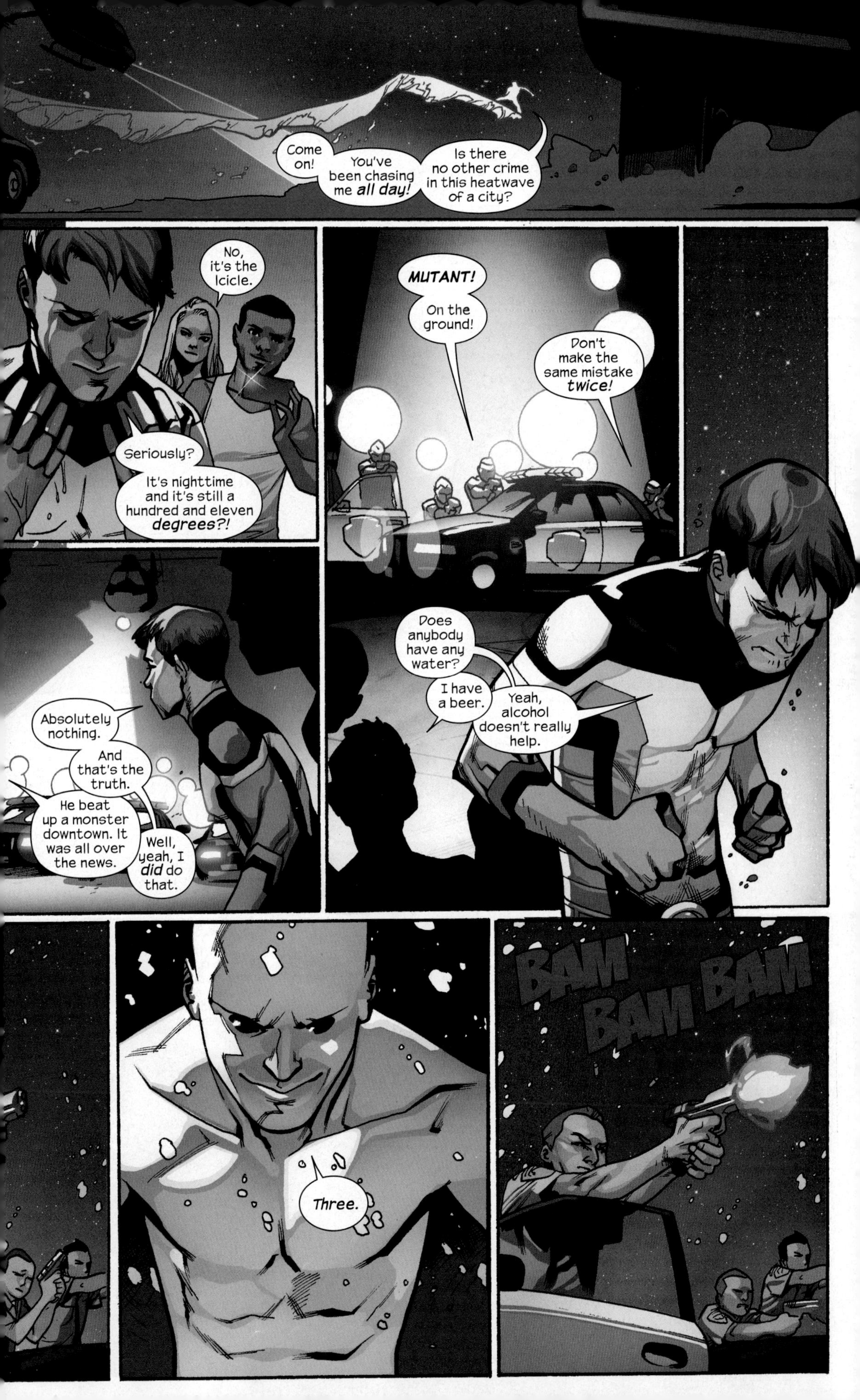
Come on!
You've been chasing me all day!
Is there no other crime in this heatwave of a city?
No, it's the Icicle.
Seriously?
It's nighttime and it's still a hundred and eleven degrees?!
MUTANT!
On the ground!
Don't make the same mistake twice!
Absolutely nothing.
And that's the truth.
He beat up a monster downtown. It was all over the news.
Well, yeah, I did do that.
Does anybody have any water?
I have a beer.
Yeah, alcohol doesn't really help.
Three.
BAM
BAM BAM

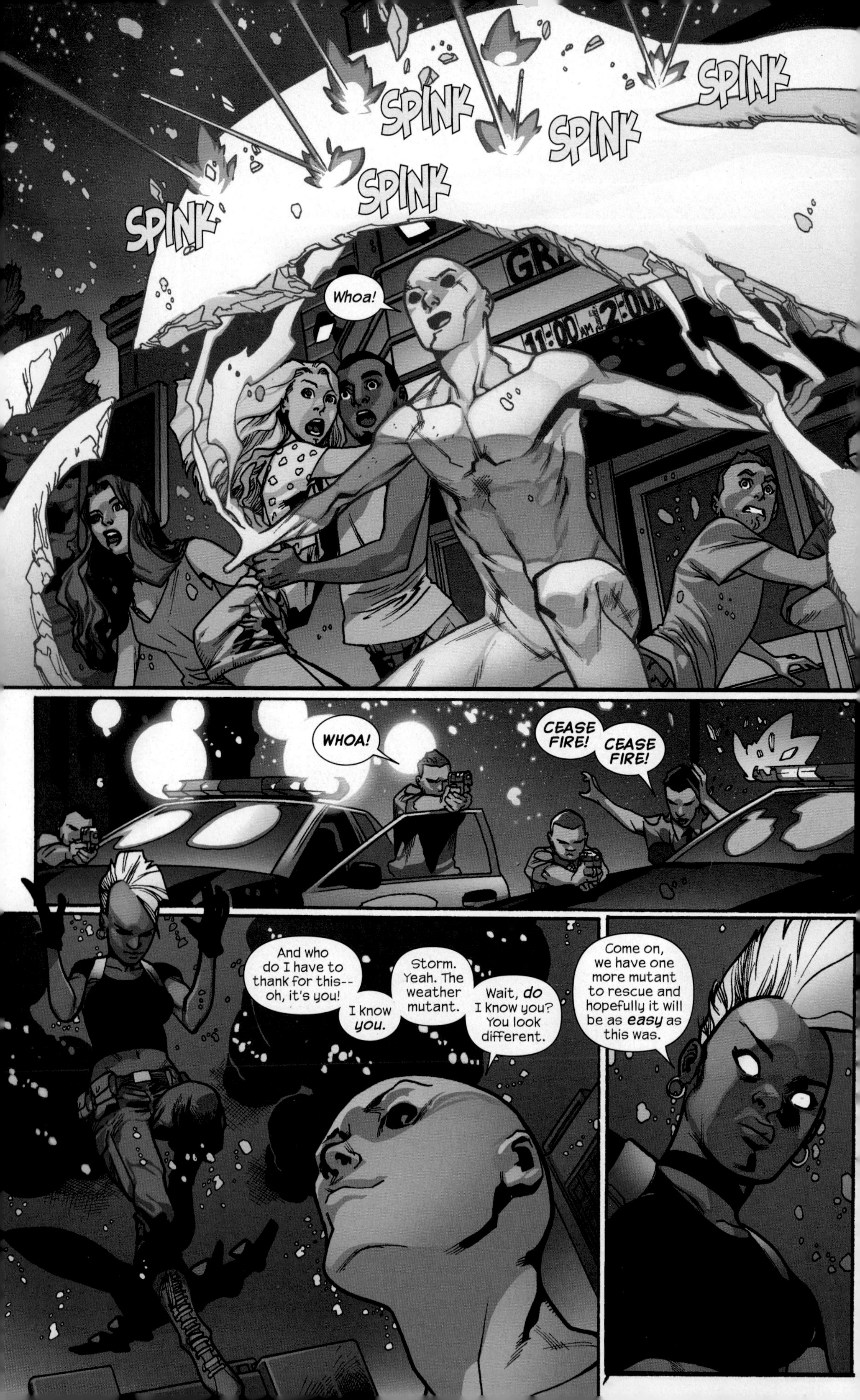
SPINK
SPINK
SPINK
SPINK
SPINK
SPINK
Whoa!
GRA
11:00 AM 12:00
WHOA!
CEASE FIRE!
CEASE FIRE!
And who do I have to thank for this-- oh, it's you!
I know *you.*
Storm. Yeah. The weather mutant.
Wait, *do* I know you? You look different.
Come on, we have one more mutant to rescue and hopefully it will be as *easy* as this was.

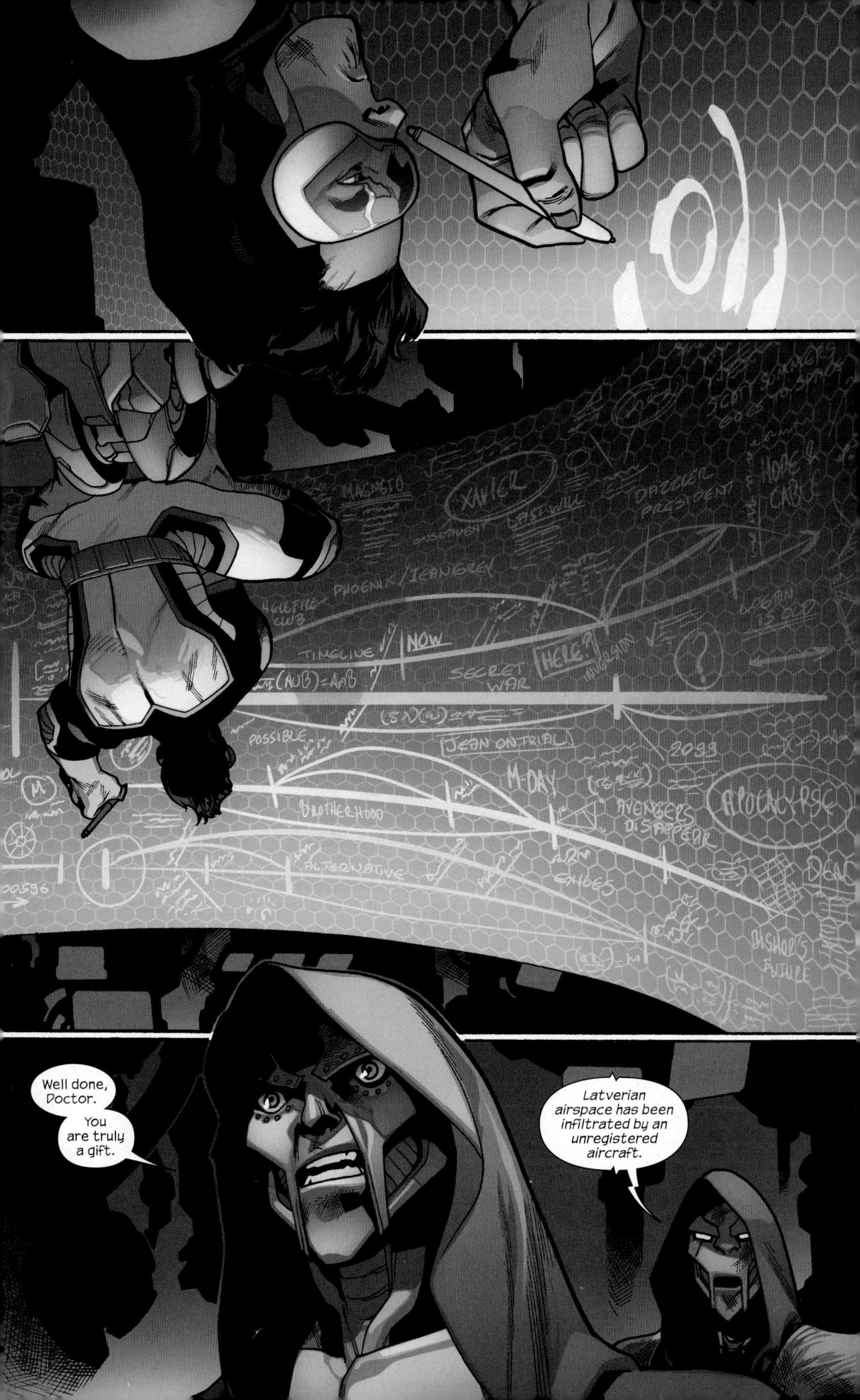
MAGNETO
XAVIER
LAST WILL
ONSLAUGHT
DAZZLER PRESIDENT
HOPE CABLE
PHOENIX/JEAN GREY
HELLFIRE CLUB
TIMELINE
NOW
SECRET WAR
HERE?
LOGAN IS OLD
POSSIBLE
JEAN ON TRIAL
2099
M-DAY
BROTHERHOOD
AVENGERS DISAPPEAR
APOCALYPSE
ALTERNATIVE
EXILES
BISHOP'S FUTURE
Well done, Doctor.
You are truly a gift.
Latverian airspace has been infiltrated by an unregistered aircraft.

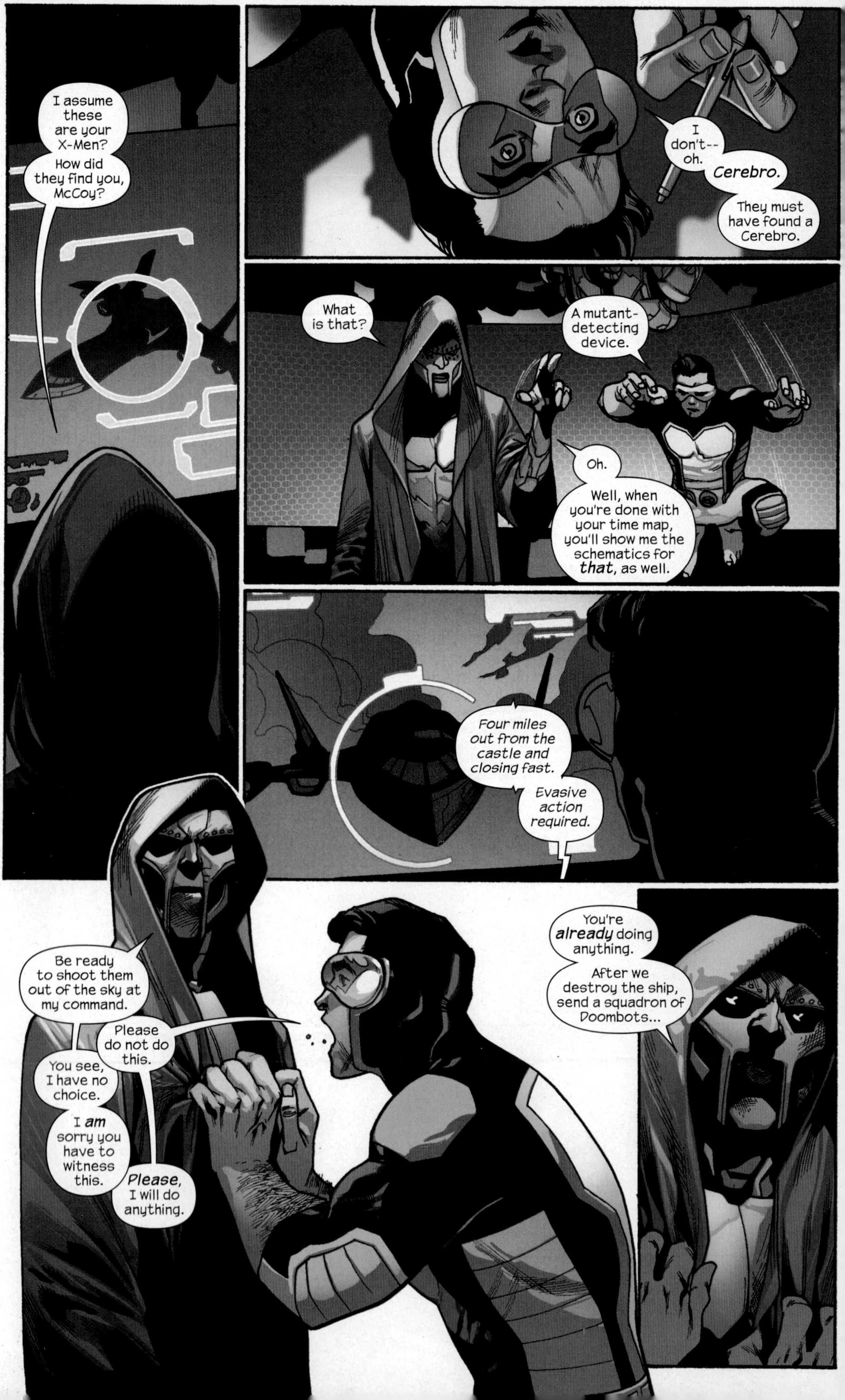
I assume these are your X-Men?
How did they find you, McCoy?
I don't-- oh.
Cerebro.
They must have found a Cerebro.
What is that?
A mutant-detecting device.
Oh.
Well, when you're done with your time map, you'll show me the schematics for *that*, as well.
Four miles out from the castle and closing fast.
Evasive action required.
Be ready to shoot them out of the sky at my command.
Please do not do this.
You see, I have no choice.
I *am* sorry you have to witness this.
Please, I will do anything.
You're *already* doing anything.
After we destroy the ship, send a squadron of Doombots...

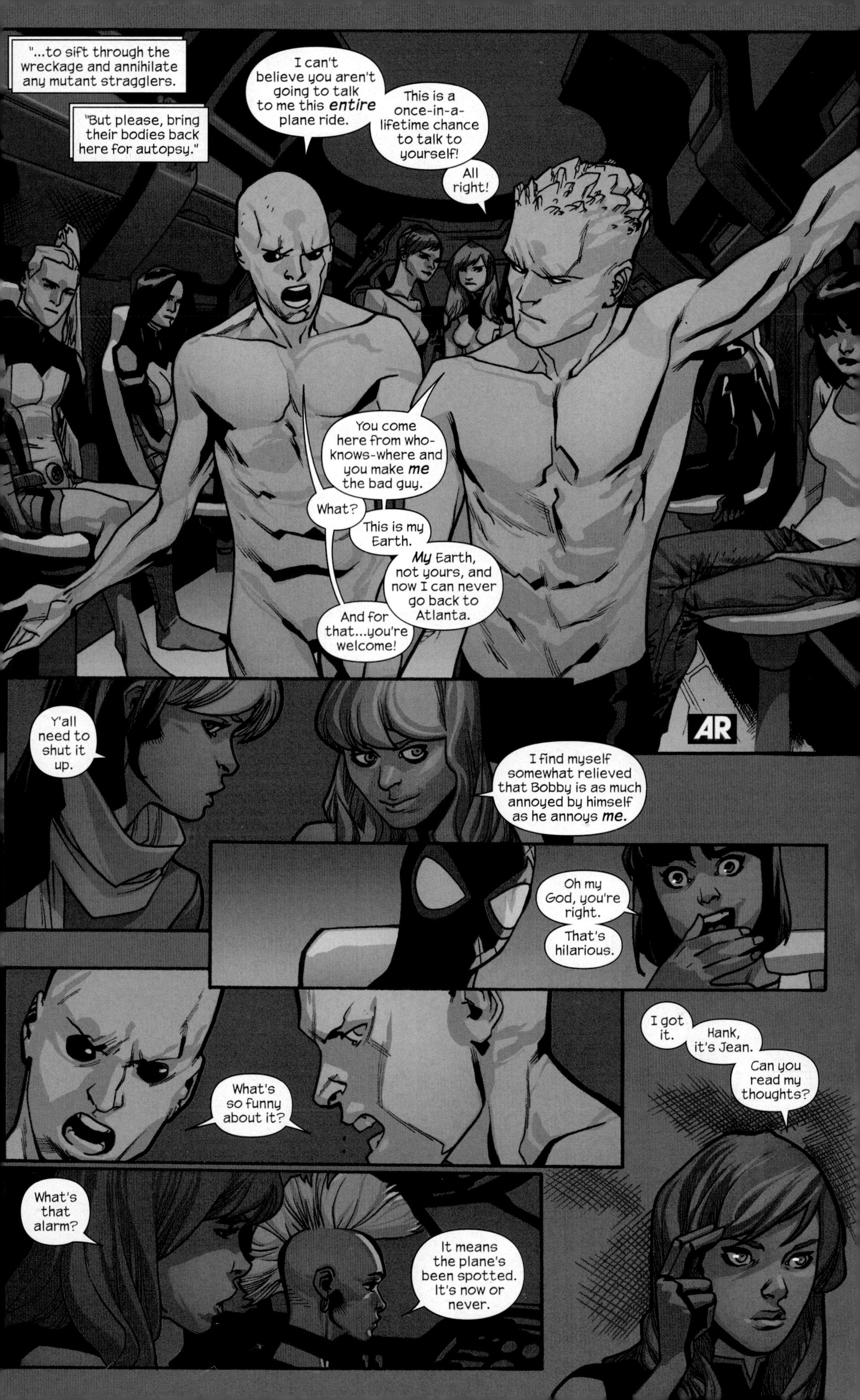
"...to sift through the wreckage and annihilate any mutant stragglers.
"But please, bring their bodies back here for autopsy."
I can't believe you aren't going to talk to me this *entire* plane ride.
This is a once-in-a-lifetime chance to talk to yourself!
All right!
You come here from who-knows-where and you make *me* the bad guy.
What?
This is my Earth.
My Earth, not yours, and now I can never go back to Atlanta.
And for that...you're welcome!
AR
Y'all need to shut it up.
I find myself somewhat relieved that Bobby is as much annoyed by himself as he annoys *me.*
Oh my God, you're right.
That's hilarious.
What's so funny about it?
I got it.
Hank, it's Jean.
Can you read my thoughts?
What's that alarm?
It means the plane's been spotted. It's now or never.

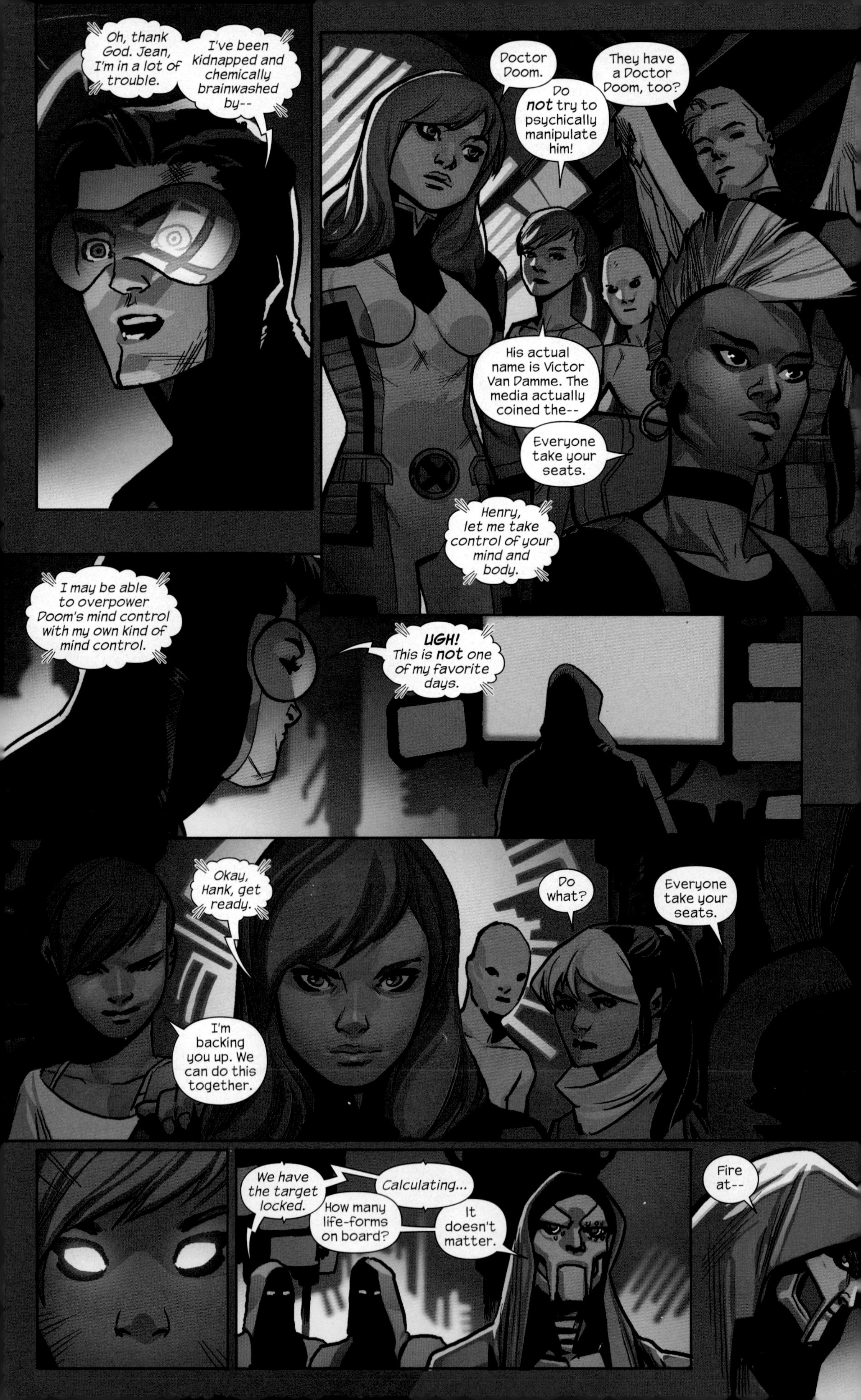

Oh, thank God. Jean, I'm in a lot of trouble.
I've been kidnapped and chemically brainwashed by--
Doctor Doom.
Do **not** try to psychically manipulate him!
They have a Doctor Doom, too?
His actual name is Victor Van Damme. The media actually coined the--
Everyone take your seats.
Henry, let me take control of your mind and body.
I may be able to overpower Doom's mind control with my own kind of mind control.
UGH! This is **not** one of my favorite days.
Okay, Hank, get ready.
I'm backing you up. We can do this together.
Do what?
Everyone take your seats.
We have the target locked.
Calculating...
How many life-forms on board?
It doesn't matter.
Fire at--

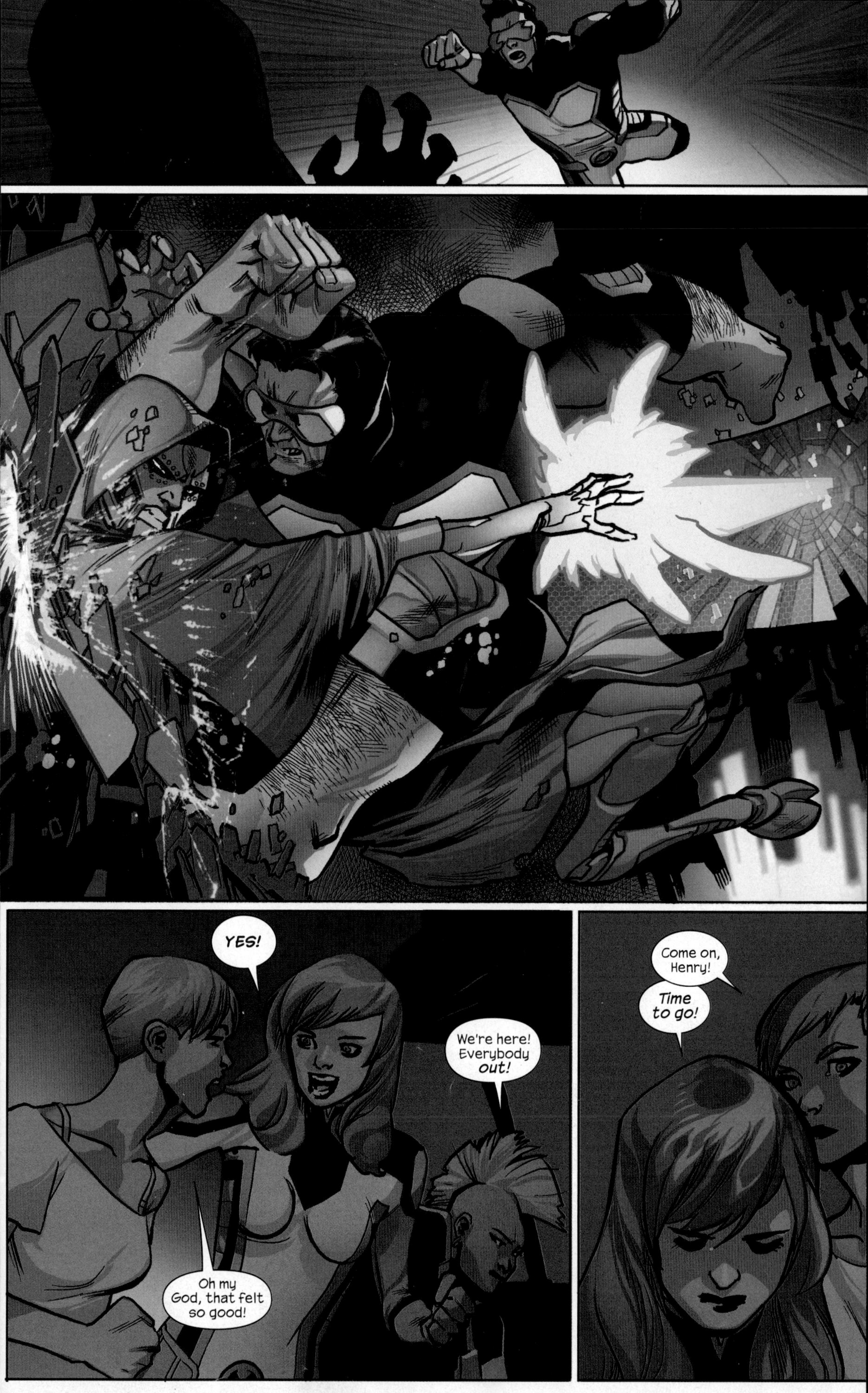
YES!
We're here! Everybody out!
Oh my God, that felt so good!
Come on, Henry!
Time to go!

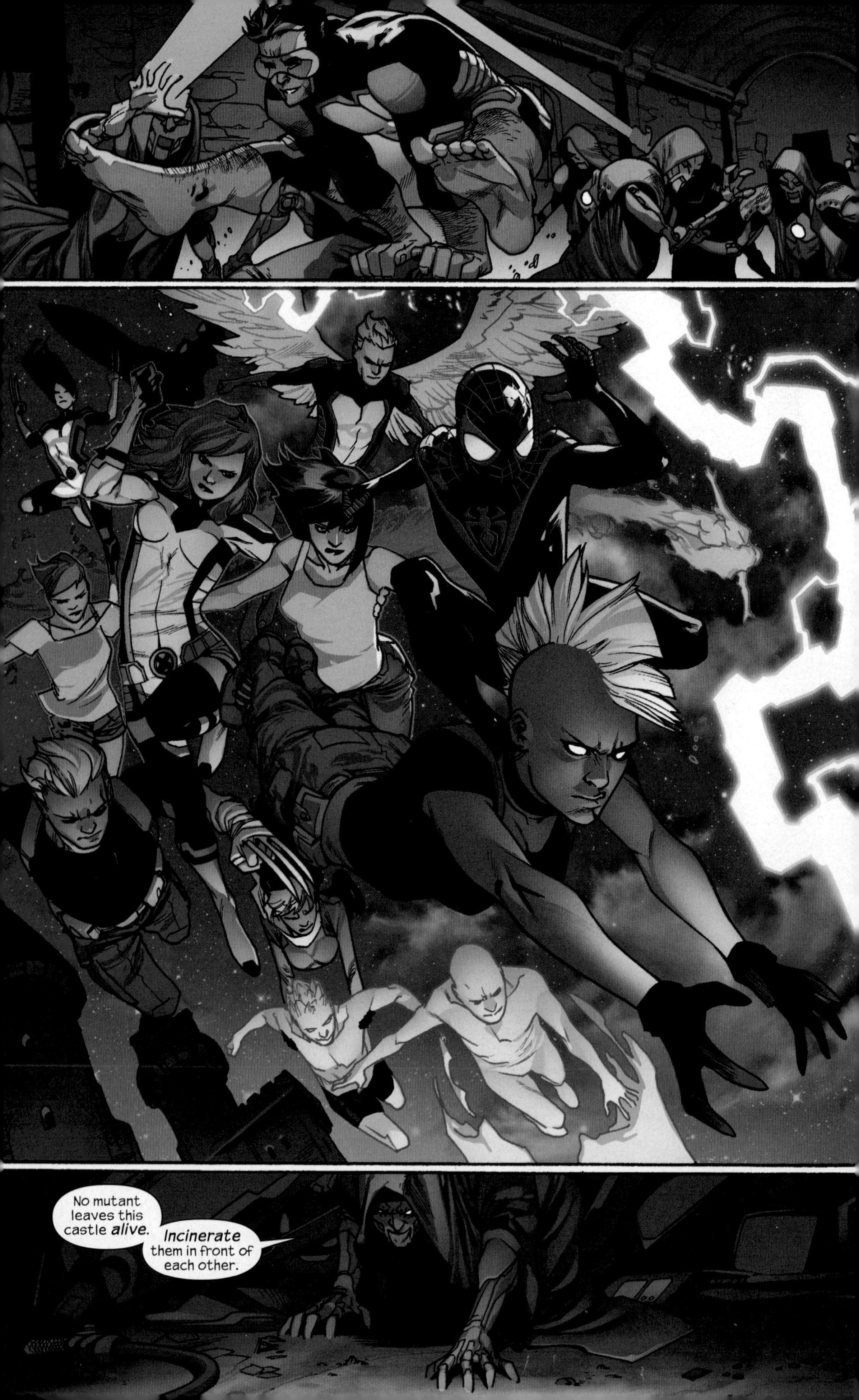
No mutant leaves this castle *alive*.
Incinerate them in front of each other.

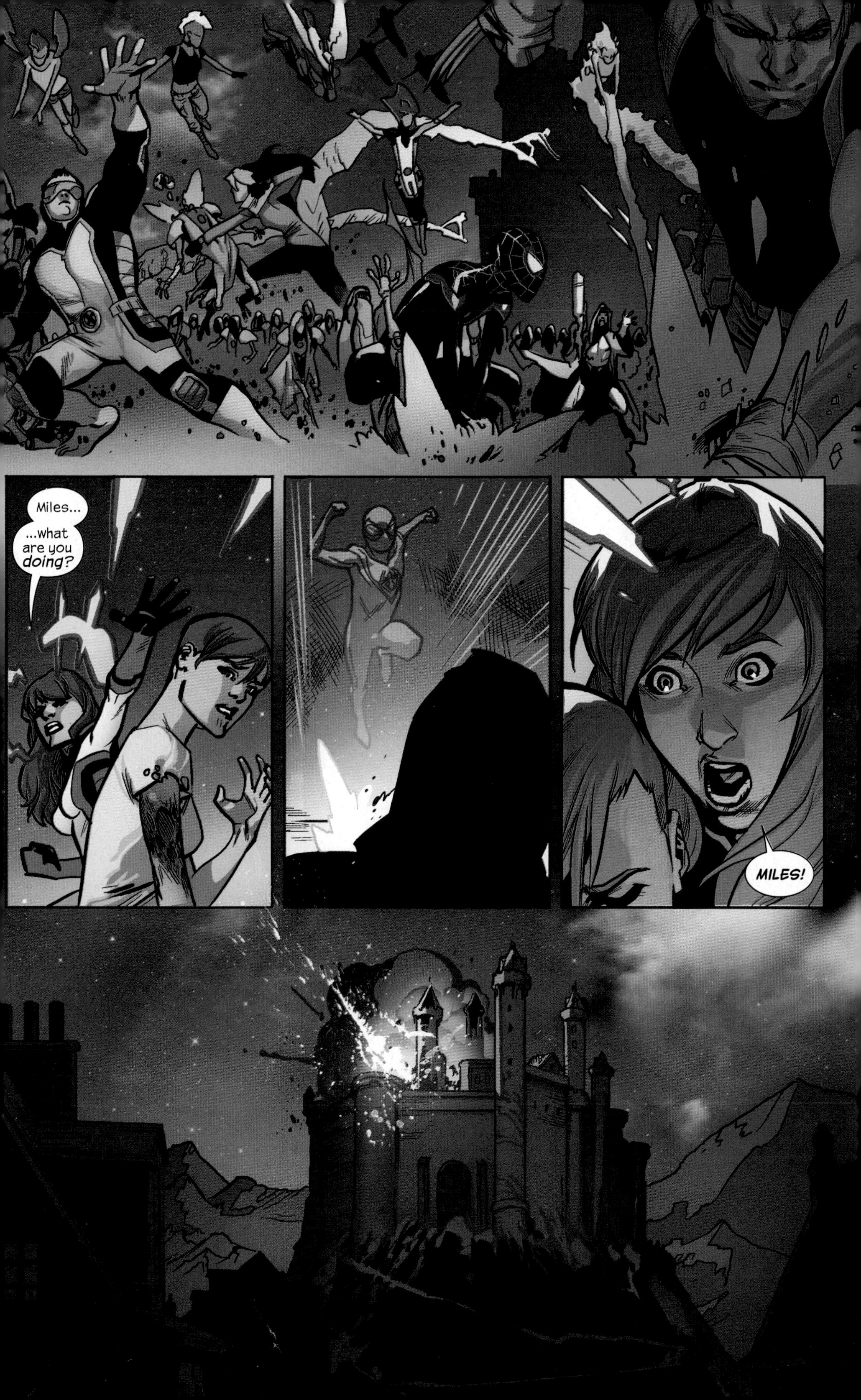
Miles...
...what are you *doing?*
MILES!

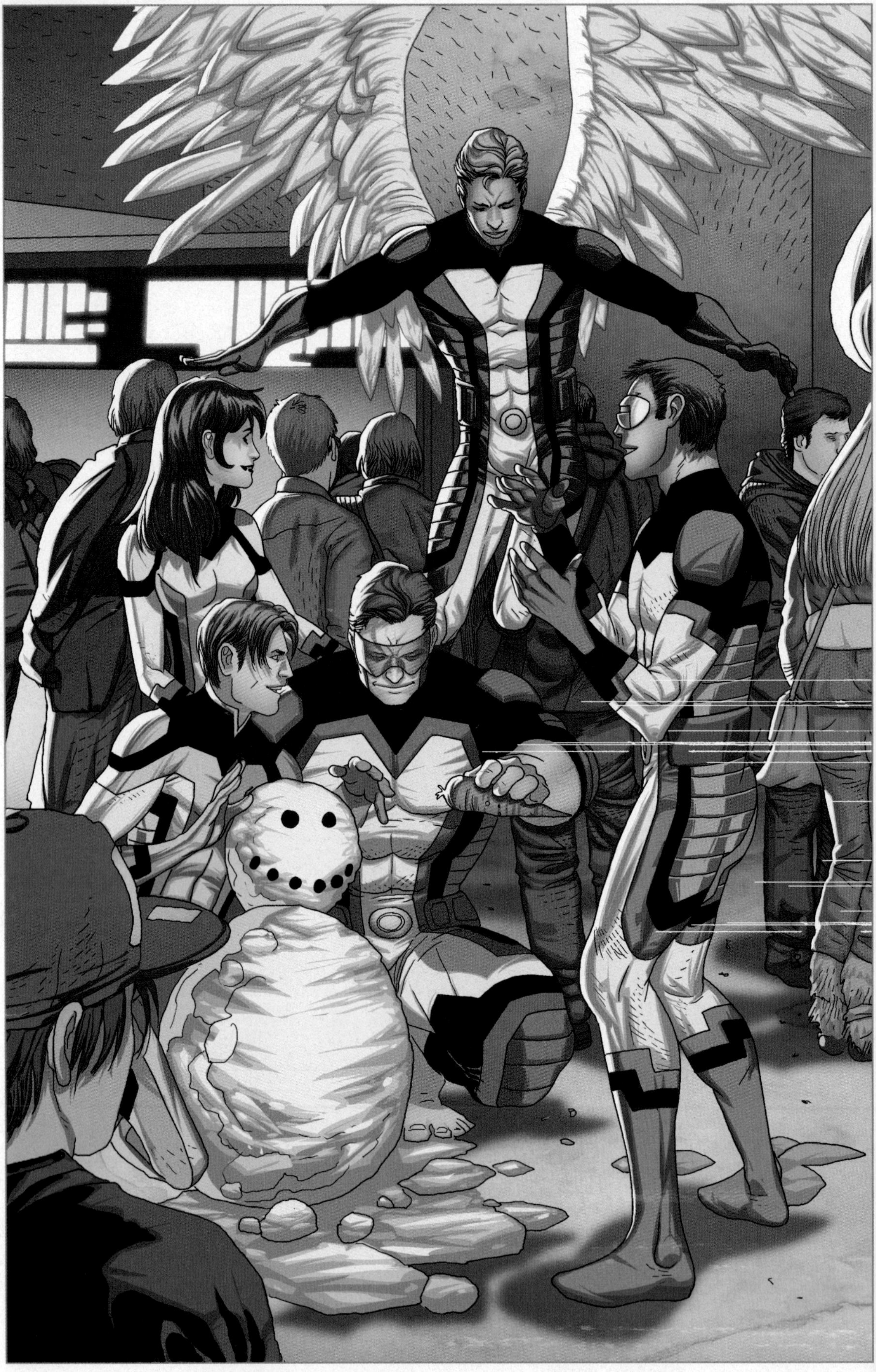

ALL-NEW X-MEN #35 WELCOME HOME VARIANT
BY SALVADOR LARROCA & ISRAEL SILVA

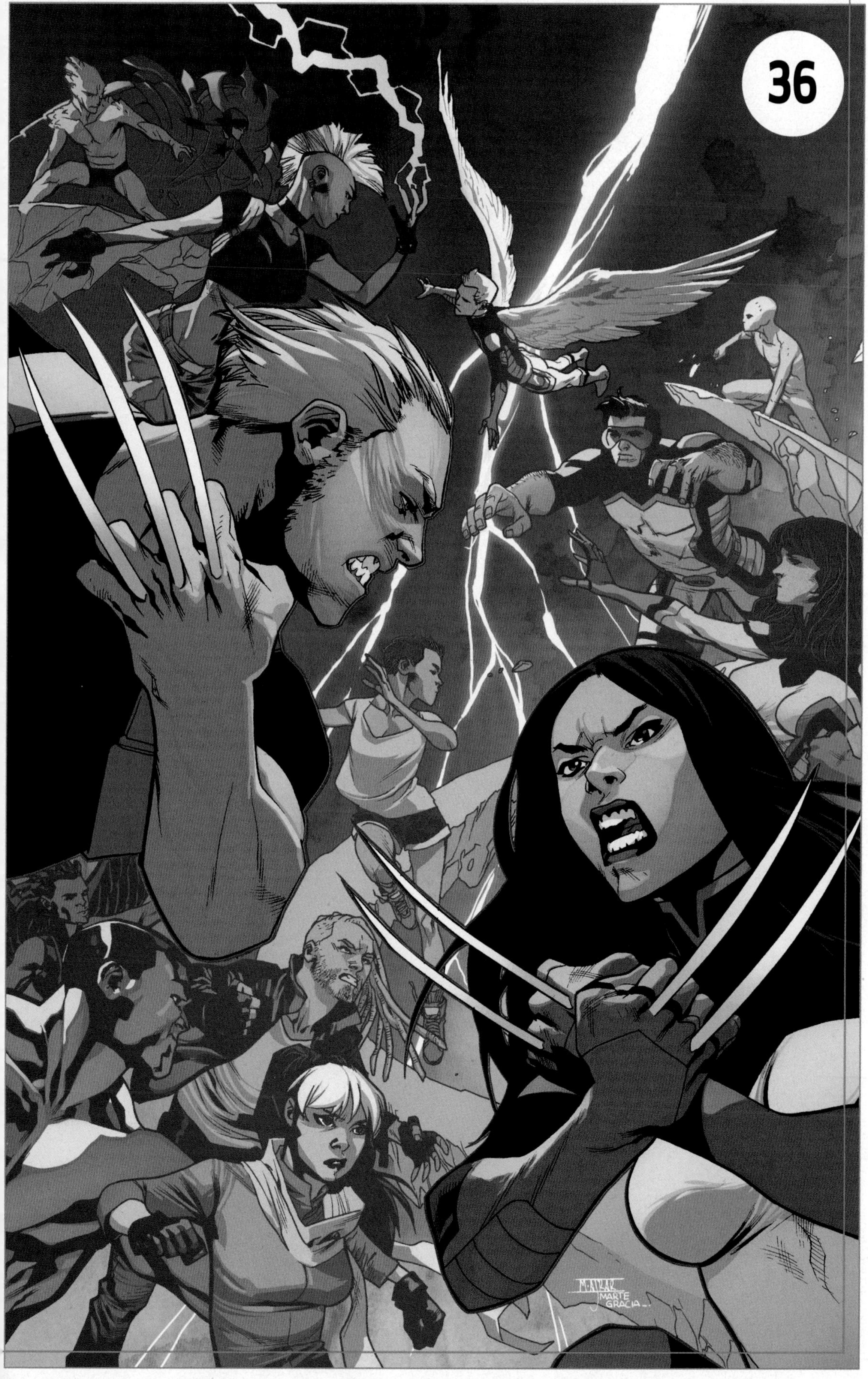
36
MARTE GRACIA

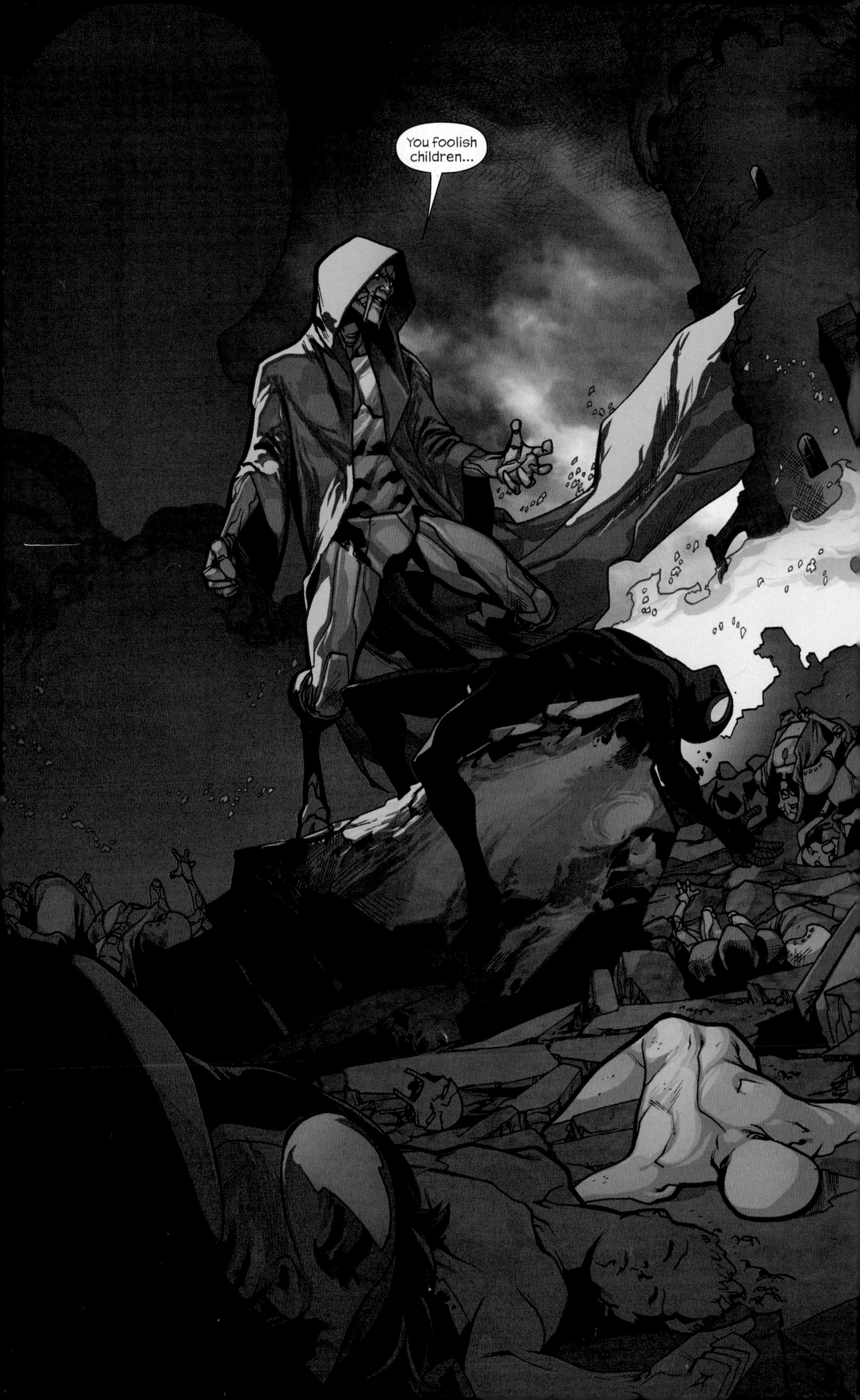
You foolish children...

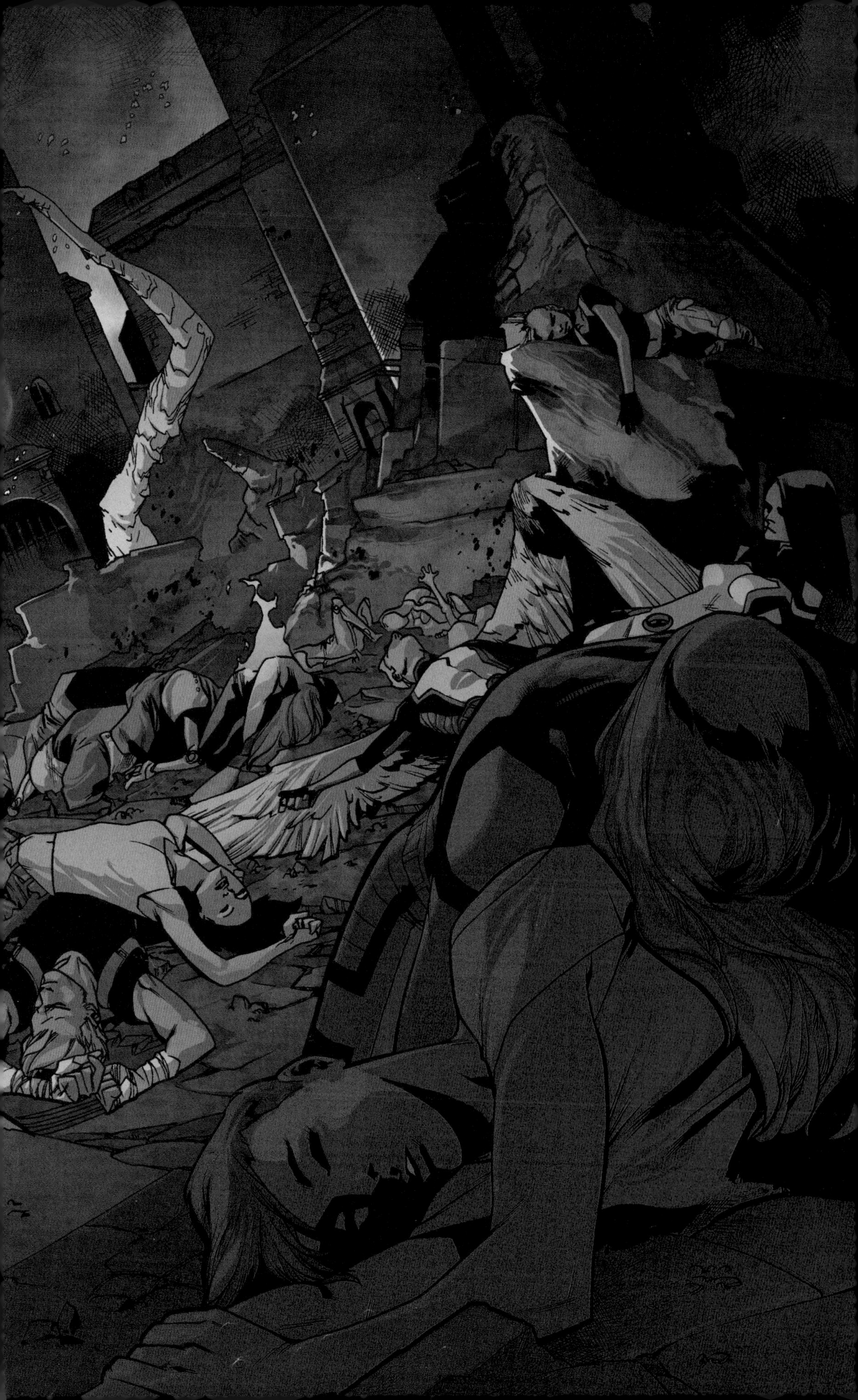

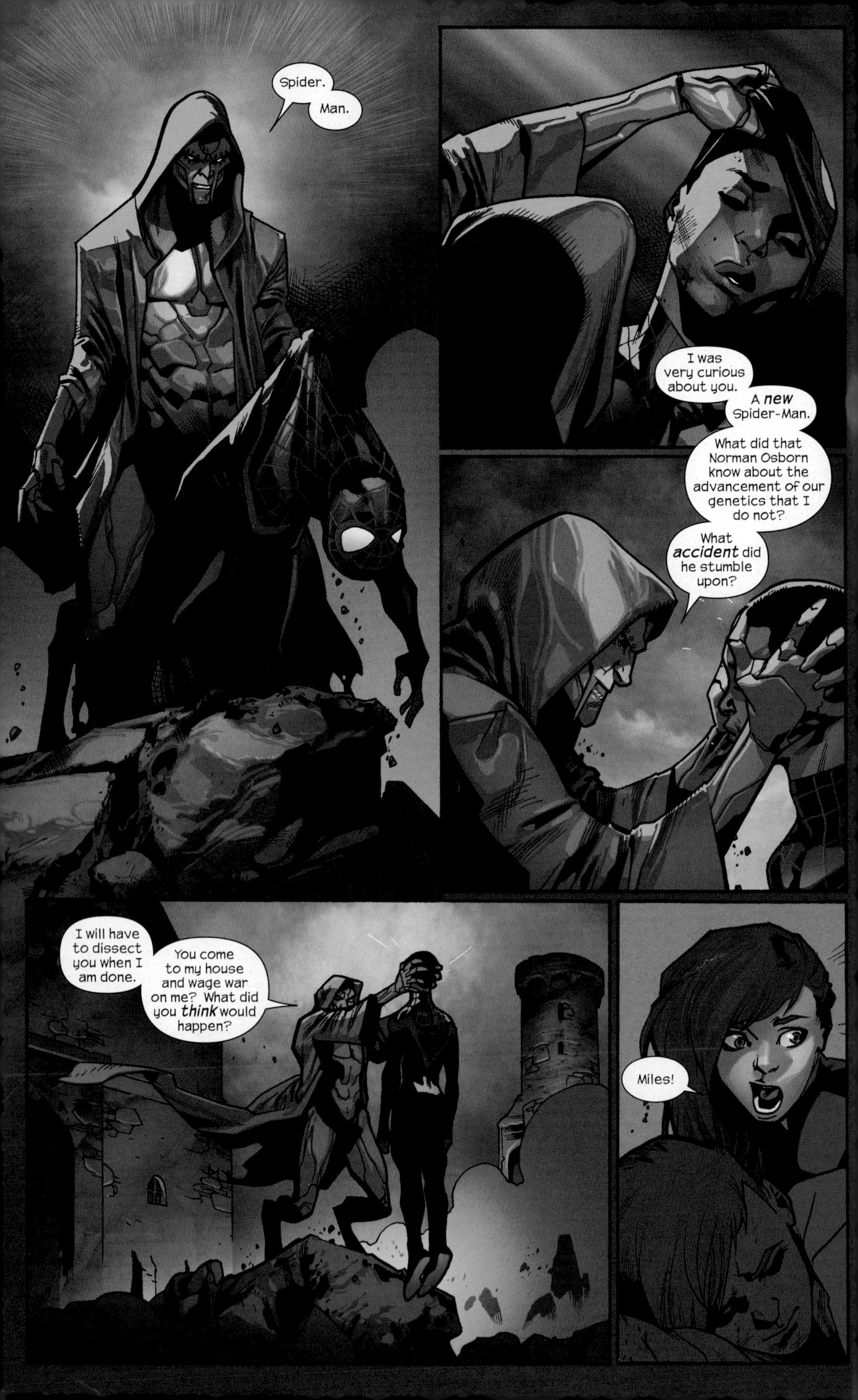
Spider.
Man.
I was very curious about you.
A new Spider-Man.
What did that Norman Osborn know about the advancement of our genetics that I do not?
What accident did he stumble upon?
I will have to dissect you when I am done.
You come to my house and wage war on me? What did you think would happen?
Miles!

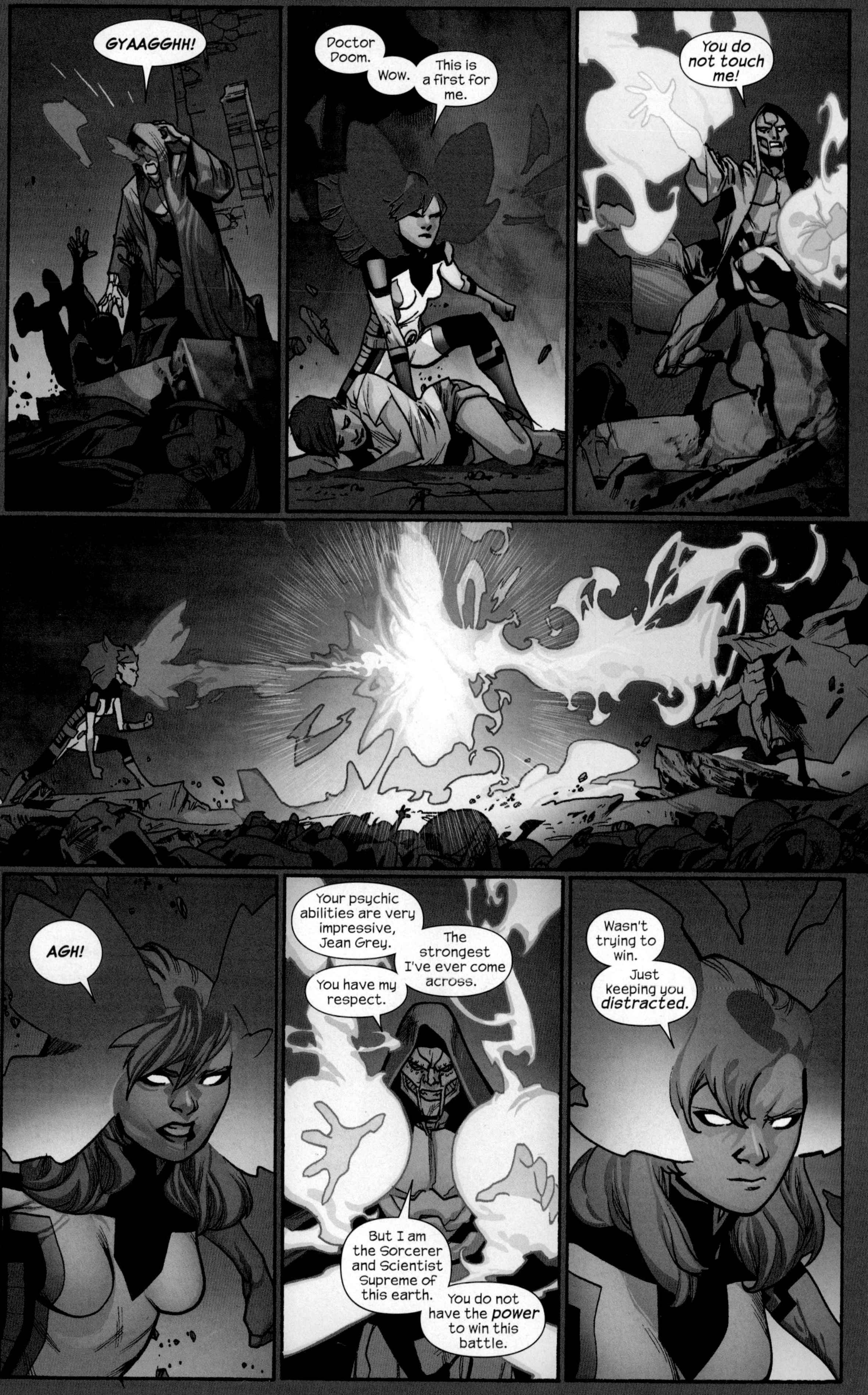
GYAAGGHH!
Doctor Doom.
Wow.
This is a first for me.
You do not touch me!
AGH!
Your psychic abilities are very impressive, Jean Grey.
The strongest I've ever come across.
You have my respect.
But I am the Sorcerer and Scientist Supreme of this earth.
You do not have the *power* to win this battle.
Wasn't trying to win.
Just keeping you *distracted*.

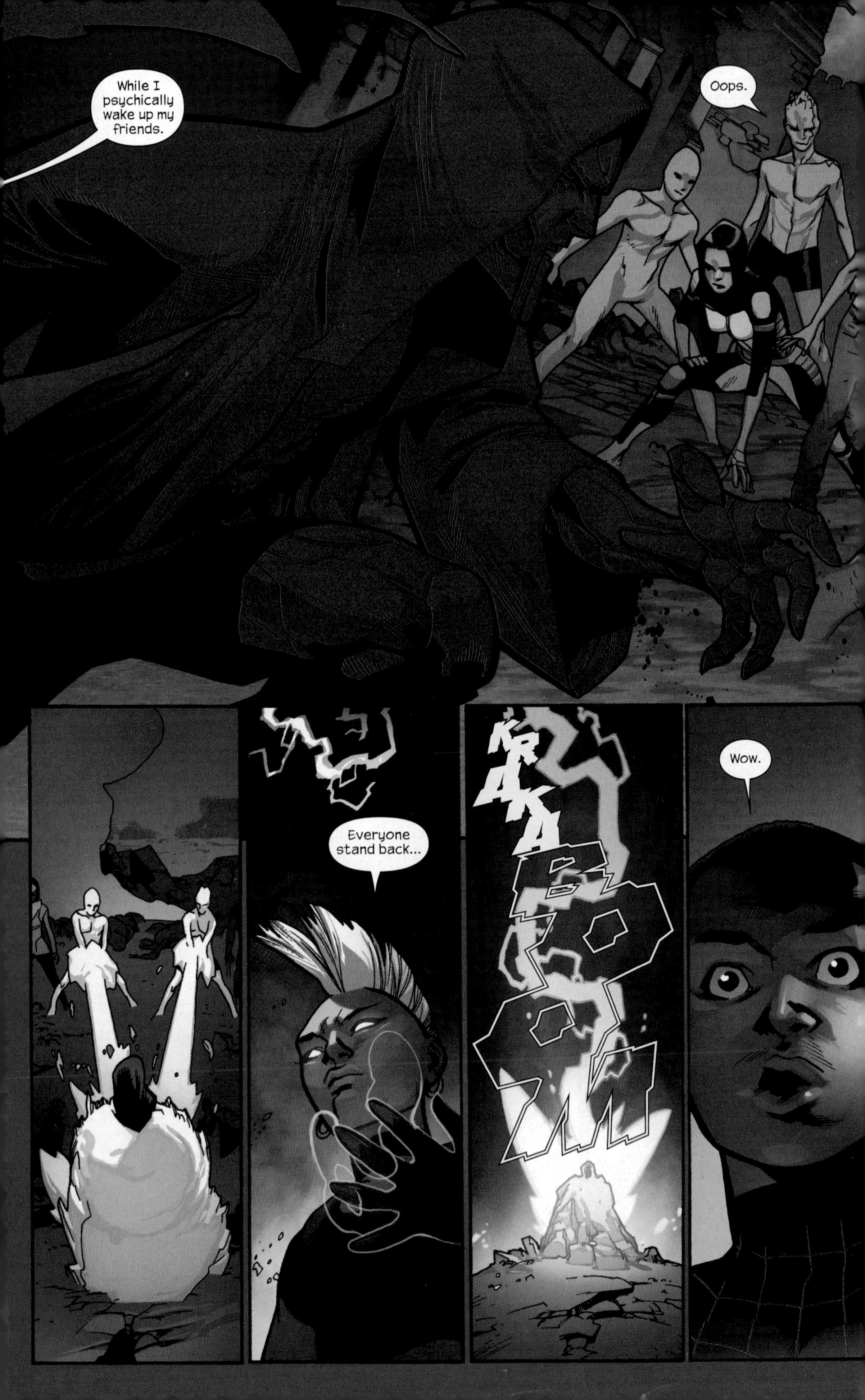
While I psychically wake up my friends.
Oops.
Everyone stand back...
KRAKABOOM
Wow.

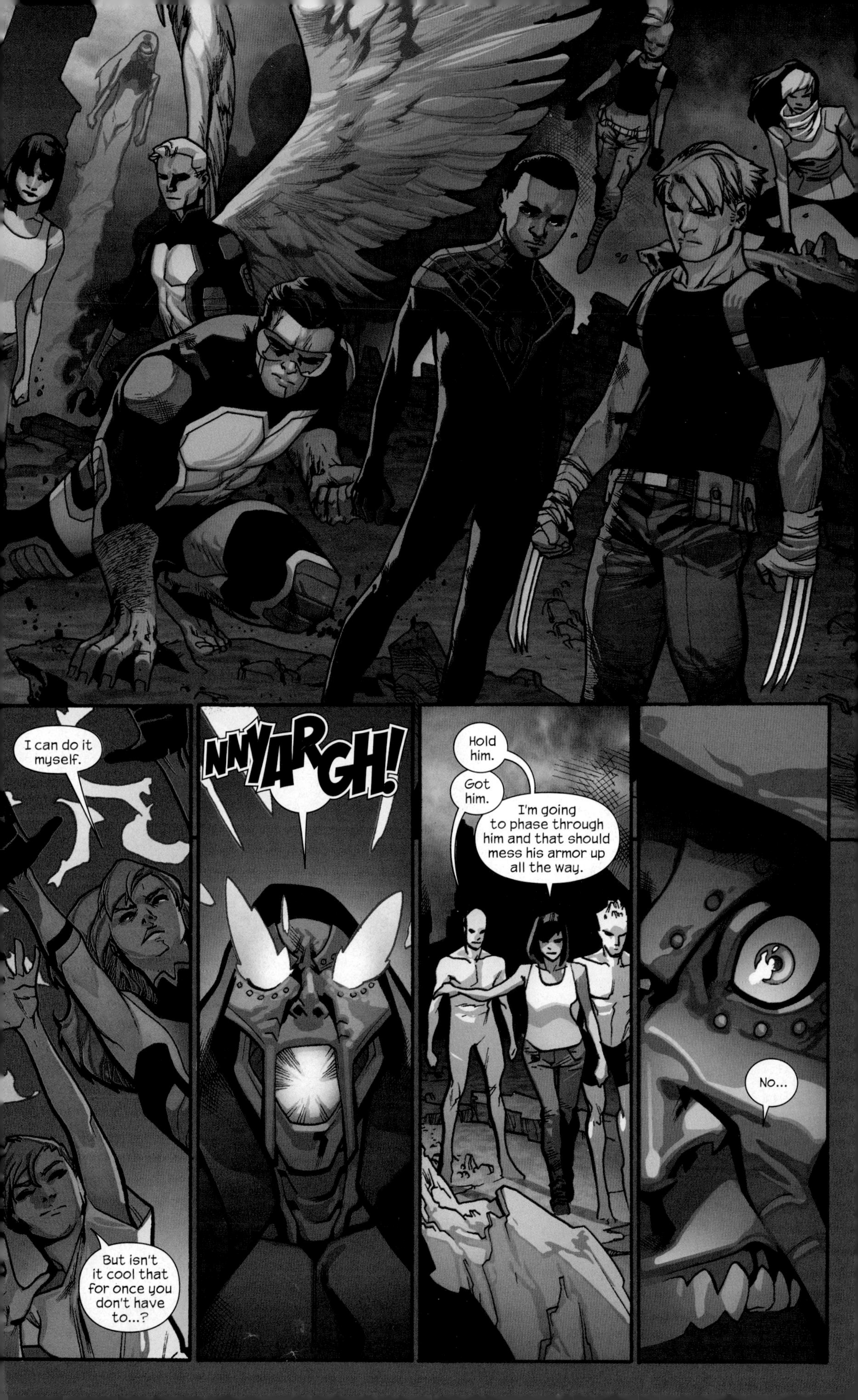

I can do it myself.
But isn't it cool that for once you don't have to...?
NNYARGH!
Hold him.
Got him.
I'm going to phase through him and that should mess his armor up all the way.
No...

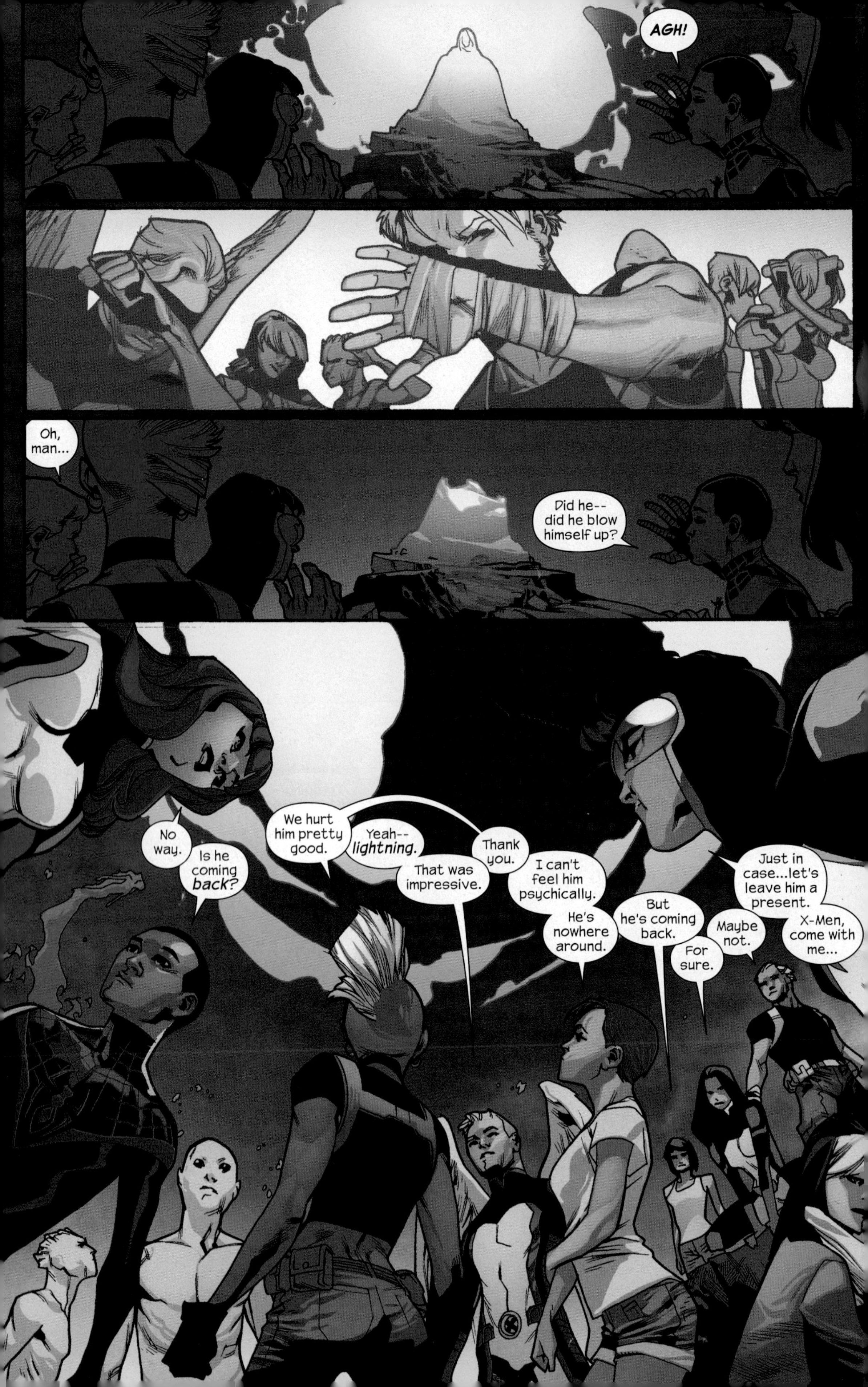
AGH!
Oh, man...
Did he-- did he blow himself up?
No way.
Is he coming back?
We hurt him pretty good.
Yeah-- lightning.
That was impressive.
Thank you.
I can't feel him psychically.
He's nowhere around.
But he's coming back.
For sure.
Maybe not.
Just in case...let's leave him a present.
X-Men, come with me...

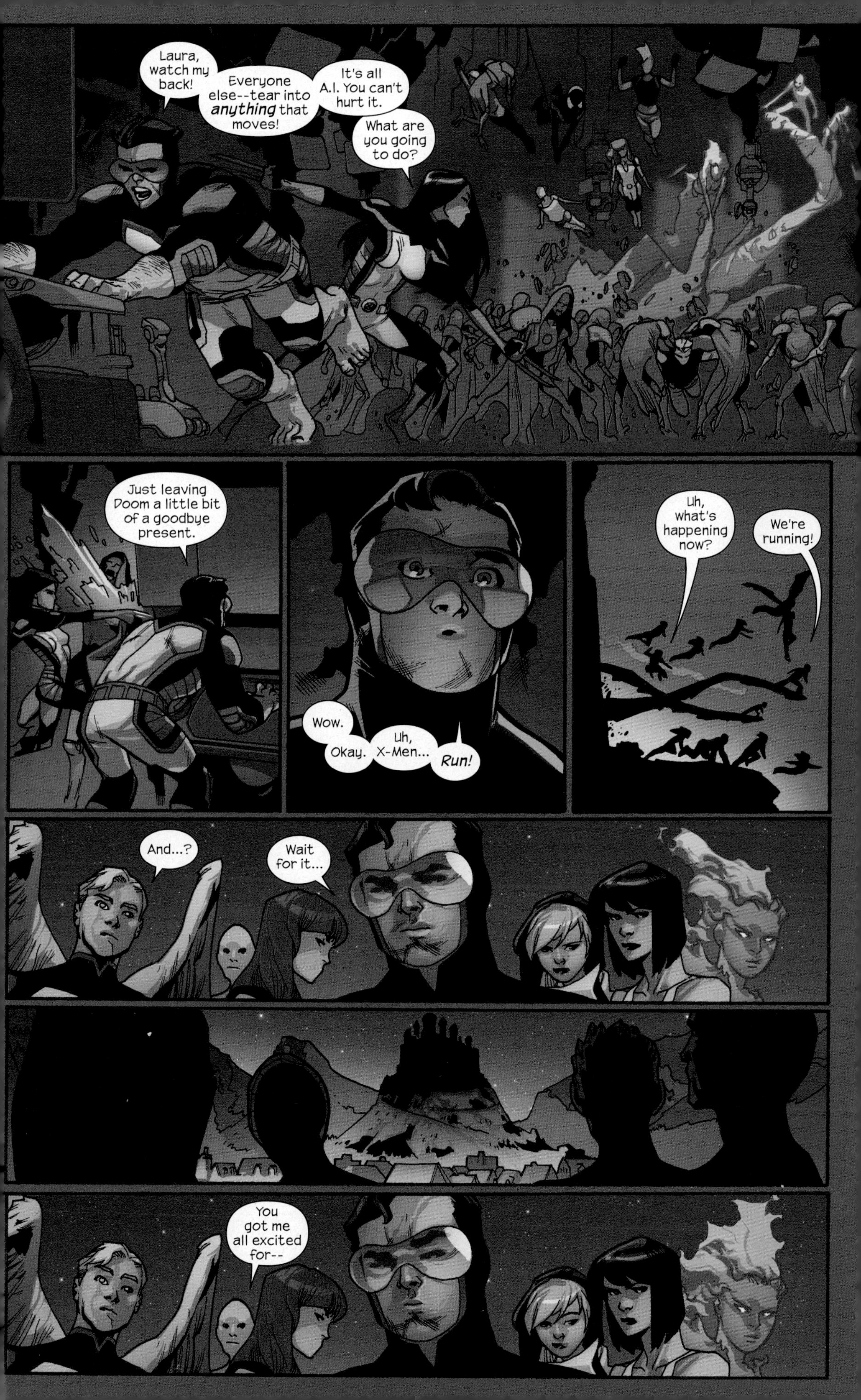

Laura, watch my back!
Everyone else--tear into *anything* that moves!
It's all A.I. You can't hurt it.
What are you going to do?
Just leaving Doom a little bit of a goodbye present.
Wow.
Okay.
Uh, X-Men...
Run!
Uh, what's happening now?
We're running!
And...?
Wait for it...
You got me all excited for--

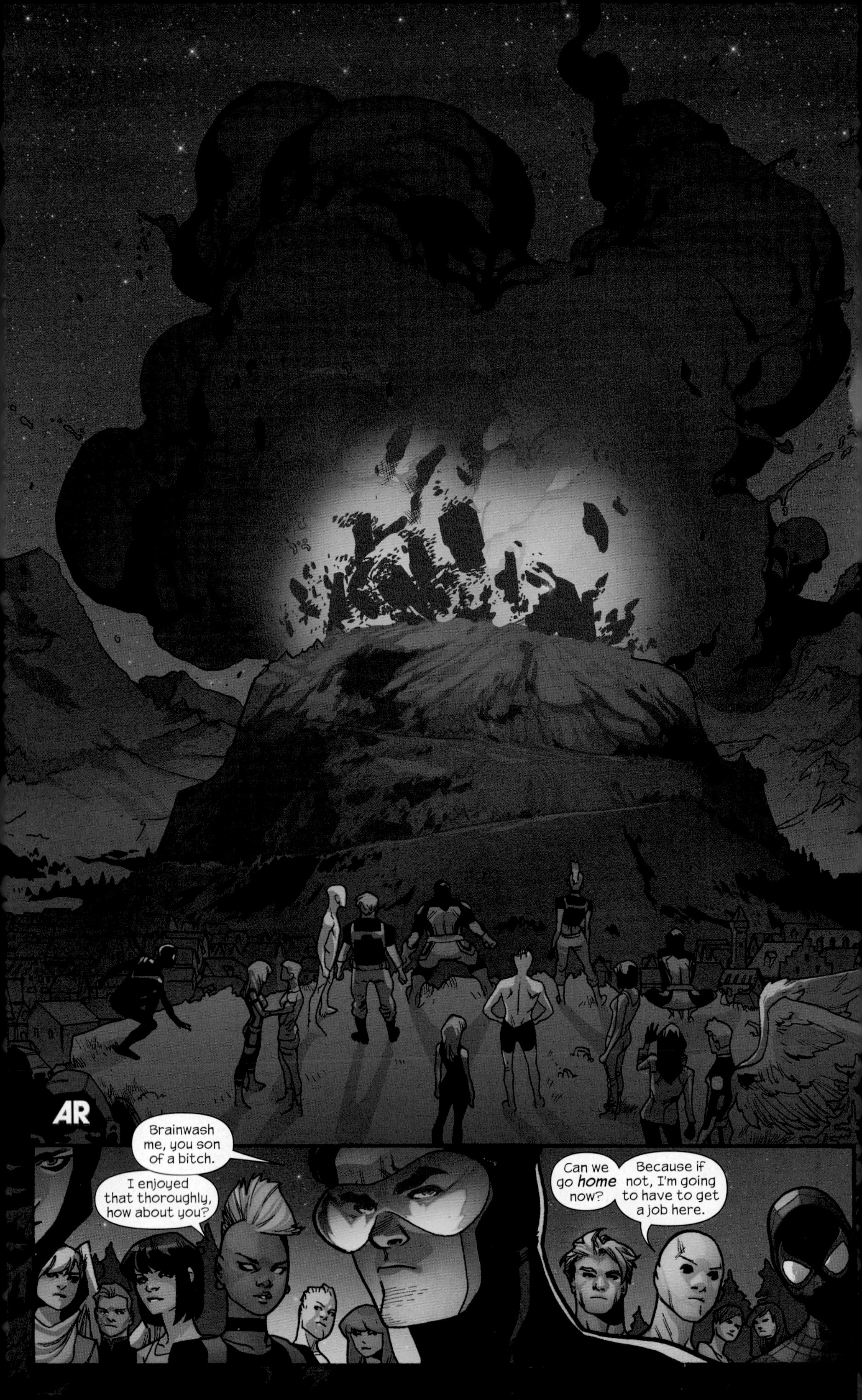
AR
Brainwash me, you son of a bitch.
I enjoyed that thoroughly, how about you?
Can we go *home* now?
Because if not, I'm going to have to get a job here.

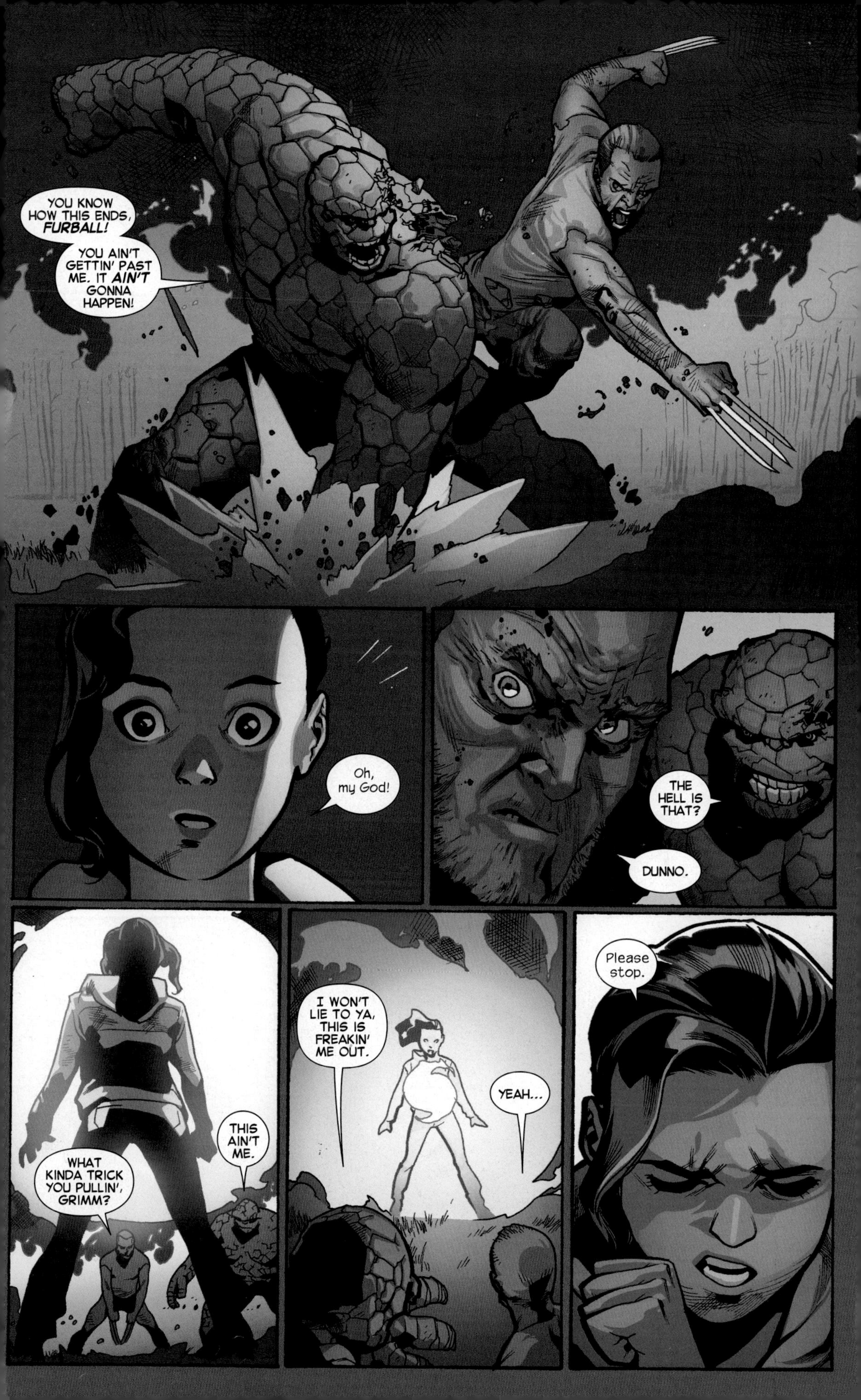
YOU KNOW HOW THIS ENDS, **FURBALL!**
YOU AIN'T GETTIN' PAST ME. IT **AIN'T** GONNA HAPPEN!
Oh, my God!
THE HELL IS THAT?
DUNNO.
WHAT KINDA TRICK YOU PULLIN', GRIMM?
THIS AIN'T ME.
I WON'T LIE TO YA, THIS IS FREAKIN' ME OUT.
YEAH...
Please stop.

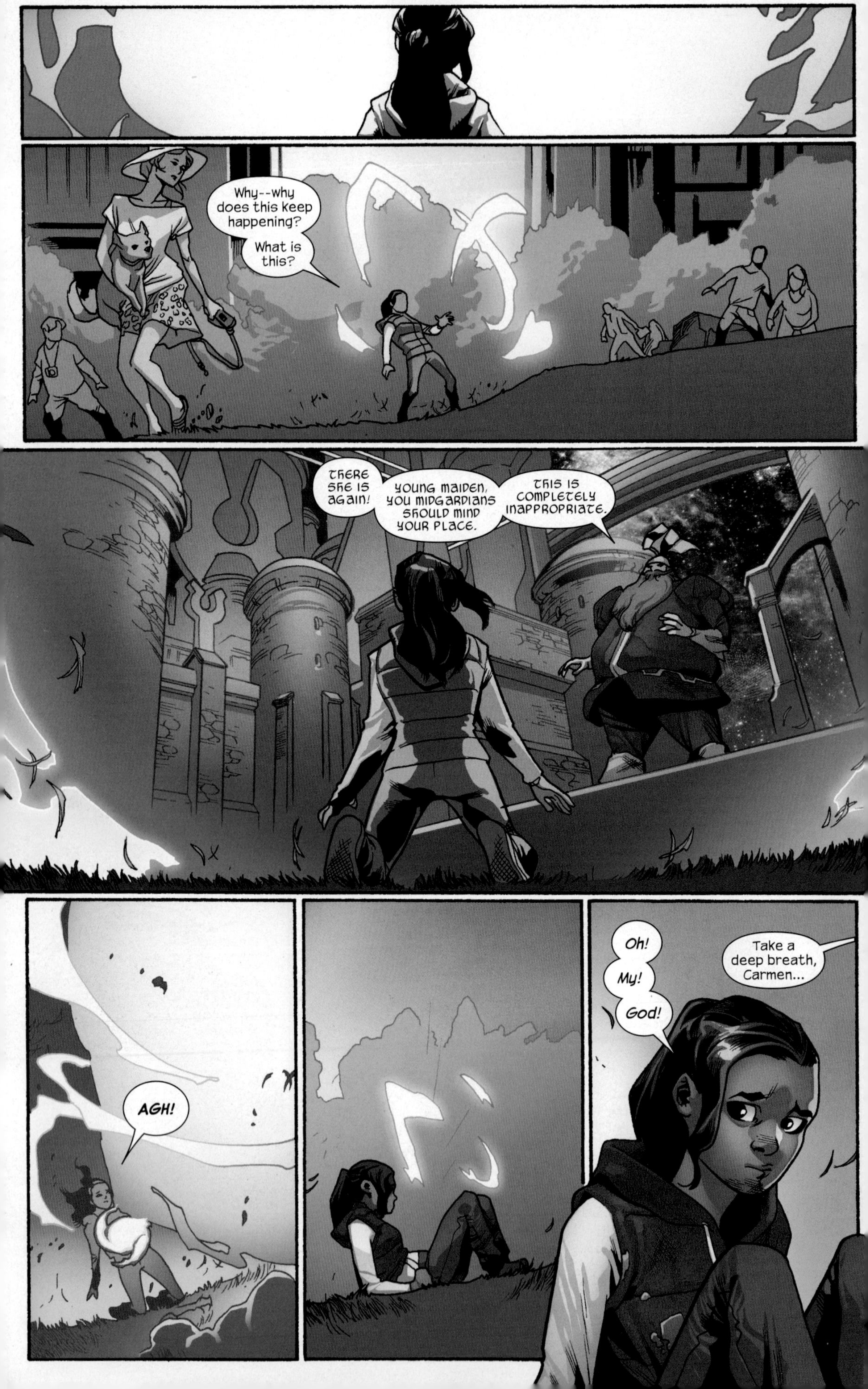
Why--why does this keep happening?
What is this?
THERE SHE IS AGAIN!
YOUNG MAIDEN, YOU MIDGARDIANS SHOULD MIND YOUR PLACE.
THIS IS COMPLETELY INAPPROPRIATE.
AGH!
Oh!
My!
God!
Take a deep breath, Carmen...

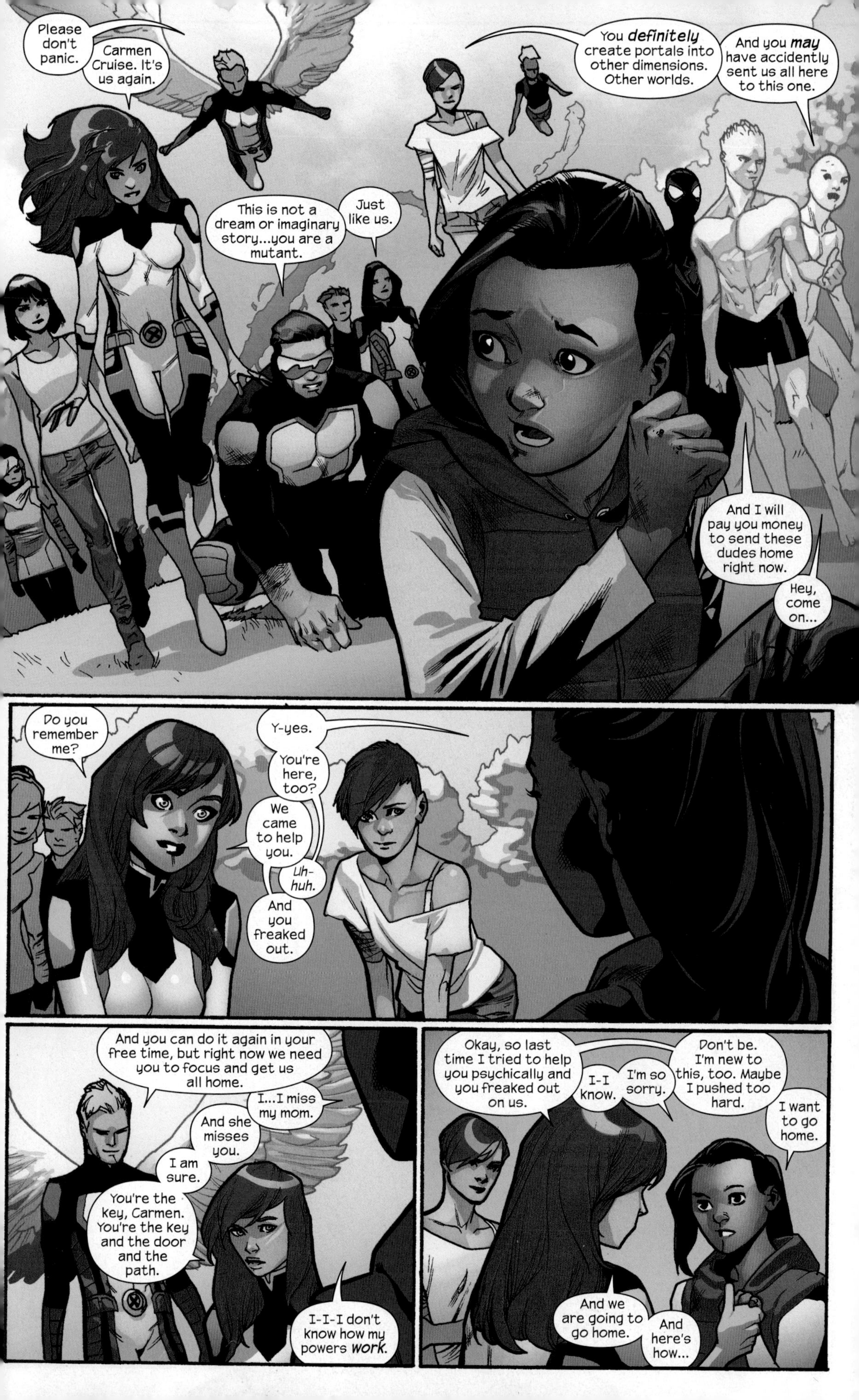
Please don't panic.
Carmen Cruise. It's us again.
You *definitely* create portals into other dimensions. Other worlds.
And you *may* have accidently sent us all here to this one.
This is not a dream or imaginary story...you are a mutant.
Just like us.
And I will pay you money to send these dudes home right now.
Hey, come on...
Do you remember me?
Y-yes.
You're here, too?
We came to help you.
Uh-huh.
And you freaked out.
And you can do it again in your free time, but right now we need you to focus and get us all home.
I...I miss my mom.
And she misses you.
I am sure.
You're the key, Carmen. You're the key and the door and the path.
I-I-I don't know how my powers *work*.
Okay, so last time I tried to help you psychically and you freaked out on us.
I-I know.
I'm so sorry.
Don't be. I'm new to this, too. Maybe I pushed too hard.
I want to go home.
And we are going to go home.
And here's how...

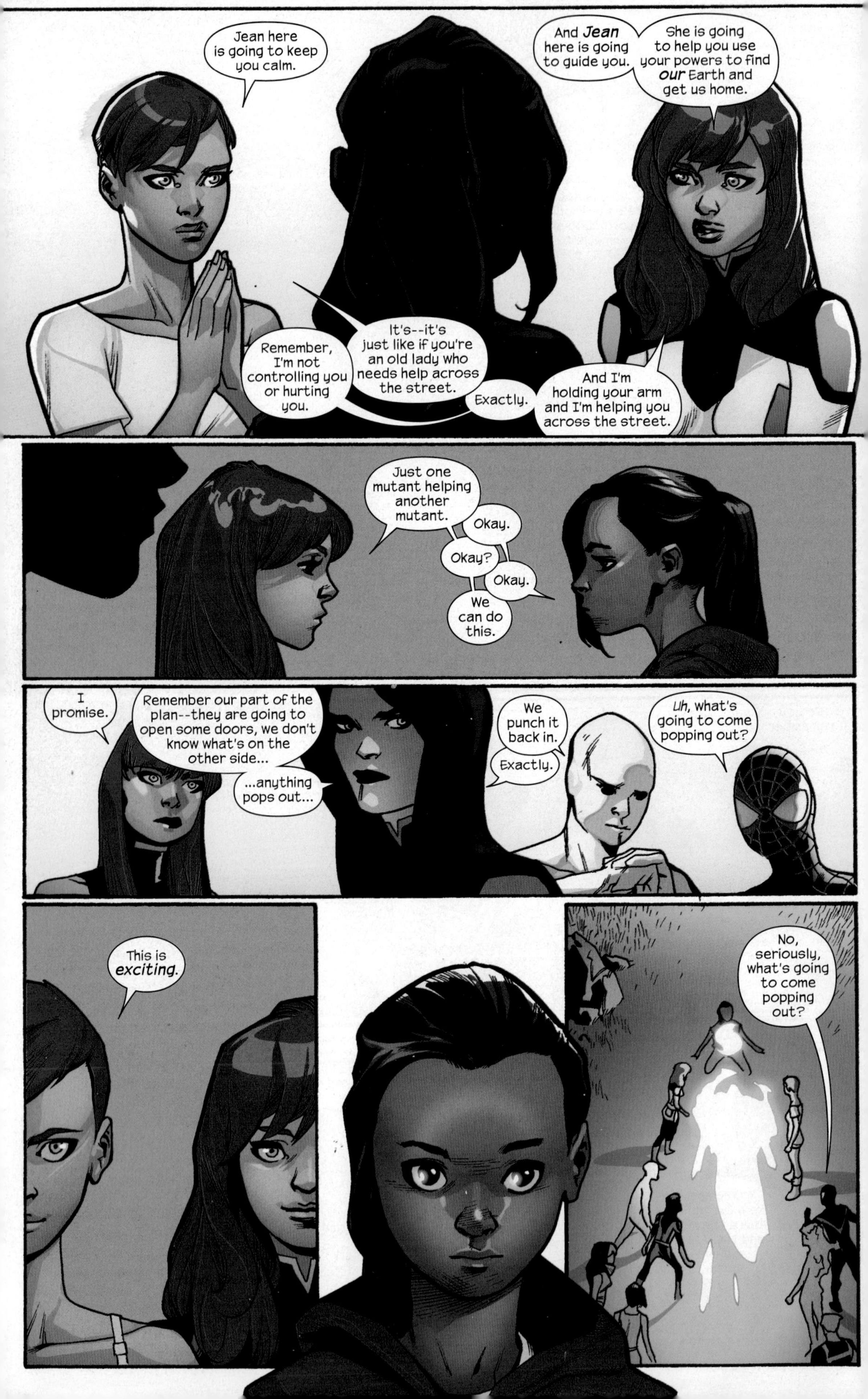
Jean here is going to keep you calm.
And Jean here is going to guide you.
She is going to help you use your powers to find our Earth and get us home.
Remember, I'm not controlling you or hurting you.
It's--it's just like if you're an old lady who needs help across the street.
Exactly.
And I'm holding your arm and I'm helping you across the street.
Just one mutant helping another mutant.
Okay.
Okay?
Okay.
We can do this.
I promise.
Remember our part of the plan--they are going to open some doors, we don't know what's on the other side...
...anything pops out...
We punch it back in.
Exactly.
Uh, what's going to come popping out?
This is exciting.
No, seriously, what's going to come popping out?

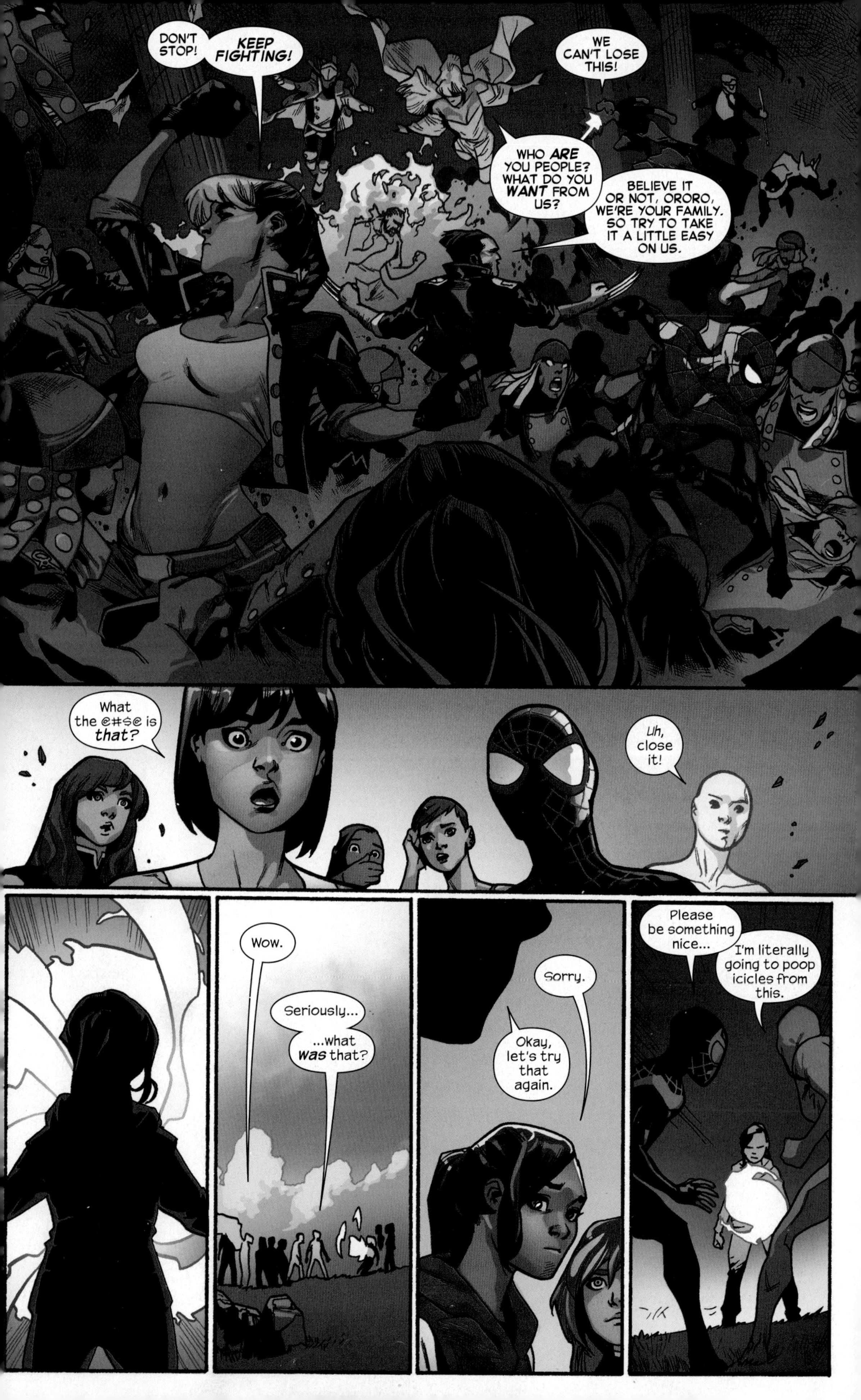
DON'T STOP!
KEEP FIGHTING!
WE CAN'T LOSE THIS!
WHO ARE YOU PEOPLE? WHAT DO YOU WANT FROM US?
BELIEVE IT OR NOT, ORORO, WE'RE YOUR FAMILY. SO TRY TO TAKE IT A LITTLE EASY ON US.
What the @#$@ is that?
Uh, close it!
Wow.
Seriously...
...what was that?
Sorry.
Okay, let's try that again.
Please be something nice...
I'm literally going to poop icicles from this.

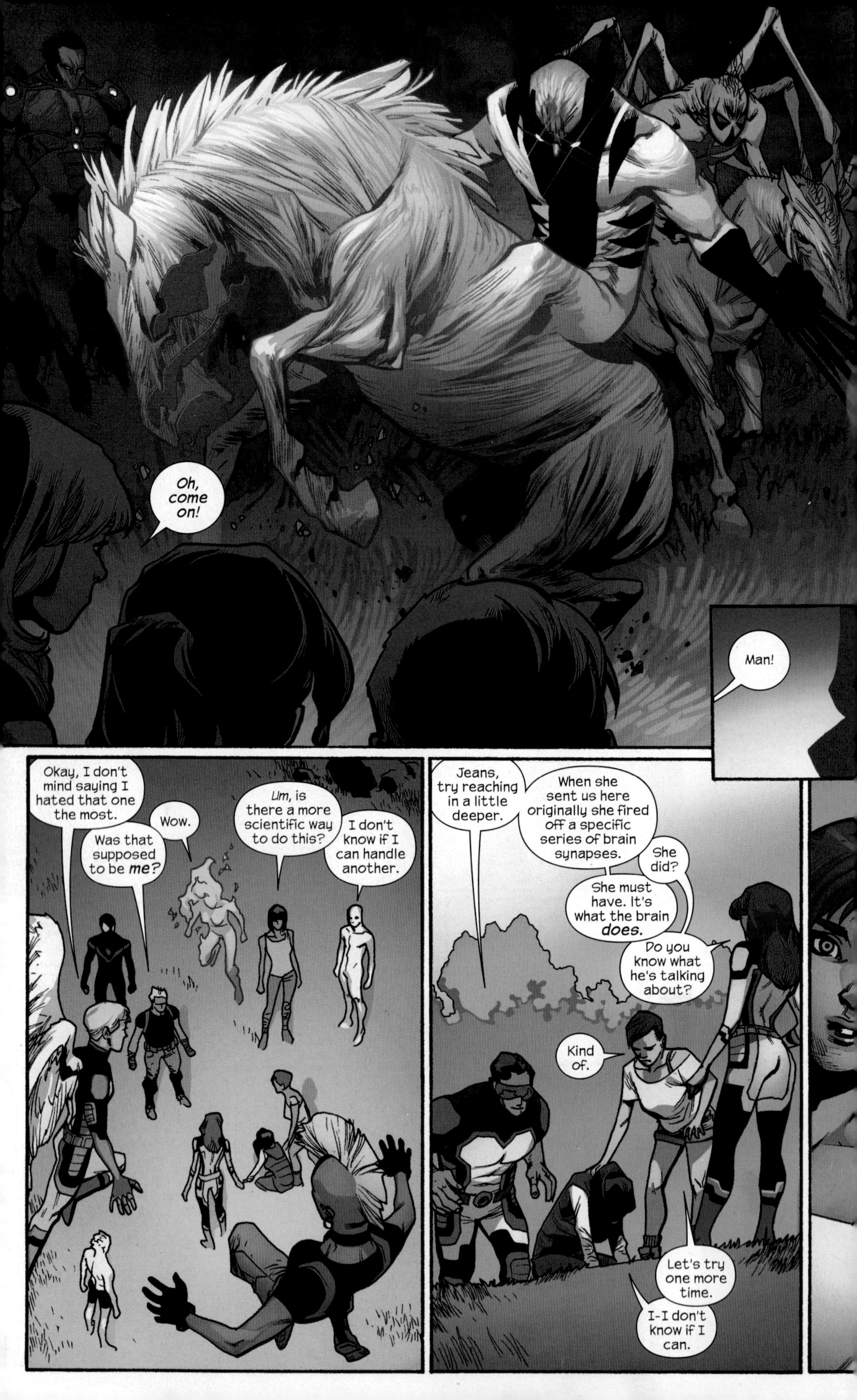
Oh, come on!
Man!
Okay, I don't mind saying I hated that one the most.
Wow.
Was that supposed to be *me*?
Um, is there a more scientific way to do this?
I don't know if I can handle another.
Jeans, try reaching in a little deeper.
When she sent us here originally she fired off a specific series of brain synapses.
She did?
She must have. It's what the brain *does.*
Do you know what he's talking about?
Kind of.
Let's try one more time.
I-I don't know if I can.

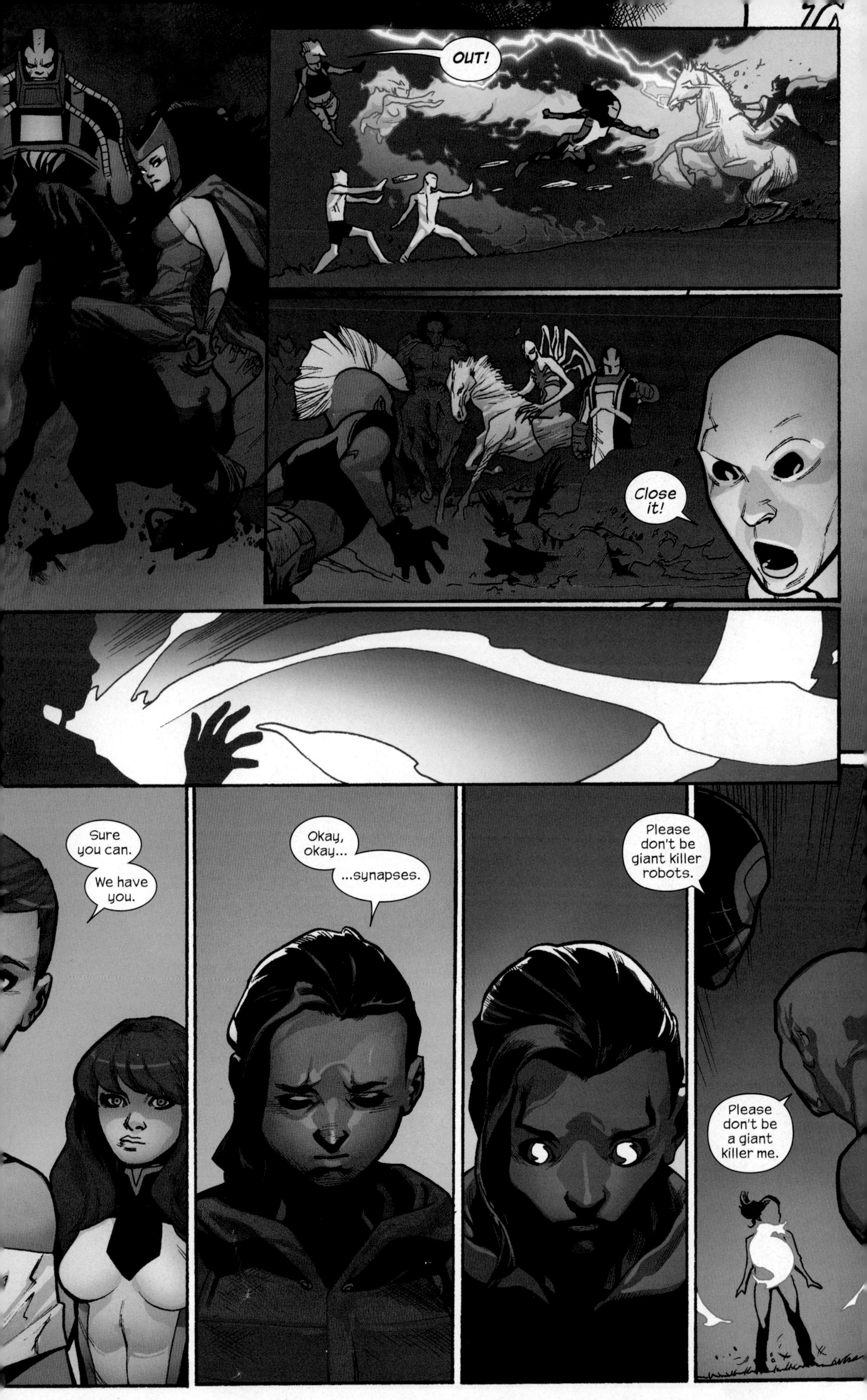
OUT!
Close it!
Sure you can.
We have you.
Okay, okay...
...synapses.
Please don't be giant killer robots.
Please don't be a giant killer me.

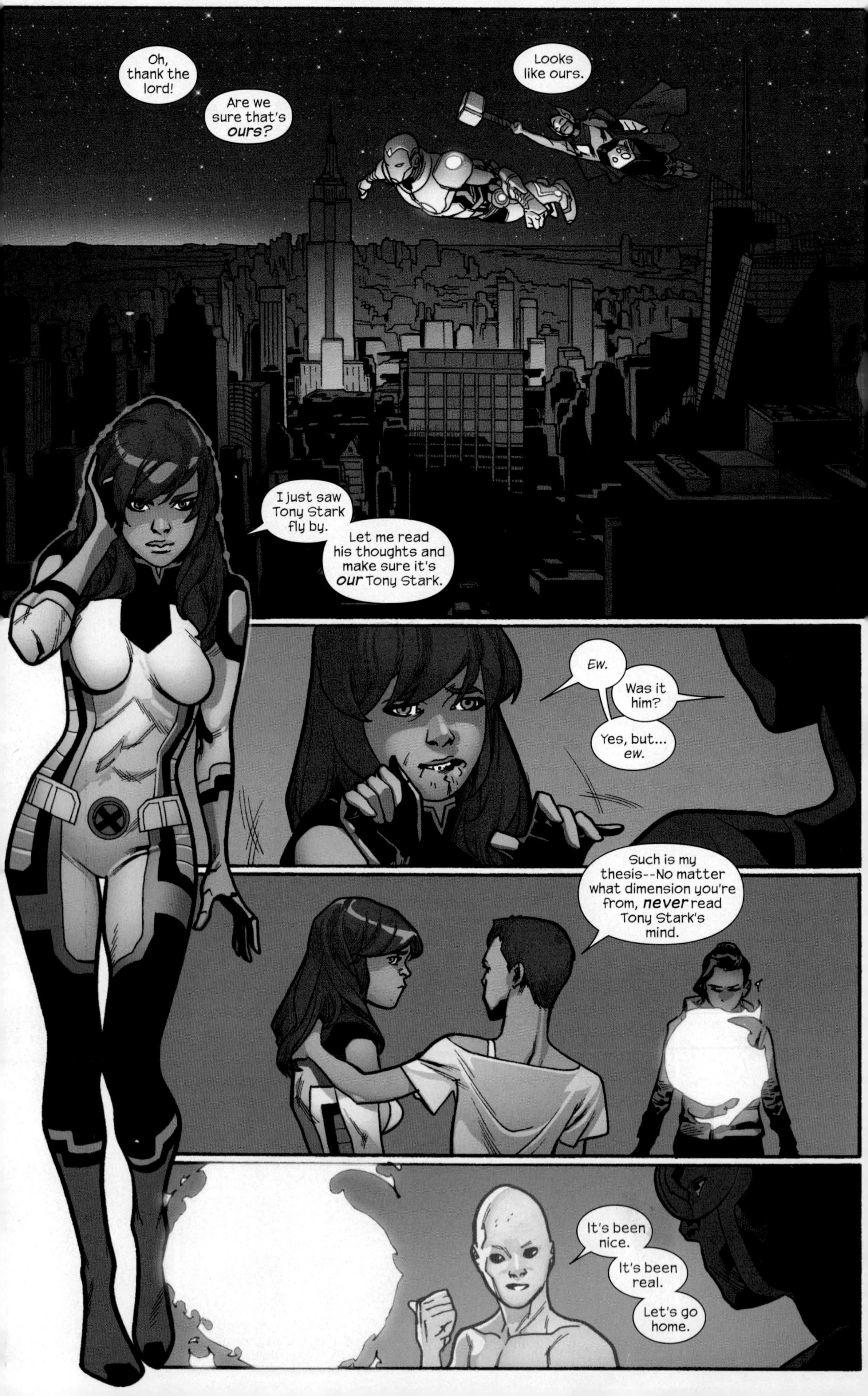

Oh, thank the lord!
Are we sure that's *ours?*
Looks like ours.
I just saw Tony Stark fly by.
Let me read his thoughts and make sure it's *our* Tony Stark.
Ew.
Was it him?
Yes, but... *ew.*
Such is my thesis--No matter what dimension you're from, ***never*** read Tony Stark's mind.
It's been nice.
It's been real.
Let's go home.

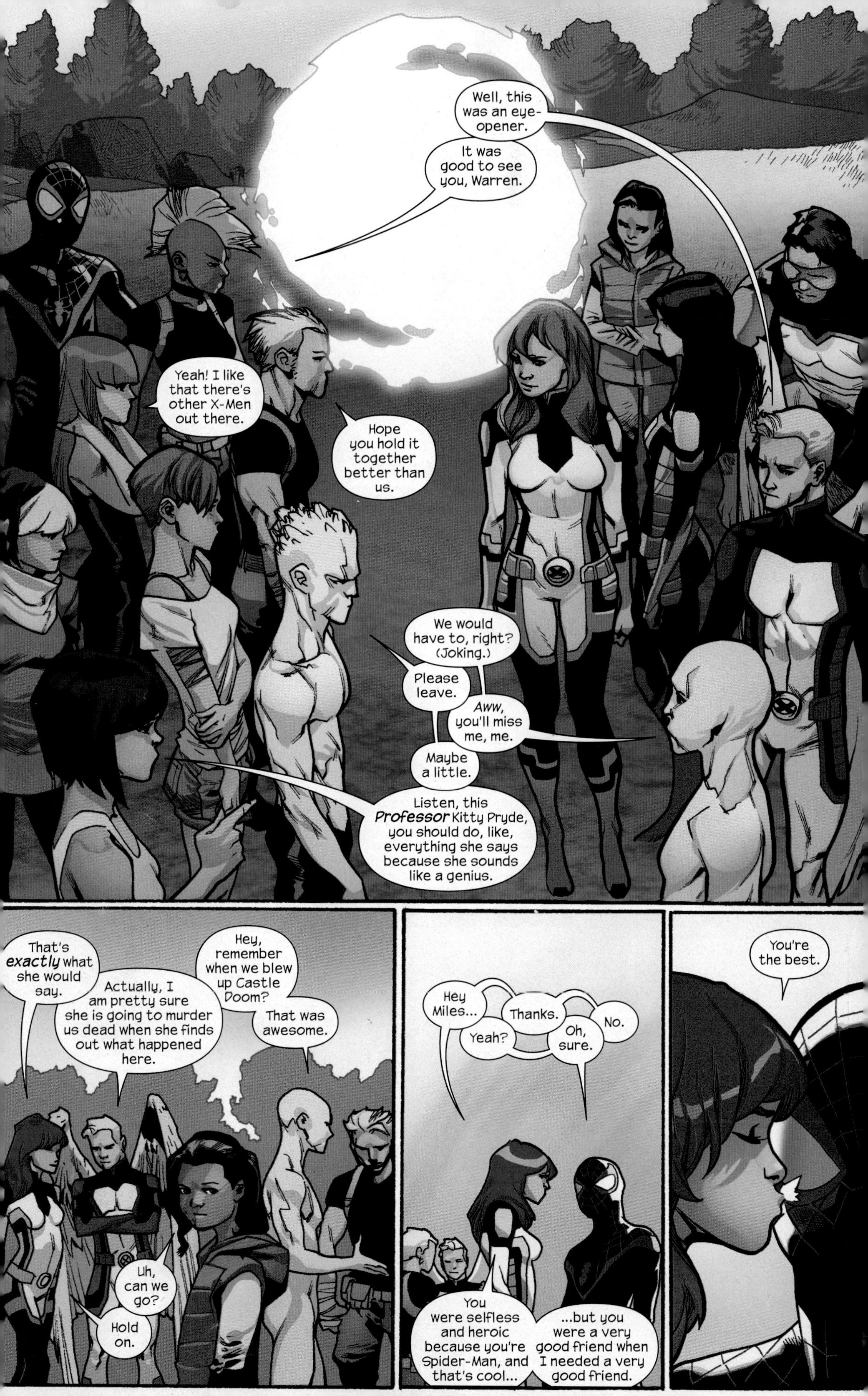
Well, this was an eye-opener.
It was good to see you, Warren.
Yeah! I like that there's other X-Men out there.
Hope you hold it together better than us.
We would have to, right? (Joking.)
Please leave.
Aww, you'll miss me, me.
Maybe a little.
Listen, this *Professor* Kitty Pryde, you should do, like, everything she says because she sounds like a genius.
That's *exactly* what she would say.
Actually, I am pretty sure she is going to murder us dead when she finds out what happened here.
Hey, remember when we blew up Castle Doom?
That was awesome.
Uh, can we go?
Hold on.
Hey Miles...
Yeah?
Thanks.
Oh, sure.
No.
You were selfless and heroic because you're Spider-Man, and that's cool...
...but you were a very good friend when I needed a very good friend.
You're the best.

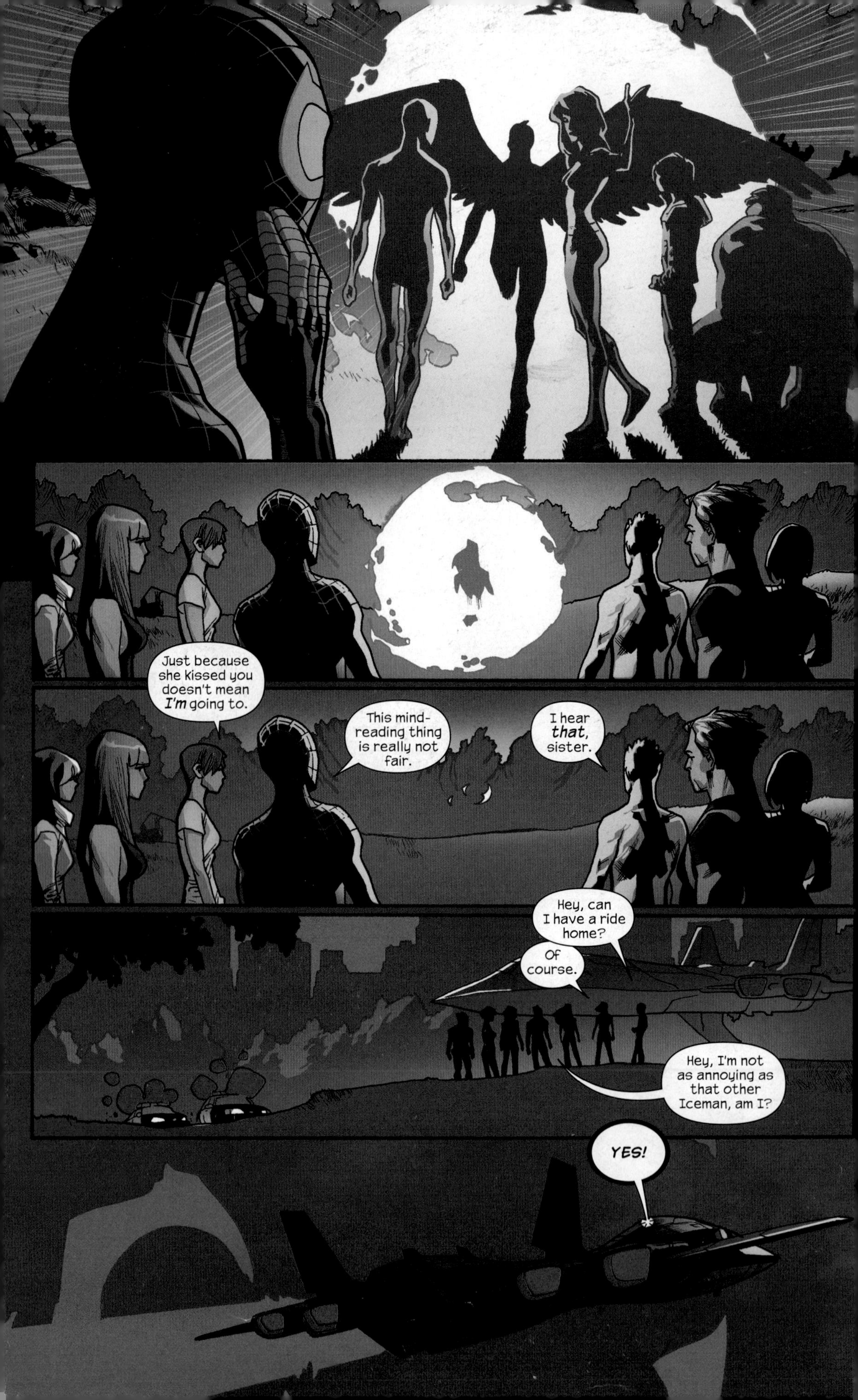
Just because she kissed you doesn't mean *I'm* going to.
This mind-reading thing is really not fair.
I hear *that*, sister.
Hey, can I have a ride home?
Of course.
Hey, I'm not as annoying as that other Iceman, am I?
YES!

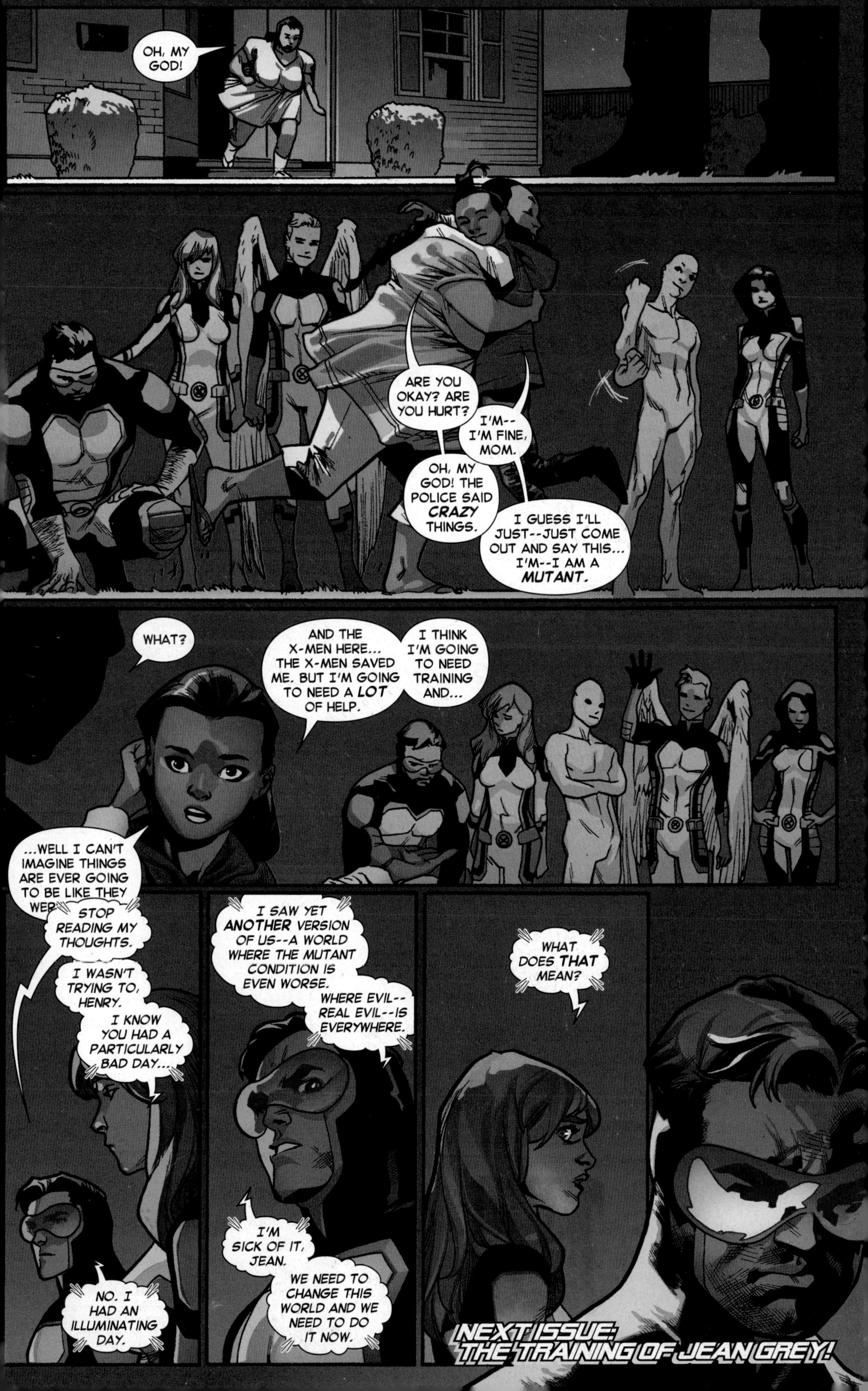
OH, MY GOD!
ARE YOU OKAY? ARE YOU HURT?
I'M-- I'M FINE, MOM.
OH, MY GOD! THE POLICE SAID CRAZY THINGS.
I GUESS I'LL JUST--JUST COME OUT AND SAY THIS... I'M--I AM A MUTANT.
WHAT?
AND THE X-MEN HERE... THE X-MEN SAVED ME. BUT I'M GOING TO NEED A LOT OF HELP.
I THINK I'M GOING TO NEED TRAINING AND...
...WELL I CAN'T IMAGINE THINGS ARE EVER GOING TO BE LIKE THEY WER
STOP READING MY THOUGHTS.
I WASN'T TRYING TO, HENRY.
I KNOW YOU HAD A PARTICULARLY BAD DAY...
NO. I HAD AN ILLUMINATING DAY.
I SAW YET ANOTHER VERSION OF US--A WORLD WHERE THE MUTANT CONDITION IS EVEN WORSE.
WHERE EVIL-- REAL EVIL--IS EVERYWHERE.
I'M SICK OF IT, JEAN.
WE NEED TO CHANGE THIS WORLD AND WE NEED TO DO IT NOW.
WHAT DOES THAT MEAN?
NEXT ISSUE: THE TRAINING OF JEAN GREY!

TO ACCESS THE FREE MARVEL AUGMENTED REALITY APP THAT ENHANCES AND CHANGES THE WAY YOU EXPERIENCE COMICS:

1. Download the app for free via marvel.com/ARapp

2. Launch the app on your camera-enabled Apple iOS® or Android™ device*

3. Hold your mobile device's camera over any cover or panel with the AR graphic

4. Sit back and see the future of comics in action!

*Available on most camera-enabled Apple iOS® and Android™ devices. Content subject to change and availability.

ALL·NEW X·MEN

AR INDEX

TO REDEEM YOUR CODE FOR A FREE DIGITAL COPY:

1. GO TO MARVEL.COM/REDEEM. OFFER EXPIRES ON 3/18/17.

2. FOLLOW THE ON-SCREEN INSTRUCTIONS TO REDEEM YOUR DIGITAL COPY.

3. LAUNCH THE MARVEL COMICS APP TO READ YOUR COMIC NOW!

4. YOUR DIGITAL COPY WILL BE FOUND UNDER THE *MY COMICS* TAB.

5. READ & ENJOY!

YOUR FREE DIGITAL COPY WILL BE AVAILABLE ON

TMA3AP2YCVIZ